Apple Pro Training Series

Logic 6

Martin Sitter
Robert Brock

Apple
Certified

Apple Pro Training Series: Logic 6
Martin Sitter and Robert Brock
Copyright © 2004 by Martin Sitter and Robert Brock

Published by Peachpit Press. For information on Peachpit Press books, contact:

Peachpit Press
1249 Eighth Street
Berkeley, CA 94710
(510) 524-2178
Fax: (510) 524-2221
http://www.peachpit.com
To report errors, please send a note to errata@peachpit.com.
Peachpit Press is a division of Pearson Education.

Editor: Serena Herr
Production Editor: Connie Jeung-Mills
Project Editors: Karen Ohlson and Suki Gear
Technical Editor: Victor Gavenda
Copy Editors: Karen Seriguchi and Elissa Rabellino
Interior Design: Frances Baca
Compositor: David Van Ness
Indexer: Jack Lewis
Cover design and illustration: Frances Baca

ISBN 0-321-20040-3
9 8 7 6 5 4 3 2 1

Printed and bound in the United States of America

Martin Sitter: *This book is dedicated to House Music.*

Robert Brock: *To my wife, Susan—I am so lucky to have married the most amazing person I have ever met.*

Acknowledgments:

Martin Sitter:

Special thanks to Patty Montesion, for keeping me in mind.

Thanks also to Aimee Mackey, for an important introduction.

Thanks to Bryan Low, of AnnexPro.com, for lending me cool stuff.

A deep debt of gratitude to Rennie "Dubnut" Foster, Scott Newton, Matt Densham, Sally Malloy, David Meyer, Brent Charmichael, Jon V., Levi, Matty, Jay Lev, Degree, Koosh, Lori the HiFi Princess, Tiger D'hula, Bill-e and all the other DJ/producers that made Victoria the place to be throughout the '90s, and still to this day.

Robert Brock:

Thanks to Martin Sitter and everyone at Peachpit Press for helping me discover the process of making this book; to Kirt Hamm, creator of the Conservatory of Recording Arts & Sciences, a phenomenal institution where one can learn as much as one teaches; and to Chris Bailey, fellow logician and digital department brother—as always, your input has proved invaluable.

Contents at a Glance

ENVIRONMENT

Table of Contents

*** **★ BUILDING A SONG FROM SCRATCH ★**
(START - CHAPTERS 6-16)

IMPORTING

SETTING TEMPO

REGIONS (EDITING)

OBJECTS
(Creating the ARRANGEMENT)

★(BUILDING A SONG - CONT'D) →

***

✳ BUILDING A SONG FROM SCRATCH ✳

(CONT'D)

✳(CONT'D) →

★ ★ ★

★ BUILDING A SONG FROM SCRATCH ★
(CONCLUSION)

FINISHING
(and)
EXPORTING

RECORDING

(CONFIGURATIONS
SURROUND
SOUND

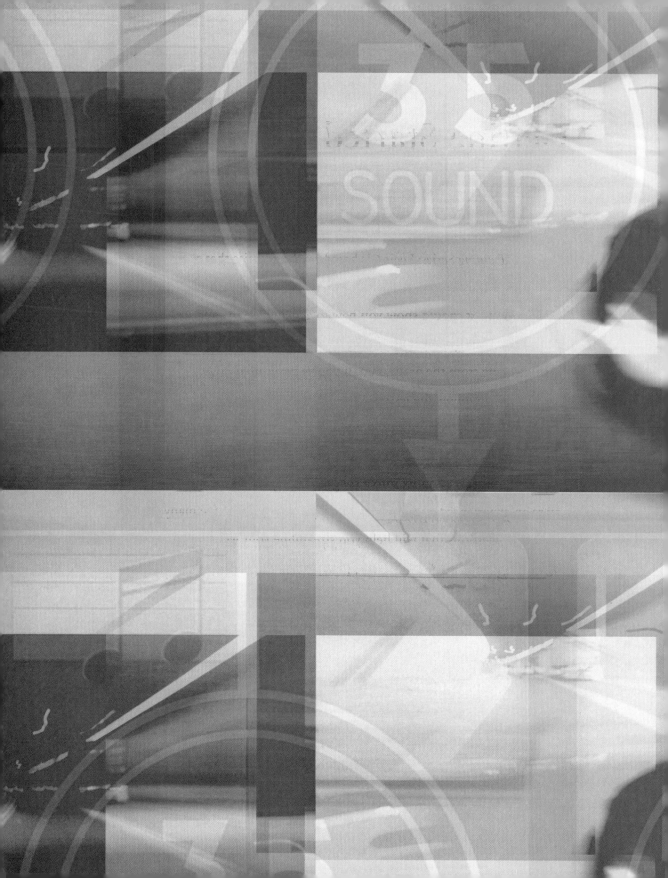

Introduction
Getting Started

Apple Pro Training Series: Logic 6 is based on the premise that a
technical book should be more than a tour of menus, commands,
and windows—it should show you how to actually use the application. In this book, you will learn how to use Logic 6 by building a
complete song from the ground up. If you've never used Logic
before, you can follow the lessons to see how a song is made:
importing audio, arranging audio and MIDI to create a composition, mixing volume levels and pan positions, and adding DSP
effects that turn a good mix into a song that really shines. And if
you're an experienced audio professional, you'll appreciate the many
tips and suggestions that will help you streamline your workflow in
Logic and get the most out of the application.

Will you be able to make a hit track with Logic? Well, there's an old saying: "Many are called, but few are chosen." In the past this was very true, because only the few could afford the equipment necessary for creating professional digital audio. That's the difference Logic 6 brings. In this one application you now have access to synthesizers, a sampler, a sequencing engine, a multitrack audio recorder, and DSP effects that are among the best the industry has to offer. So while many are still called, for the first time in the history of audio production the many now have the power to create the hits of tomorrow.

The Methodology

This book is designed to be an introduction to Logic and is not meant for those who have a lot of experience using this program. Video editors, audio hobbyists, and music producers switching to Logic from other sequencing programs will have the most to gain by reading this book.

This doesn't mean that the book's lessons are basic in nature. Logic is sophisticated software, and the lessons cover all aspects of making music with it. A lot goes into making a good song, so to cover it all this book is divided into four sections:

▶ Lessons 1, 2, and 3 lay the groundwork by introducing you to Logic, its editing windows, and some basic functions such as setting up screensets, using the Transport to play and navigate through a song, and creating personalized key commands—things you'll use throughout the book.

▶ Logic's Environment window is perhaps the single most intimidating window in the program, and it is arguably the one reason why some new users find the program difficult to learn. But this doesn't have to be the case. Lessons 4 and 5 break down these barriers by walking you through the process of customizing Logic to make it work in your studio. In the course of these two lessons you'll learn how to select synthesizers and use audio channels to get sound into and out of Logic. By the end of Lesson 5

you'll have created your own personalized Autoload song that opens every time you launch Logic, and this Autoload song will be perfectly configured to interact with your studio's MIDI devices.

▶ The remaining lessons build an actual song from the ground up! You start by importing MIDI and audio files, then use Logic's editing windows to modify those imported files into an arrangement. Finally, you'll mix the song, add DSP effects to sweeten the sound, and finish by bouncing out a master version of your song that can be recorded to a CD-R or distributed as an MP3 over the Internet.

▶ With the popularity of products like Final Cut Pro and DVD Studio Pro, there can be no doubt that video is an important part of Apple's Pro application line, and these days 5.1 surround is the hot-ticket item. If you're a video editor looking to add polish to your creations, 5.1 surround is a good way to go. Logic 6 is a fantastic 5.1 surround sound editor, and this book contains a bonus lesson that shows you exactly how to set up Logic to create those immersive soundscapes you've been dreaming of.

About the Apple Pro Training Series

Apple Pro Training Series: Logic 6 is part of the official training series for Apple Pro applications developed by experts in the field. The lessons are designed to let you learn at your own pace. If you're new to Logic, you'll learn the fundamental concepts and features you'll need to master the program. If you've been using Logic for a while, you'll find that this book teaches many advanced features, including tips and techniques for using the latest version of Logic.

Although each lesson provides step-by-step instructions for creating a specific project, there's room for exploration and experimentation. It is recommended that you follow the book from start to finish or at least complete the first five chapters before skipping around. Each lesson concludes with a review section summarizing what you've covered.

System Requirements

Before beginning to use *Apple Pro Training Series: Logic 6,* you should have a working knowledge of your computer and its operating system. Make sure that you know how to use the mouse and standard menus and commands and also how to open, save, and close files. If you need to review these techniques, see the printed or online documentation included with your system.

> **NOTE ►** This book is designed for Logic Platinum 6. However, except for the exercise on Automation Curves and the bonus lesson on 5.1 surround mixing, Logic Gold and Logic Audio users will be able to follow most of the exercises without a problem. Where a feature is not available to Logic Gold or Logic Audio users, it is noted in the steps.

Basic system requirements for Logic 6 include:

- ► Mac OS 9.1 or higher (however, this book covers only OS X)
- ► Mac OS X 10.2 or higher
- ► 604/250 MHz or better
- ► 128 MB of RAM or more
- ► CD/DVD drive
- ► Free USB port for XSKey
- ► Low latency audio interface such as the Emagic EMI 2|6 or EMI 6|2
- ► Separate hard disk and MIDI interface recommended

Installing Logic

The CD-ROM that accompanies this book includes a full 30-day license of Logic Platinum 6. Use the following guidelines to install and start your copy of Logic Platinum on a Macintosh OS X 10.2 system.

> **NOTE ►** Instructions for installing Logic 6 under Mac OS 9 are provided on the CD-ROM.

Requesting Your 30-Day Hardware Key

Before you can use your free 30-day Logic 6 license, you must obtain a 30-day hardware key (XSKey) from Peachpit Press.

1   Launch your Web browser and go to
www.peachpit.com/applepro/logickey.

2   Follow the online instructions to order your hardware key. Fulfillment
will take up to ten business days within the United States.

Installing Logic under Mac OS X

Important: You must have administrator privileges to install Logic under
Mac OS X. Also, do not run the installation program with your hardware
key (XSKey) inserted into a USB port.

1   Insert the *APTS Logic 6* CD-ROM into your computer's CD-ROM
drive.

2   Go to the Software folder and double-click the **Logic Platinum
6.1.dmg** file.

The Logic Platinum 6.1 volume icon is created, and it opens to reveal
two folders, named Mac OS X and Mac OS 9.

3   Double-click the Mac OS X folder.

The **Logic Platinum 6 Install** icon appears in the Mac OS X window.

4   Double-click the **Logic Platinum 6 Install** icon.

The Install Logic and Authenticate windows appear.

5   In the Authenticate window, enter your name and password or phrase.

6   In the Install Logic window, follow the onscreen instructions. Choose
the Easy Install option.

7   When the installation process is complete, click the Restart button to reboot your computer.

8   Now, insert your XSKey into any USB port on your computer, or on a USB hub connected to your computer.

9   Start the Logic application by navigating to /Applications/Logic 6 Series/ and double-clicking the **Logic Platinum 6.1.0** icon.

Copying the Logic Lesson Files

The *Apple Pro Training Series: Logic 6* CD-ROM includes folders containing the lesson files used in this course. Each lesson has its own folder, and you should copy these folders to your hard drive to use the files for the lessons. The companion disc also contains a folder called Course Media. Inside this folder you will find all the source audio and MIDI files used in the lessons.

[handwritten margin notes: Program disc — Source (audio & MIDI files) disc (Step 4 below)]

To install the Logic Lesson files:

1   Insert the *Apple Pro Training Series: Logic 6* CD-ROM into your CD-ROM drive.

2   Create a folder on your hard drive and name it Logic Lessons.

3   Drag the Lessons folder from the CD into the Logic Lessons folder on your hard drive.

4   If possible, drag the Course Media folder from the CD onto a hard disk (or disk partition) called Audio. If you don't have a hard disk called Audio, drag the Course Media folder into the Logic Lessons folder on your hard drive.

MORE INFO ► *These lessons were created with the Course Media folder on a hard disk named Audio. Logic 6 uses absolute links to reference media files to songs, so to preserve the references between the lesson song files and the source media, it helps to copy the Course Media folder to a hard disk (or disk partition) called Audio. This is, however (not) mandatory—Logic 6 will search for media files it can't find. However, if you (do) have a hard disk named Audio, copy the Course Media folder there to make opening lesson files easier.*

Resources

Apple Pro Training Series: Logic 6 is not intended as a comprehensive reference manual, nor does it replace the documentation that comes with the Logic application. For comprehensive information about program features, refer to these resources:

- The Reference Guide. Accessed through the Logic Help menu, the Reference Guide contains a complete description of all features.
- Emagic's Web site: www.emagic.de.
- The Emagic Infoweb: www.emagic.de/support/infoweb/.

Apple Pro Certification Program

The Apple Pro Training and Certification Programs are designed to keep you at the forefront of Apple's digital media technology while giving you a competitive edge in today's ever-changing job market. Whether you're an editor, graphic designer, sound designer, special effects artist, or teacher, these training tools are meant to help you expand your skills.

Upon completing the course material in this book, you can become an Apple Pro by taking the certification exam at an Apple Authorized Training Center. Certification is offered in Final Cut Pro 3, DVD Studio Pro 2, Shake 3, and Logic 6. Successful certification as an Apple Pro gives you official recognition of your knowledge of Apple's professional applications while allowing you to market yourself to employers and clients as a skilled, pro-level user of Apple products.

To find an Authorized Training Center near you, go to www.apple.com/software/pro/training.

For those who prefer to learn in an instructor-led setting, Apple also offers training courses at Apple Authorized Training Centers worldwide. These courses, which use the Apple Pro Training Series books as their curriculum, are taught by Apple Certified Trainers and balance concepts and lectures with hands-on labs and exercises. Apple Authorized Training Centers for Pro products have been carefully selected and have met Apple's highest standards in all areas, including facilities, instructors, course delivery, and infrastructure. The goal of the program is to offer Apple customers, from beginners to the most seasoned professionals, the highest quality training experience.

1

Lesson 1
The Workspace

This lesson serves as a general primer to get you into the swing of using Logic's workspace. In the following steps you'll explore all of the windows that make up Logic, and along the way you'll learn a few important tricks and techniques that make working with Logic easier. Even if you have a bit of experience with the program, take the time to work through this lesson's steps. Don't forget: This book is a front-to-back tutorial that uses Logic to build an actual song. Many of the concepts in these early chapters are vital to later lessons, so to be properly prepared, don't miss a step. With that in mind, let's explore the editing windows that combine to give Logic its immense power over sound.

Launching Logic

Installing Logic creates a folder named Logic 6 Series in Mac OS X's Applications folder, located at the root level of your startup disk (the startup disk is the one that contains your system software). Inside the Logic 6 Series folder you'll see several other folders and files. Let's open it up now and take a look around.

"EXS"

1. In the ~~Finder~~, locate the Logic 6 Series folder and open it up.
   (Browser)

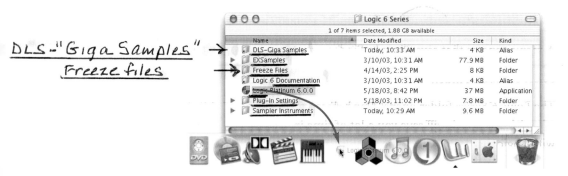

Logic 6 Series			
7 items, 1.69 GB available			
Name ▲	Date Modified	Size	Kind
▶ EXSamples	3/10/03, 10:31 AM	77.9 MB	Folder
Logic 6 Documentation	3/10/03, 10:31 AM	4 KB	Alias — *Manual*
Logic Platinum 6.0.0	5/18/03, 8:42 PM	37 MB	Application
▶ Plug-In Settings	5/18/03, 11:02 PM	7.8 MB	Folder
▶ Sampler Instruments	Today, 10:29 AM	9.6 MB	Folder

EXS Software Sampler [MARK II]

These folders are all named for the content they contain. For example, the EXS Mark II is a software sampler made by Emagic (and the preferred software sampler for use with Logic). Inside the EXSamples folder you'll find audio samples used by EXS instruments, while the instruments themselves are located inside the Sampler Instruments folder. The Plug-In Settings folder contains presets for all of Logic's DSP (digital signal processing) plug-ins, plus any saved settings for third-party AV plug-ins. Of course, the most obviously important file in this folder is Logic Platinum 6.0.0, because clicking its Logic application icon launches Logic. But don't do that yet. Let's make the Logic application easy to find by putting it in your computer's ~~Dock~~. *(Desktop)*

2. Drag the Logic application icon to the Dock and drop it there.

DLS –"Giga Samples"
Freeze files

Logic 6 Series			
1 of 7 items selected, 1.88 GB available			
Name ▲	Date Modified	Size	Kind
DLS–Giga Samples	Today, 10:33 AM	4 KB	Alias
▶ EXSamples	3/10/03, 10:31 AM	77.9 MB	Folder
▶ Freeze Files	4/14/03, 2:25 PM	8 KB	Folder
Logic 6 Documentation	3/10/03, 10:31 AM	4 KB	Alias
Logic Platinum 6.0.0	5/18/03, 8:42 PM	37 MB	Application
▶ Plug-In Settings	5/18/03, 11:02 PM	7.8 MB	Folder
▶ Sampler Instruments	Today, 10:29 AM	9.6 MB	Folder

3 Close the Logic 6 Series folder.

Placing the Logic application icon in the Dock has advantages beyond making it easier to find. As you continue to grow with Logic, there's a good chance you'll end up using Emagic's EXS sampler quite a bit. This sampler's instruments and sample files (or aliases to them) are all stored in the EXSamples and Sampler Instruments folders, which you'll often need to access. Even if you don't use the EXS, the Logic 6 Series folder contains a Documentation folder with PDFs that hold valuable information. As a result, you will need to open the Logic 6 Series folder quite often. With the Logic application in the Dock, this becomes a simple process.

★
Emagic →
EXS Sampler

★
"PDF" →
(Documentation)

EX SAMPLES and
Sampler INSTRUMENTS
FOLDER"

NOTE ▶ Emagic's EXS sampler is a software sampler perfectly designed to work with Logic. In fact, it's so well designed that if you're making music with Logic, it's essential! But don't take our word for it—a 28-day demo of the EXS sampler is included with this book (along with demos of all Emagic's software instruments), so open it up and see for yourself.

4 Hold the Control key at the bottom-left corner of your computer's keyboard, and then click and hold the Logic application icon in the Dock.

"Show
IN
Finder"

A menu appears that says Show In Finder.

5 Select Show In Finder.

The Logic 6 Series folder opens! Don't discount the power of this simple trick, because it will save you a lot of time in your future work with Logic.

⑥ Close the Logic 6 Series folder, then single-click the Dock's Logic Application icon.

Logic opens, and the default workspace appears on your computer's monitor.

NOTE ► The *workspace* is the name for all of Logic's editing windows combined. It's the *space* you *work* in as you make music.

handwritten notes: WORKSPACE

handwritten notes: "Untitled ARRANGE"

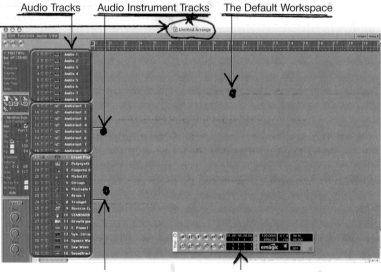

Audio Tracks   Audio Instrument Tracks   The Default Workspace

GM MIDI Tracks   Transport Window

handwritten notes: (Generic WORKSPACE) BASICS
handwritten notes: (MIDI) External devices and LOGIC CUSTOMIZATION

Logic's default workspace represents a *generic* studio with 8 audio tracks, 8 audio instrument tracks, and 16 MIDI tracks representing all the MIDI channels found on a General MIDI (GM) synthesizer. This is an adequate base for working in Logic, but it could be better. For example, your studio probably has more than one synthesizer. You may also have a few digital-effects units and perhaps even a sampler or two. Logic's default workspace is not set up to communicate with these extra MIDI devices, so you need to customize the workspace to better represent your studio. In Lessons 4 and 5 you will do just that—you'll take this generic workspace and customize it to exactly reflect the setup of your studio. In fact, the song that you'll explore in this lesson has a customized workspace, as you'll see in the next exercise.

> **NOTE** ▶ *General MIDI (GM) is a protocol developed by Roland that defines the type, name, and order of synthesizer sound programs. GM was an early attempt at standardizing the way synthesizers make sound, but as time passed, it became obvious that music producers wanted more sounds than the GM sound set offered. Today, few synthesizers adhere to the GM sound set. However, there are notable exceptions, such as the QuickTime synthesizer that comes as part of OS X.*

[handwritten margin note:] ★ General MIDI ("GM" standard Synthesis Sounds)

Opening a Song File

There are several ways to open a Logic song file. For example, you can drag a song file and drop it onto the Logic application icon (in either the Finder or the Dock), or double-click a song file in any Finder window.

[handwritten margin note:] ★ FINDER IS "Look in" box of Windows

With Logic running, a common way to open a song file is to use the File > Open command located in Logic's main menu bar. To follow along with this lesson, use these steps to open the **01-The_Workspace-Start** song file:

1   Choose File > Open.

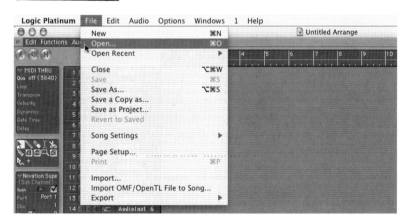

NOTE ▶ The File > Open Recent option offers a convenient way of opening songs you've recently been working on. If you select this option, a submenu listing recently opened songs appears. You may now instantly open a song by clicking its name in this submenu, which saves you from having to locate the file on your hard disks.

Logic's default song should still be open in the background, so a dialog appears asking if you'd like to close the currently open song before opening the new one.

Logic lets you work on several songs at one time, which often comes in handy. For example, you can cut and paste MIDI or audio regions between songs, or compare the DSP settings of a finished song against those of a song you're working on. But for now, let's concentrate on one song at a time.

2   Click the Close button.

The default song closes, and an Open dialog appears.

3   Navigate to the file named **01-The_Workspace-Start**, and click Open.

A dialog appears alerting you that an audio file used in this song cannot be located.

NOTE ▶ The file not found may be different than the file listed in the following figure.

This is a dialog you'll see time and time again as you work through this book's lessons, but don't worry—it's an easy problem to solve. Here's what's happening: Logic uses *absolute links* to reference audio files, which means that it locates files by following the file's disk name > folder name > filename. Because your computer's hard disks are very likely named differently from the one used to produce these lessons, you will have to search for audio files whenever you open a song that has audio in it. Luckily, this is a simple process!

4   Click the Search button.

Logic automatically searches your hard disks and finds all files that have the same name as the missing one.

5   Select the file you want to use.

Unless you've copied this book's sample files to several different places on your hard disks, only one file should be found. If several files are found (as in the figure above) you'll have to choose the correct one by examining the file paths beside the search dialog's Select buttons.

The **01-The_Workspace-Start** song opens.

TIP ▶ If you copy the Course Media folder of this book's companion CD-ROM, and place it on a hard disk (or disk partition) named Audio, you will not have to relink the audio files.

Getting to Know the Arrange Window

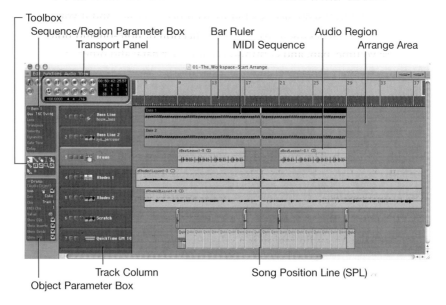

Toolbox
Sequence/Region Parameter Box   Bar Ruler   Audio Region
Transport Panel   MIDI Sequence   Arrange Area

Track Column   Song Position Line (SPL)
Object Parameter Box

Can you see sound? With Logic, you can. A soundscape is more or less an aural painting, filled with emotion and colored by experience in much the same way as a painting hung on the wall reflects the mood of the artist when she picked up her brush. In a painting, the artist arranges strokes and dabs of color across a canvas to make a visual picture. In Logic, you arrange strokes and dabs of sound across the Arrange widow to make a song. The Arrange window is your sound canvas. It's also Logic's main editing window.

Let's take a brief look at the various parts of the Arrange window.

The Transport Panel The Transport panel holds buttons used to control Logic's playback and recording functions.

The Arrange Area The heart of the Arrange window is the Arrange area. This large rectangular space occupies most of the Arrange window, and it has one function only: It's used to arrange MIDI sequences and/or audio regions together, to make a song.

MIDI Sequences MIDI sequences are little boxes that contain a collection of MIDI data. A MIDI sequence is a tightly wrapped package, and if you open one up by double-clicking it, you'll see a collection of note-on and note-off messages; volume, pan, and continuous controller data; and other information (such as sysex messages) that tell a synthesizer how to play notes.

It's important to note that MIDI sequences do not contain sounds! The sounds all sit in your synthesizers. Think of a player piano in an Old West saloon. In this device, a roll of paper with holes punched in it cycles through the piano. The punched-out holes represent note information that tells the player piano which keys to press and when to press them. If your synthesizer is a player piano, MIDI sequences are the rolls of punched paper that tell it which keys to press.

Audio Regions An audio region is a selected area of an audio file. Like MIDI sequences in the Arrange window, audio regions look like horizontal boxes. But there's a difference: While MIDI sequences hold MIDI data that plays your MIDI devices, audio regions point to digital audio files stored on your hard disks. This can be audio recorded directly into Logic through your sound card, audio imported from a folder on your hard disk or a CD, or even converted MP3 files downloaded from the Internet (the OS X version of Logic 6 will happily import and export MP3 files, which makes it easier than ever to share and publish your songs on the Web).

The Bar Ruler The Bar Ruler is divided into bars and beats. It's your song's timeline. As the song plays, the Bar Ruler works in conjunction with the Song Position Locator (SPL) to help you determine the current playback position in your song.

The Track Column In Logic, all MIDI sequences and audio regions are recorded and arranged on horizontal lines called *tracks.* These tracks are listed vertically, from the top of the Arrange window toward the bottom. Toward the left edge of the Arrange window there is a column displaying the names of your song's tracks—this is called the Track column.

The Sequence/Region Parameter box and the Object Parameter box These boxes update to show you information about MIDI sequences and audio regions selected in the Arrange area. There are a lot of settings in these boxes, each with a unique purpose, so let's defer the discussion of these boxes until the appropriate lessons later in this book.

The Toolbox MIDI sequences and audio regions sometimes need to be erased, cut, or combined together. The tools for these jobs can be found in the Arrange window's toolbox. There are many tools in this box, and each is designed for a specific purpose. The functions of most of these tools are obvious from their icons, and you'll discover how to use each one as you work through this book's lessons. In this lesson, we'll stick to some general tips about selecting tools quickly and efficiently.

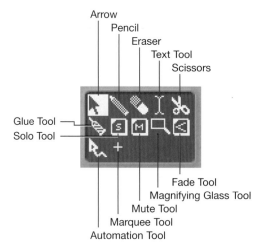

Selecting Tools

Selecting tools from the toolbox is every bit as easy as you'd expect—just move the pointer over the tool and click it! But still, there are some tricks you can use to make selecting tools quicker. Let's explore a few of them now.

NOTE ▶ The following tricks work in all editing windows that have a toolbox.

1 In the toolbox, click the Pencil, and then move the pointer over the Arrange area.

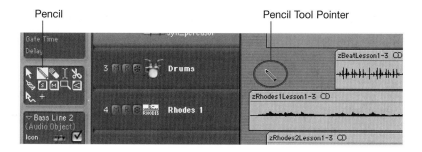

Toolbox tools are designed to work on Arrange area objects, so the selected tool does not appear until you move the pointer into the Arrange area.

Logic gives you access to both a main tool and a secondary tool. The main tool is the one currently selected and highlighted in the toolbox. The secondary tool is reserved for any function you use often and is accessed by holding down the Command key. For example, if you're constantly returning to the toolbox to grab the Glue tool, save yourself some time by assigning the Glue tool as your secondary tool, and it will become available each time you press the Command key. Let's assign the Glue tool as the secondary tool now.

2 Hold down the Command key and select the Glue tool.

3 Move the pointer over the Arrange area.

The pointer still shows the Pencil tool.

4   Press Command.

While you hold down Command, the pointer turns into the Glue tool.

To save yourself the effort of moving the pointer all the way over to the toolbox, you can open the toolbox right under the pointer's current position in the Arrange area by holding down the Escape key.

5   With the pointer over the Arrange area, press the Escape key.

The toolbox opens under the pointer.

Press the Escape key to open the toolbox under the pointer.

You can select a tool from this floating toolbox by either clicking it or pressing a number key.

6   Press the 3 key.

The floating toolbox disappears, and the pointer turns into the Eraser tool.

7   Press Escape to open the floating toolbox, and then press the 1 key to select the Arrow tool.

Once again the floating toolbox disappears, and the pointer turns into the Arrow tool. You will need the Arrow tool for the rest of this lesson's exercises, so leave it selected.

Exploring the Transport Panel

The Transport panel contains buttons that control Logic's playback and record functions. These buttons look similar to the control buttons on a cassette deck or recordable audio CD player, and indeed, they work exactly the same way. The Transport panel's other displays are used to edit your song's tempo, move the SPL (Song Position Line), or set up loop boundaries for cycle playback and record modes, as you'll learn in Lesson 2, "Using The Transport."

Let's use the Transport panel controls to start and stop playback of your song.

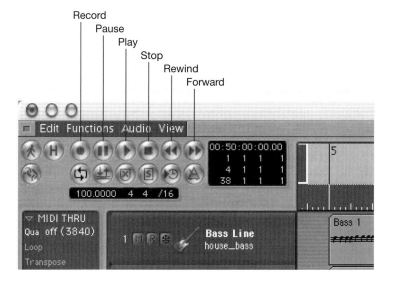

1   Click the Transport's Play button to begin playing back the song.

The song plays.

2   Click the Stop button to stop playback.

The song stops.

Feel free to play and stop the song at any time as you explore the various sections of this lesson. After all, Logic is meant to make music, and hearing the song is a big part of the process!

Getting to Know the Editing Windows

The Arrange window is your entrance into Logic. It's the center of this program, and the window from which all editing decisions are initiated. The rest of Logic's editing windows are all used to either add or affect the MIDI sequences and audio regions arranged in this window. You've already explored the Arrange window and seen what its various parts do, so let's now turn our attention to Logic's editing windows.

A First Look at the Track Mixer

The Track Mixer is a virtual mixing console used to position Logic's tracks "in the mix," or give tracks their own unique place in the aural picture you're painting. Using this window, you can change a track's volume or panorama (pan) position, insert DSP effects like reverb or dynamic range compression (audio and virtual instrument tracks only), or mute and solo individual tracks. The Track Mixer is explored in detail in Lesson 11, "Basic Mixing," but for now let's open it up and take a quick look.

1   To open the Track Mixer, choose Windows > Open Track Mixer (Cmd-2).

The Track Mixer opens.

The Track Mixer is used to mix the sound of audio and MIDI tracks together. The Track Mixer is an adaptive window that mirrors the number and order of tracks in the Arrange window. For example, the Track Mixer currently has seven channels, each corresponding to an Arrange window track. Each time you add a track to the Arrange window, it automatically appears in the Track Mixer. If you delete a track from the Arrange window, it also disappears from the Track Mixer.

2   Click the red Close button in the top-left corner of the Track Mixer to close it.

A First Look at the Event List

The Event List presents a catalog of song events, such as MIDI note events or region start events. This editor replaces the graphic interface of the other editors with a straightforward list displaying a progression of song events over time, and it's covered in Lesson 10, "Exploring the MIDI Editors."

1 To open the Event List, choose Windows > Open Event List.

The Event List opens.

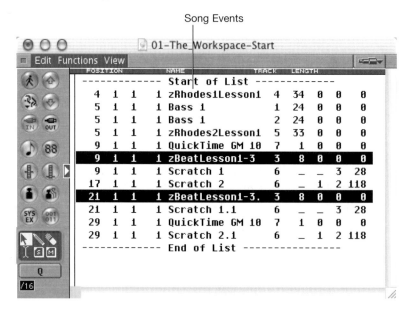

The Event List's display area currently shows the start times of all the Arrange window's MIDI sequences and audio regions. Notice that two events are currently selected. The selected events reflect the Objects selected in the Arrange window (depending on the Objects selected in the Arrange window, you might have different events selected than the ones displayed in the figure above).

2   In the Event List, click the first Bass 1 event.

The Bass 1 event is selected—and the Bass 1 MIDI sequence is also selected back in the Arrange window, as you can tell by the black highlight across its top. This demonstrates an important feature of the Event List: When you select an event in one window, the same event is also selected in all other open editing windows. This feature really helps you keep track of what you're editing and where, when the workspace gets crowded with several open editors.

3   Select a few other events, and watch as the corresponding objects are selected in the Arrange area.

4   Close the Event List.

A Quick Look at the Score Edit Window

If you're coming to Logic from a formal music background, you'll feel right at home in the Score Edit window (the Score editor). This editor uses traditional music notation (staffs and notes) as an interface for programming and editing MIDI sequences. Using Logic's Print function, you can even print out complete musical scores of the MIDI sequences you program in Logic (including sequences created with any of Logic's other MIDI editing windows).

Due to its reliance on music notation, the Score editor is suited to a small subset of Logic users—those who can read music. If you can't read music, don't let this scare you, because *you don't need to!* Logic's other editors graphically display notes and note events, so there's no need to ever get into music theory. In the next few steps you'll open the Score editor and take a look around, but this will be one of the few times you'll see the Score editor in these lessons.

1   In the Arrange area, select the Bass 1 MIDI sequence.

The Score editor is a MIDI editor. Before you open it, it's best to have a MIDI sequence selected so that Logic knows what MIDI data to display.

2   Choose Windows > Open Score (Cmd-3).

The Score editor opens to display the Bass 1's MIDI data as notes in a musical score.

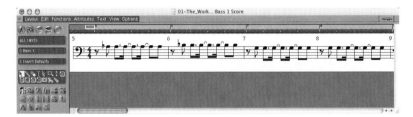

3   Close the Score editor, and click the Arrange area's background to make sure that no objects are selected in the Arrange area.

4   Once again, choose Windows > Open Score (Cmd-3).

The Score editor reopens, but this time it displays three lines of notes. These lines represent the notes from each of the song's three MIDI tracks. This demonstrates another important point about Logic's MIDI editors: If no MIDI sequence is selected when you open a MIDI editor, the editor shows the MIDI data of *all* the song's MIDI sequences, together (the exception to this rule is the Hyper Editor, as you'll learn in Lesson 10, "Exploring the MIDI Editors"). This is a great technique to keep in mind, because it allows you to compare or edit the MIDI data of more than one sequence at the same time.

5   Close the Score editor.

A First Look at the Hyper Editor

The Hyper Editor is a very specialized editor that displays control-change messages, but it can also be used to program drum sequences. This editor is covered in Lesson 10, "Exploring the MIDI Editors."

1 Select the first MIDI sequence in the QuickTime track (Track 7).

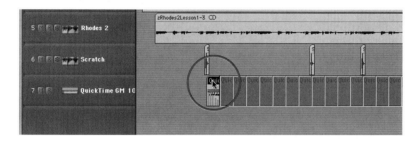

Unlike the other MIDI editors, the Hyper Editor will not open unless a MIDI sequence is selected in the Arrange area, so this is an important step.

2 Choose Windows > Open Hyper Edit (Cmd-5).

The Hyper Editor opens.

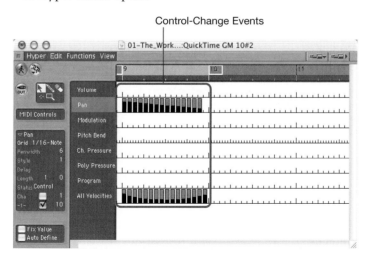

In the Hyper Editor, control-change events are displayed as vertical beams with a black bottom and gray top. The line dividing the top and bottom sections determines the value of the event. In an exercise above, you used the Transport to play your song. And you may have noticed that this QuickTime track is actually a hi-hat line. Let's check out the hi-hat line using a special layer of the Hyper Editor.

3   On the left edge of the Hyper Editor, click and hold the box that says MIDI Controls.

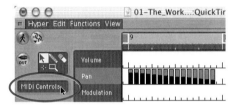

This is the Hyper Editor's Layer box, and clicking it opens the Layer menu. (Layers are officially known as Hypersets, so you may encounter this term as well.) Right now the Layer menu holds two selections: MIDI Controls and GM Drum Kit.

4   Choose GM Drum Kit.

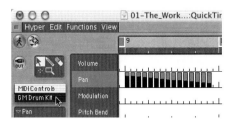

The Hyper Editor changes to display GM MIDI drum events.

5   Scroll down the list until you see the events on the Closed HH line.

These are the MIDI sequence's hi-hat hits.

6   Close the Hyper Editor.

A First Look at the Matrix Editor

The Matrix editor displays notes as rectangles along a piano keyboard, and unless you're coming to Logic from a traditional music background (in which case you might prefer the Score editor), the Matrix editor will be your primary MIDI editing window. Like the other MIDI editors, the Matrix editor is examined in detail in Lesson 10, "Exploring the MIDI Editors."

1 Select the Bass 1 MIDI sequence, and then choose Windows > Open Matrix Edit (Cmd-6).

The Matrix editor opens.

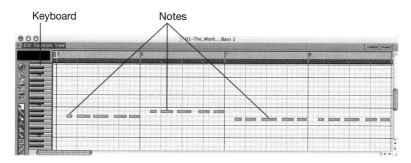

A MIDI controller keyboard provides the most common way of entering notes into Logic, and the Matrix editor obligingly provides a keyboard along its left edge. In the Matrix Editor's display area, note events (notes) look like colored rectangles, and their positions along the keyboard show you exactly which notes they represent.

2 Close the Matrix editor.

NOTE ▶ As with the Score editor, if no MIDI sequence is displayed when you open the Matrix editor, it defaults to show the note events for all of your song's MIDI sequences.

A First Look at the Environment

The Environment is a virtual representation of your recording studio. When properly configured, Logic's Environment contains a separate Instrument Object to represent each MIDI device in your studio. New Logic users find the Environment to be Logic's most intimidating window, and this window alone is responsible for Logic's undeserved reputation as a difficult program to learn. This is likely because the default workspace's environment is filled with objects you simply don't need. It's too confusing! In this book, we strip the Environment down to the raw essentials and let you build your own customized Environment that exactly reflects the setup of your studio (this process is covered in Lessons 4 and 5). In a few short lessons you'll feel completely at home working in the Environment, but before getting too deep into this very important window, let's open it up and take a quick look around.

There are several ways to open the Environment. For example, you can choose Windows > Open Environment or press Cmd-8 to pop it open onscreen. However, the Environment window has many layers, and opening it from the Windows menu provides very little control over which layer will appear onscreen (typically, the last layer edited will be the one that is shown). To make sure your screen looks like the figures below, let's open the Environment using a slightly different technique.

1   In the Arrange window's Track column, double-click the Drums track.

   The Environment window opens to show several channel strips. Notice that the Drums channel strip is selected. This is the channel that corresponds to the track you double-clicked in the Arrange window.

The Environment primarily acts as Logic's ears and mouth: It listens for incoming audio/MIDI information, which it then transmits into Logic's sequencer, and it also speaks, or sends audio/MIDI information back out to your synthesizers, samplers, and sound card. It's extremely important to understand that the Environment is Logic's link to the outside world, because without the Environment, Logic could not communicate with your studio's external devices.

The Environment itself is organized into layers, much the same as the Hyper Editor. Layers are selected using the Environment's Layer box, which is located directly under the toolbox in the top-left corner. You can switch layers by making a selection from the Environment's Layer menu.

2 Click and hold the Environment's Layer box.

The Layer menu appears.

3   From the Layer menu, choose QuickTime Synt.

The Audio layer is replaced by the QuickTime Synt layer. This layer holds the QuickTime Synth Object responsible for the song's hi-hat line (you are going to build this layer in Lesson 4).

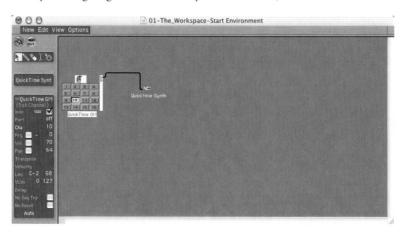

4   Close the Environment window.

A First Look at the Audio Window

The Audio window holds and organizes all of your song's audio files. You can also use this window to rename audio files and regions, to optimize files by deleting unused portions, to move files from one hard disk to another, and to change your song's sampling rate. But most important of all, the Audio window is used to add audio files from your hard disks to your song, a process that's fully covered in Lesson 6, "Using Prerecorded Media."

Let's look at how this window displays information about audio tracks.

1   Choose Audio > Audio Window (Cmd-9).

The Audio window opens. As mentioned above, the Audio window displays your song's audio files. These files are represented by thin horizontal rectangles that have a triangle on their left edge. If you click the triangle, it twirls down and the Audio file expands to show its audio regions.

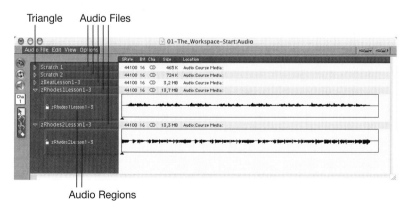

2   Click the triangle beside the **zBeatLesson1-3** audio file.

The triangle twirls down, and its audio region is displayed. These are the two audio regions in the Arrange window's Drums track.

3   Click **zBeatLesson1-3**'s first region.

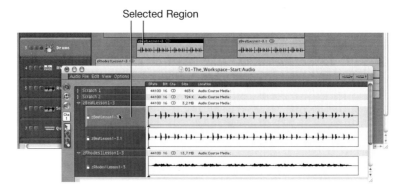

The region is selected, and back in the Arrange window the first Object in the Drums track is also selected. As you might have guessed, this is exactly the same region in both windows! You saw this interconnection between Logic's editing windows a few exercises ago when selecting events in the Event List. As your songs become more complex, with dozens or even hundreds of different Objects crowding the editing windows, you'll find this interconnectivity an invaluable way to locate Objects in Logic's various editing windows.

4   Close the Audio window.

A First Look at the Sample Edit Window

The Sample Edit window (Sample editor) is used to adjust the length and anchor points of your song's audio regions. This window lets you make sample-accurate edits to audio files, which means the Sample editor gives you such precise control that you can actually even edit the individual samples that make up your audio files. This comes in handy when you need to make tight drum loops or edit pops and clicks out of audio recordings.

Let's open this window and take a look.

1   An audio region must be selected before the Sample editor will open, so in the Arrange window select the first audio region in the Drums track.

2   Choose Audio > Sample Editor (or simply double-click on the selected region).

The Sample editor opens. You'll notice right away that this window provides a very accurate view of the region's waveform—and indeed, that's its purpose! It's the Sample editor, and it lets you zoom right down to the individual sample level of any audio region in your song.

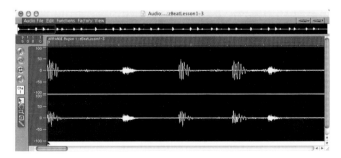

NOTE ▶ With version 6, Logic is now capable of sample-accurate display of waveforms right in the Arrange window. However, it's often much more convenient to use the Sample editor to make precise edits to audio regions, because it saves you from having to zoom in on objects in the Arrange window and then zoom back out after you've made your edits.

3   Close the Sample editor.

Using Screensets

Screensets are customized window combinations you create and assign to your keyboard's number keys. Efficiently using screensets is one secret to mastering Logic. Time is money, and screensets save you time. So do screensets save you money? Well, only if you use them!

NOTE ▶ You may ask yourself, why bother? Isn't it just as easy to open windows as needed and close them when you're done? The short answer is, no. Screensets exactly recall the screen positions of windows, their zoom values, and even the type of tool selected. As a simple example, Screenset 6 could show the Matrix editor with the Pencil tool enabled, while Screenset 16 shows the same Matrix editor but with the Velocity tool enabled. By alternately switching between Screenset 6 and 16, you can flip back and forth between tools (editing notes and velocities) without returning the pointer to the Matrix editor's toolbox to select the next tool. Add in different zoom values, and you've unleashed some true screenset power.

Let's check out some screensets that are already set up in the song you are working on.

1   Press the 2 key.

The Track Mixer appears on your screen. If you look in the menu bar, you'll notice the number 2 to the right of the word Windows. This indicates that you are currently looking at Screenset 2.

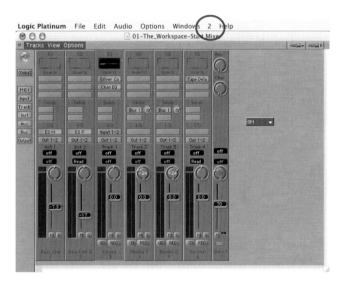

2 Press the number keys in order, from 3 to 9, and check out each screenset.

These first nine screensets match the order of the editing windows as listed in the Windows menu, with one extra—Screenset 9 is the Audio window. Throughout this book's lessons you will often use these screensets when accessing Logic's editing windows, so don't change them!

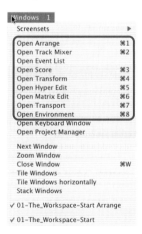

Creating a Screenset

As you saw above, the first nine screensets are used to open Logic's individual editing windows, providing a fast way to call up editing windows when you need them. Of course, this means that any custom screensets you create will need to be saved to the double-digit numbers, starting at 11.

There are a few things to keep in mind when creating screensets. First, a value of 0 is not allowed, which means that screensets 0, 10, 20, 30, and so on are not available. Second, to call screensets above 9, you must hold down the Control key as you type in the number. But other than that, using double-digit screensets is just as easy as using the first nine. Let's practice now by creating a custom screenset and assigning it to Screenset 11.

> **NOTE** ▶ Logic lets you store up to 90 different screensets per song.

1   Hold down the Control key and press 1 and then 1 again.

Screenset 11 appears on your screen—sort of! Screenset 11 is currently empty, but if you look beside the Windows menu, you'll see the number 11, so you know you're in the right place.

2   Choose Audio > Audio Window (Cmd-9).

3   Choose Windows > Open Arrange (Cmd-1).

You should now have both the Audio and Arrange windows open in Screenset 11.

4   Choose Windows > Tile Windows horizontally.

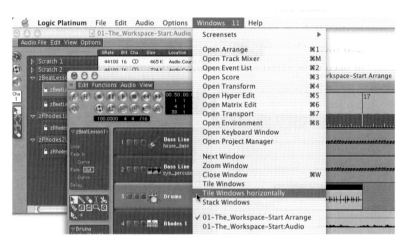

The Windows are tiled, with the Arrange window on top and the Audio window on the bottom. This is a common screenset used for adding audio to the Arrange window, and you'll learn how to use this screenset in Lesson 6, "Using Prerecorded Media."

Congratulations! You've just created a screenset.

5   Press the 1 key.

Screenset 1 opens to show just the Arrange window.

6   Hold down Control, and press 1 and then 1 again.

Screenset 11 reappears just as you left it, with the Arrange window tiled above the Audio window.

Copying a Screenset

As you edit in Logic, from time to time you'll create a window layout that is really useful. To save it for later use, copy the window layout to its own screenset by following the steps in this excercise.

1   Press 1 to select Screenset 1.

The Arrange window opens.

2   Choose Windows > Open Matrix Edit.

The Matrix editor opens.

3   Position the Arrange window and Matrix editor so that you can clearly see both.

4   Choose Windows > Screensets > Copy Screenset.

A copy of your current screenset is stored in the Clipboard.

5   Hold down Control, and press 1 and then 2 to open Screenset 12.

6   Choose Windows > Screensets > Paste Screenset.

Screenset 1 is pasted into Screenset 12.

7   Press 1 to open Screenset 1, and close the Matrix editor.

Now, Screenset 1 returns to showing just the Arrange window.

8   Hold down Control, and press 1 and then 2.

Screenset 12 opens to show the Arrange window and Matrix editor.

NOTE ▶   You can also copy screensets by holding down Ctrl-Shift and pressing the screenset number. Two-digit screensets are copied using key commands Ctrl-Shift-1 and then 1 (while holding down Ctrl-Shift), through Ctrl-Shift-9 and then 9 (while holding down Ctrl-Shift).

Locking a Screenset

Locking a screenset ensures that it can't be permanently altered. Under normal conditions, if you change the layout of a screenset, the changes are automatically stored. By locking the screenset, you can make changes to the layout, but each time you return to that screenset, you'll return to the original, and not the altered layout.

To try out this feature, let's lock Screenset 11.

1   Hold down Control, and press 1 and then 1 again to go to Screenset 11.

The Arrange and Audio windows appear.

2   Choose Windows > Screensets > Lock Screenset (Shift-L).

In Logic's main menu bar, a dot appears before the screenset number (beside the Windows menu). This indicates that this screenset is locked.

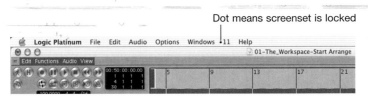

3 While still in Screenset 11, choose Windows > Tile Windows (not "Tile Windows horizontally").

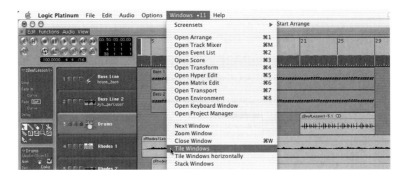

The Arrange and Audio windows tile vertically on the screen. Oops! The Arrange window displays tracks, which by their very nature are wide and short. This screen layout makes it hard to see the Arrange window's tracks, and consequently it's not that useful. Thank goodness you locked Screenset 11:

4 Hold down Control and press 1 and then 1 again to recall the locked Screenset 11.

The windows revert back to the way Screenset 11 was when you locked it.

NOTE ▸ To unlock the screenset, choose Windows > Screensets > Lock Screenset (Shift-L) again.

5 Press 1 to return to Screenset 1.

What You've Learned *✷CHAPTER 1 SUMMARY✷*

✓ Placing the Logic application icon in the ~~Dock~~ makes it easy to find when you want to launch Logic. Ctrl-clicking the Logic application in the Dock lets you quickly open the folder that contains the Logic application.

✗DOCK = (Windows)
DESKTOP ✗

✓ Pressing the Escape key opens a floating toolbox under the pointer. To select a tool from the floating toolbox, use your computer keyboard's number keys.

✓ To open any of Logic's editing windows except the Audio and Sample windows, use the Windows menu. The Audio and Sample windows are located in the Audio menu.

✓ The Arrange window is Logic's primary editing window, and the one from which all editing decisions are initiated. This window is used to arrange the sequences and regions that combine to make your song.

✓ The Track Mixer is a virtual mixing console used to position Logic's tracks "in the mix." Using this window, you can change a track's volume or panorama (pan) position, insert DSP effects like reverb or dynamic range compression, and mute and solo individual tracks.

✓ The Event List presents a catalog of song events, such as MIDI note events or region start events. This editor replaces the graphic interface of the other editors with a straightforward list displaying a progression of song events over time.

✓ The Score editor uses traditional music notation (staffs and notes) as an interface for programming and editing MIDI sequences.

✓ The Hyper Editor displays control-change messages, but it can also be used to program drum sequences.

✓ The Matrix editor displays notes as beams stretched across a piano keyboard, and it shows the length, position, and velocity of each note in a MIDI sequence.

✓ The Environment is a virtual representation of your recording studio. When properly configured, Logic's Environment contains a separate Instrument Object to represent each MIDI device in your studio.

(Cont'd) ⟶

✓ The Audio window holds and organizes all of your song's audio files.

✓ The Sample editor is used to adjust the lengths and anchor points of your song's audio regions.

✓ Screensets are customized window combinations you create and assign to your keyboard's number keys.

2

Start	02-The_Transport-Start
Complete	02-The_Transport-Finished
Time	Approximately 30 minutes
Goals	Learn how to read the various Transport displays
	Transport the Song Position Line (SPL) to different points in your song
	Use the Transport to play, pause, and stop your song
	Set left and right locators to define a cycle region
	Use the Cycle mode to loop the playback of a certain part of your song
	Experiment with Skip mode

Using the Transport

The Transport contains all of Logic's playback and record functions, and it can be thought of as the control area used to *transport* you to various points in your arrangement. In the last lesson you got a brief introduction to the Transport panel in the top-left corner of the Arrange window, and you used it to play and stop the song, but Logic also contains a dedicated window, called the Transport window, that contains all of the same functions as the Arrange window's Transport panel, plus a few more. In this lesson you are going to learn about all of the Transport's functions—all, that is, except the ones that govern recording (the Transport's recording functions are detailed in Lesson 15, "Recording").

Exploring the Transport Window

The Transport window, or Transport bar, is like mission control for your song. This window contains all the buttons and displays that play the song, pause it, enable recording, and display what part of the song you're currently listening to. It's a complex little window with many important areas, so let's open it up and take a quick orientation tour.

1   Open the file named **02-The_Transport-Start**.

This file is located on the CD-ROM that came with this book, and you should have already copied this CD-ROM's contents to your computer's hard disk, as described in the "Getting Started" section.

2   Choose Windows > Open Transport to open the Transport window (Cmd-7).

The Transport window opens. This window is an example of a floating window, which means it always sits above all the other editing windows, ensuring that the song's playback controls are always at your fingertips when needed (with the exception of another floating window, that is).

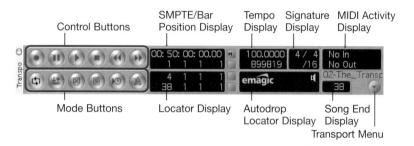

This is a dynamic window that can change size and shape to display only the functions you need to see. For example, if you're across the room playing a keyboard, you can increase the size of the entire Transport, or even just certain displays, such as the Bar or SMPTE display.

3 In the Transport's lower-right corner, click and hold the triangle button.

The Transport menu appears.

4 From the Transport menu, choose Size > 3.

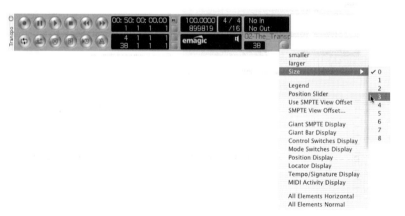

The Transport window becomes larger.

5 From the Transport menu, choose Giant Bar Display.

The Giant Bar display is a great visual aid if you're far away from the computer but still need to follow the Bar display as Logic progresses through your song (or if you forgot to bring your glasses to the studio!). Keep this in mind if you're across the studio playing a synthesizer.

6 From the Transport's pop-up menu, choose Legend.

The Transport window reverts to its normal display, but with a twist: Now, most of the Transport window's parts are named. This is a good option to use while learning about the Transport, so let's leave it enabled for the remainder of this lesson.

Exploring the Transport Panel

The Transport panel occupies the top-left corner of the Arrange window. By default, this area is disabled, but you can turn it on using the Arrange window's View menu. When enabled, the Transport panel gives you access to many of the Transport window's functions from directly within the Arrange window. The main benefit of using the Transport panel instead of the Transport window is that you don't have a floating window obscuring certain areas of your screen. However, you also don't have access to several Transport functions, such as the Autodrop Locator display, the MIDI Activity monitor, and the Song End box.

The song you're working on has the Transport panel displayed, but if you prefer using the Transport window, you can hide the Transport panel to get it out of the way. Let's check out a few important display options that let you hide all or part of the Transport panel.

1   From the Arrange window's local menus, choose View > Transport.

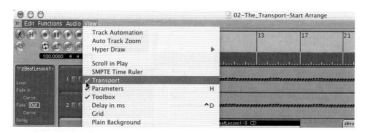

The Arrange window's Transport panel disappears.

Transport panel is hidden

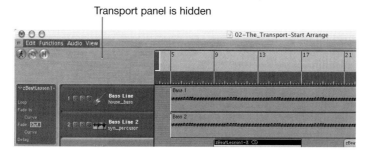

2   Choose View > Transport once again to reenable the Transport panel.

3   You can show or hide certain areas of the Transport panel by readjusting the window elements.

Window elements are all the individual elements that make up a window. For example, in the Arrange window, the Track column, Bar Ruler, and Arrange area are all window elements—and so is the Transport panel. If you'd like to see more of any one element in the window, use the following trick:

4   Position the pointer over the area where the Track column and Bar Ruler intersect.

The pointer turns into a pointed cross.

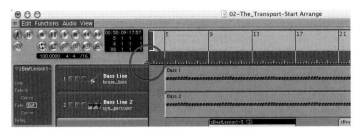

5   Click and drag up and to the left.

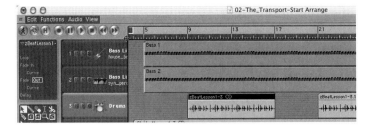

The Track column grows thinner, and fewer Transport functions are now displayed in the smaller Transport panel.

6   Return the window's elements back to their original display size so that you can see all the Transport panel's buttons and display boxes.

Moving the Song Position Locator

Song Position Locator (SPL)

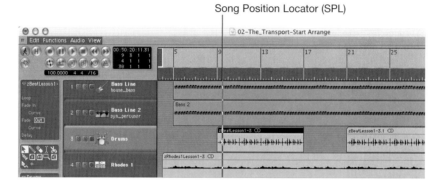

The Song Position Locator (SPL) is a thin vertical line that travels across the Arrange window as your song plays. The SPL has one function only: It shows you the current playback position of your song. As you audition various parts of your song, such as intros, choruses, and breakdowns, you will need to move the SPL to the area you want to hear. This is an interactive process—move the SPL, listen, move the SPL, listen again. In fact, as basic as it may seem, moving the SPL is an important editing technique, and Logic provides you with several ways to do it.

Using the SMPTE/Bar Position Display

The Transport's SMPTE/Bar Position display offers the most precise method of moving the SPL, because it lets you type in an exact song position for the SPL to jump to. Available in both the Transport panel and Transport window, this display is made of two separate sets of numbers: the Bar Position display and the SMPTE display.

SMPTE/Bar Position display
in Transport panel

SMPTE/Bar Position display
in Transport window

The Bar Display Songs are measured in bars and beats. Obligingly, the Bar Position display shows your current song position in bars and beats, and also allows a greater degree of resolution by breaking bars into divisions and ticks.

While bars and beats are basic music concepts, divisions and ticks are a bit more confusing. The Bar display's Division number is governed by the Transport's Division setting, and the Division setting tells Logic to divide each bar a certain number of times. For example, with a Division setting of 16, each bar is divided into 16 parts, which are equivalent to sixteenth notes. Each beat is a quarter note, and there are four sixteenth notes in a quarter note, so each beat in the Bar display is further divided into four parts. These four parts are reflected in the Bar display's Division number. With a division setting of 32, the Bar display's division value can be used to divide each quarter note into eight parts, and so on. (Don't worry if you find this confusing, because you won't often have to enter division values into the Bar display.)

If the Division setting doesn't offer a fine enough degree of resolution, you can also dial a tick number into the Bar display. At $\frac{1}{3840}$ of a bar, ticks are the smallest bar subdivision offered by Logic.

> **NOTE** ▶ Later when you learn about quantization in Logic, you'll see that the *quantization off* setting has the number 3840 printed beside it. This reflects the fact that with quantization turned off, notes are still quantized to the nearest $\frac{1}{3840}$ of a bar, which is the finest timing resolution offered by Logic.

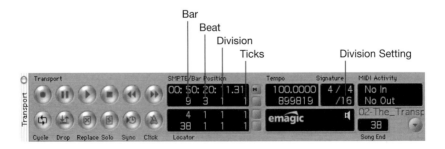

The SMPTE Display The SMPTE display shows the SPL's position in minutes and seconds, and for most music makers, that's the only useful part of this display. However, the SMPTE display is really designed for Logic users who are spotting sound to video, because this display is actually showing SMPTE timecode.

SMPTE (Society of Motion Picture and Television Engineers) timecode is used for determining time points in a video stream. Video displays a series of still pictures over time. Each picture is called a *frame,* and as the frames flip by, they create the effect of motion. Because video is a frame-based medium, its smallest degree of resolution is a single frame. Consequently, the SMPTE display shows hours, minutes, seconds, frames, and subframes.

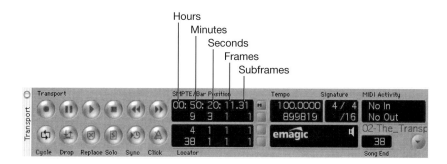

> **MORE INFO** ▶ *Broadcast video has two major competing standards: NTSC (National Television Standards Committee) and PAL (Phase Alternation Line). The standard you use is dependent on the country you live in. In NTSC countries, video progresses at a frame rate of 29.97 frames per second (fps), while PAL countries use a frame rate of 25 fps. Keep this difference in mind when reading the frame portion of the SMPTE display.*

Now that you know how to read the SMPTE/Bar Position display, it's time to try using it to move the SPL.

1   In the Transport's SMPTE/Bar Position display (in either the Transport window or the Arrange window's Transport panel—it doesn't matter which), double-click the Bar display.

A text field appears. Let's move the SPL to the beginning of the song, at bar 4.

2   Type *4*-space-*1*-space-*1*-space-*1*, and press Return.

The SPL jumps to bar 4, beat 1, division 1, tick 1, which is the very beginning of bar 4 (make sure to use a space between the numbers; otherwise the SPL will jump to bar 4111 instead of the beginning of bar 4).

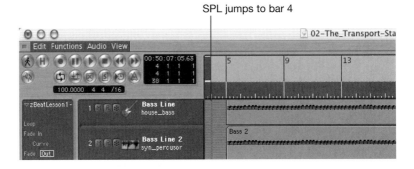

To save time while moving the SPL, Logic lets you avoid typing in all four position numbers. If you only want to jump to the beginning of bar 7, for example, you don't need to type *7 1 1 1* into the Bar display—just type *7* and press Return. Similarly, to jump to bar 7, beat 2, type *7 2*, and press Return.

3   Double-click the Bar display, type *7*, and press Return.

The SPL jumps to the beginning of bar 7.

4   In the Transport, click and hold the Bar display's beat value, and then drag up or down to change the value.

As you drag, the beat value changes and the SPL moves back and forth across the Arrange window.

5   Click the Transport's Forward button a few times.

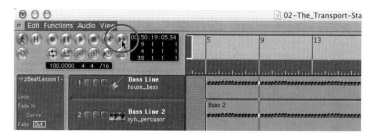

The SPL jumps from bar to bar across the Arrange window. The same thing happens if you click the Rewind button. This is a great trick for quickly stepping forward or backward by a few bars only.

Using the Bar Ruler

The most common way to move the SPL is to drag it along the Arrange window's Bar Ruler. The Bar Ruler has a horizontal line that divides it into two parts. The section under the line is used for moving the SPL.

1   Click in the lower section of the Bar Ruler at bar 5.

Click the lower third of the
Bar Ruler at bar 5

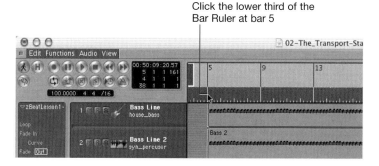

The SPL jumps to bar 5.

2   In the lower third of the Bar Ruler, click and drag left and right.

A crosshair appears as you drag, and the SPL moves back and forth across the Arrange area.

You might notice that the SPL's movement is jerky. This is because it's snapping along Logic's internal timing grid. Let's disable this snapping in the next step.

3   Hold down Control while dragging along the bottom section of the Bar Ruler.

NOTE ▶ Holding the Control key engages a finer resolution mode (which becomes more precise the more you're zoomed in). The SPL now moves smoothly across the Arrange area.

Using the Transport's Position Slider

The Transport window's position slider provides a further method of dragging the SPL forward or backward through your song. The position slider represents the length of your song as defined by its song start and song end markers (setting song start and song end markers is covered in Lesson 12, "Sweetening the Mix"). Because the position slider shows you the whole length of your song at a glance, it provides a very intuitive method for quickly navigating your arrangement.

1   From the Transport window's pop-up menu, choose Position Slider.

The position slider appears along the bottom of the Transport window.

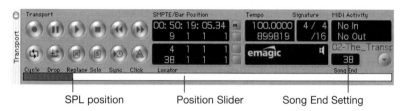

SPL position   Position Slider   Song End Setting

TIP ▶ If your song is short, you should adjust the song end marker close to the end of the Arrange area's Objects to make the position slider more accurately reflect your song's length.

2   Drag the right end of the gray area to move the position slider.

The SPL moves through your song.

NOTE ▶ The position slider is only available in the Transport window and not in the Arrange window's Transport panel.

Controlling Playback

Logic's Play, Pause, and Stop buttons function in a much more complex way than you might imagine. Of course, these buttons do exactly what they say—they play, pause, and stop your song. However, depending on how you interact with the buttons, they can play, pause, and stop in different ways.

Let's practice some of the clever maneuvers these buttons allow.

1   Place the SPL at bar 5.

2   Click the Transport's Play button.

Play Button

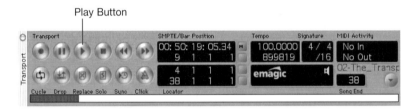

The song begins playing.

3   Click the Stop button.

Stop Button

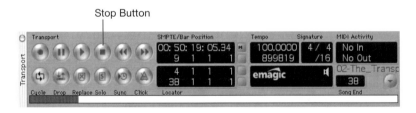

Playback stops at the SPL's current position.

NOTE ▶ The Enter key on the numeric keypad is the default key command for the Play button. The 0 key on the numeric keypad is the default key command for the Stop button. The spacebar toggles between the Start and Stop functions.

4   Click the Stop button a second time.

The SPL jumps back to the beginning of the song.

NOTE ▶ If Cycle mode is engaged, clicking Stop twice jumps the SPL to the beginning of the cycle region (Cycle mode is covered in the next exercise).

5   Click the Play button to start playback, and then click the Pause button.

Pause Button

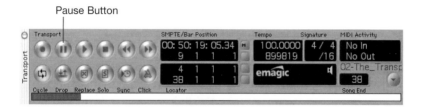

Clicking the Pause button does the same thing as clicking Stop, but with a twist—pausing playback enables Logic's Scrub mode. Scrubbing lets you hear sound while moving the SPL back and forth along the arrangement!

6   Drag along the lower section of the Bar Ruler to move the SPL left and right.

The SPL scrubs along the arrangement, and you can now hear the song as you move the SPL.

NOTE ▶ Audio and MIDI work in different ways: The audio track will raise and lower in pitch as you speed up and slow down, while scrubbing. MIDI tracks do not change pitch as you scrub.

7 Click the Pause button a second time to turn it off.

Playback continues from the SPL's current position.

8 Press the spacebar to halt playback.

9 Double-click the lower third of the Bar Ruler at bar 7.

Playback begins at bar 7.

10 Click anywhere else in the lower part of the Bar Ruler.

The SPL jumps to the clicked position, and playback continues.

11 With the song playing, double-click the lower part of the Bar Ruler to stop playback.

Using Cycle Mode

Cycle mode causes a specified section of your song to repeat over and over again. Cycle mode is particularly useful for practicing MIDI sequences before recording, editing song events as you listen to them, or driving your roommates and neighbors crazy with a continuously looping beat …

But seriously, Cycle mode lets you focus on a small section of your song as you practice or home in on exact edits—and this makes it an extremely important editing technique. For example, if you're using the Hyper Editor to program a MIDI drum sequence, Cycle mode lets you hear that sequence over and over while you arrange its drum hits.

Cycle mode uses the Transport's Cycle button in conjunction with the Locator display to set the left and right locators for the cycle (the Locator display is found in both the Transport window and Arrange window Transport panel).

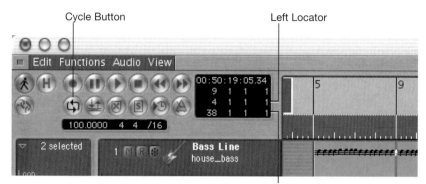

Cycle Button   Left Locator

Right Locator

In the song you're currently working on, Cycle mode is already enabled, with the left and right locators set to bar 4 and bar 38—that's the entire length of the song! If you play the song all the way through, it loops back to the beginning and then plays again. Cycle mode is a feature you'll use often while working through this book's lessons, so pay particular attention to the exercises in this section!

Setting Locators

Let's change the locators to create a new cycle region in your song.

1   In the Transport's Locator display, double-click the left locator, type *9*, and press Return.

This sets the first locator to 9 1 1 1, which defines the beginning of your cycle.

2   In the Transport's Locator display, double-click the right locator, type *17,* and press Return.

This sets the cycle's end locator to 17 1 1 1. The Transport's Cycle button is already enabled, and you may have noticed that changing the locator positions changed the length of the highlighted section in the top of the Bar Ruler. This highlighted section shows you the length of the cycle, and it's called the *cycle region.*

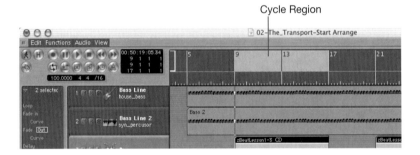

3   Press the spacebar to play your song.

The SPL begins playing from the left locator. When it hits the right locator, it jumps back to the left locator and begins playing the cycle again. The transition between locators is seamless, and you hear a continuous loop.

4   In the Transport, click Stop to halt playback, and then click the Cycle button to turn Cycle mode off (the slash [/] key also toggles Cycle mode on and off).

Defining a Cycle Region from the Bar Ruler

In the last exercise you saw that the cycle region is displayed as a highlight in the top portion of the Bar Ruler. Guess what? You don't have to use the left and right locators to set the Cycle mode's boundaries. A much quicker technique is just to drag a cycle region right into the top portion of the Bar Ruler!

1 In the Bar Ruler's top portion (above the dividing line) click and hold at bar 17, and drag to the right until you hit bar 21.

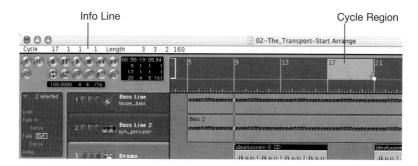

Info Line   Cycle Region

As you drag out this cycle region, a few things happen. First, the pointer turns into a Finger tool. Second, the Info Line appears.

MORE INFO ▶ *Every time you move something in Logic, the Info Line replaces the local menus of the editing window you're currently working in. The Info Line is a display that shows you information about the operation you're currently performing. For example, when you move the boundary of the cycle region, the Info Line shows you the start and length of the cycle region. If you move a MIDI sequence, the Info Line shows you the sequence's new position and length. As soon as you release the object you're moving, the Info Line disappears, replaced once again by the editing window's local menus.*

2 Press the spacebar to play the cycle region.

The song cycles between bar 17 and bar 21.

3   Click and hold the center of the cycle region, and drag right.

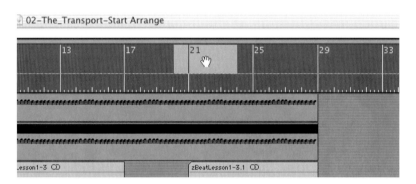

The pointer turns into a Hand tool, and the entire four-bar cycle region drags right.

4   Release the cycle region when it covers the four bars from bar 21 to bar 25.

You can adjust the boundaries of a cycle region by grabbing its lower-left or -right corner and dragging. But note that you must drag the lower portion of the corner, because dragging anywhere else moves the entire cycle region, not just the region's boundary.

5   Click the lower-right corner of the cycle region, and drag right until you get to bar 29.

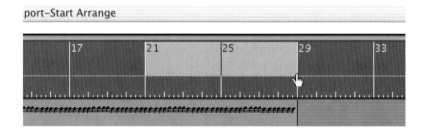

Using Skip Cycle Mode

Skip Cycle mode is like Cycle mode inverted: Instead of cycling continuously through the cycle region, Skip Cycle mode jumps right over the region
specified in the Locator display. In fact, to set up Skip Cycle mode, you actually enter the left and right locator positions in reverse! In Cycle mode, the
left locator is always earlier in the song than the right locator. In Skip Cycle
mode, the left locator is always *later* in the song than the right one.

Think of it this way: In both Cycle and Skip Cycle modes, the SPL jumps
from the right locator to the left one. In Cycle mode the right locator
comes after the left, so the SPL jumps from the right locator *back* to the
left locator *earlier* in the song. In Skip Cycle mode, the right locator comes
before the left, so the SPL jumps from the right locator *forward* to the left
locator *later* in the song. By jumping forward in the song, you skip a section of the song's content. Clear as mud? Let's do a little practice to drive
this concept home.

1   In the Transport's Locator display, double-click the left locator, type
17, and press Return.

The left locator is set to the beginning of bar 17.

2   In the Transport's Locator display, double-click the right locator, type
9, and press Return.

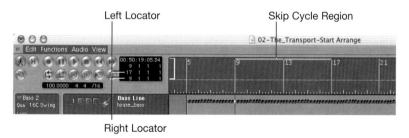

The right locator is set to the beginning of bar 9, which is *earlier* in
the song than the left locator. In the Bar Ruler, notice how the cycle
region's thick highlight has been replaced by thin gray one. This thin
gray line defines a Skip Cycle region.

3   Double-click the Bar Ruler at bar 7 to play the song from bar 7.

The song plays, but skips right over bars 9 through 17!

4   Press the spacebar to stop the song.

5   To turn off Skip Cycle mode, click once in the middle of the cycle region (this does exactly the same thing as clicking the Cycle button or pressing /).

The cycle region's highlight disappears, and Skip Cycle mode is turned off. A quick glance at the Transport's Cycle button shows that it is no longer enabled.

TIP ▶ To turn Cycle mode back on, click the top section of the Bar Ruler. Cycle mode will automatically turn on, and a cycle region will be created between the left and right locators defined by the Transport's Locator display.

What You've Learned

- Logic's Transport is used to *transport* you to various points in your arrangement, and is primarily used to control Logic's playback and recording functions.

- The Transport window's position slider shows you the whole length of your song at a glance and provides a very intuitive method for quickly navigating your arrangement.

- The Transport's Bar display shows the SPL's location in bar/beat/division/ticks, while the SMPTE display shows the SPL's location in hours/minutes/seconds/frames/subframes.

- Cycle mode defines a specific area of your song that Logic cycles through until playback is stopped.

- Skip Cycle mode is like Cycle mode inverted—instead of cycling continuously through the cycle region, Skip Cycle mode jumps right over the region defined by the left and right locators.

- Every time you move something in Logic, the Info Line replaces the editing window's local menus with information about the operation you're performing.

3

Start	03-Editing_Basics-Start
Complete	03-Editing_Basics-Finished
Time	Approximately 45 minutes
Goals	Learn how to use the telescopes to zoom in and out on the contents of an editing window
	Learn various methods of selecting Objects in Logic
	Explore active and floating windows
	Use Logic's Link functions
	Gain experience using Logic's Catch mode and Scroll in Play function
	Name Objects
	Hide tracks
	Create custom key commands to control Logic's editing functions

Lesson 3
Editing Basics

Now that you're at home in the workspace, you've seen how Logic's editing windows interrelate, and you've explored the Transport's playback functions, it's time to get a bit deeper into editing songs. This lesson explores some basic editing functions you'll use throughout this book, such as zooming in and out on an editing window's display, making selections with Logic's unique selection techniques, hiding tracks, and creating custom key commands to control Logic's editing functions. Just because these editing functions are basic, it doesn't mean they are any less important than the things you'll learn later in this book. In fact, the editing techniques you'll learn in this lesson provide a good foundation of skills you'll constantly use while using Logic. So with no further ado, let's jump straight into the editing basics.

Zooming and Magnifying

Songs in Logic can be made up of elaborate combinations of audio recordings and MIDI sequences. When you display a song in Logic's Arrange window, you have to balance the need to see all the tracks at once with the need to see the details in individual sequences and samples. Logic provides controls that let you zoom in to see more detail in your song, or zoom out to see more of your song at once. The first situation is called *zooming in,* and the second is *zooming out.*

You activate Logic's zoom functions using the telescopes in the top-right corner of the window (almost every Logic window has at least one telescope). If the window has two telescopes, the one on the left zooms the window display vertically, while the one on the right zooms it horizontally. To zoom out and see a greater overview of the window's content, click the smaller end of a telescope (the left end). To zoom in and see the window's contents in greater detail, click the larger end of the telescope (the right end).

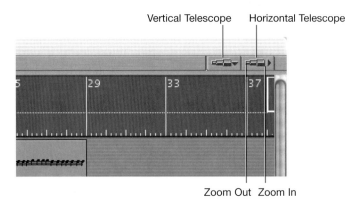

Let's experiment a bit with Logic's telescopes and Magnifying Glass (Zoom tool).

1 Open the file named **03-Editing_Basics-Start**.

2   In the Arrange window's top-right corner, click the left and right ends of the telescopes to experiment with Logic's zoom functions.

TIP ▶ The following key commands have the same functions as Logic's telescopes: Ctrl–left arrow zooms out horizontally, Ctrl–right arrow zooms in horizontally, Ctrl–up arrow zooms out vertically, and Ctrl–down arrow zooms in vertically.

You can also use Logic's Magnifying Glass tool to zoom in on a certain area of a window. Logic will then expand the selected area to fill the window.

3   Select the Magnifying Glass tool and drag a rectangle around the first audio region in the Drums track.

Magnifying Glass Tool

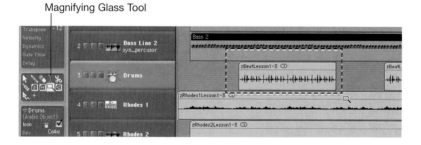

The Drums region fills the Arrange area.

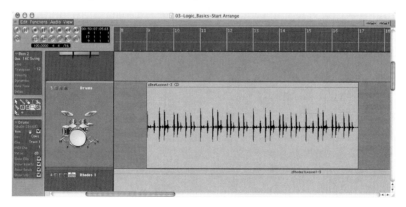

4   To revert to the premagnified state, click with the Magnifying Glass tool anywhere on the Arrange area.

The Arrange window reverts to its premagnified state.

NOTE ▶ The Magnifying Glass tool remembers multiple magnification states. If you magnify a section of the Arrange area, and then zoom in on that section, you can click the Arrange area twice to revert the Arrange area to its premagnified state.

Selecting with the Arrow Tool

Whether you're selecting notes in the Matrix editor, MIDI Objects in the Arrange window, or Objects in the Environment, Logic's selection techniques always function the same way. You can select any object at all by simply grabbing the Arrow tool and clicking the object, but there are also a few other selection techniques you should be aware of. A good understanding of these techniques greatly speeds song editing, so work carefully through the following steps, and make sure you try each one.

1   From the toolbox, grab the Arrow tool and click the first region in the Drums track.

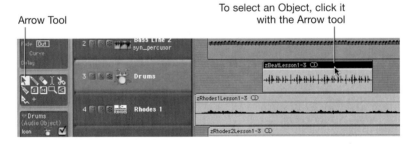

The region is selected.

2   In the Track column, click the Scratch track's name.

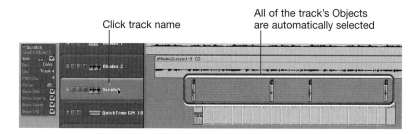

Click track name

All of the track's Objects
are automatically selected

Clicking the track name selects all Objects in that track.

TIP ▶ With Cycle mode enabled, clicking the track name selects
only events falling within the cycle region.

3   Click the Arrange window's background to deselect all Objects in the
Arrange area.

Shift-clicking lets you select noncontiguous Objects (Objects that are
not beside each other).

4   Select the second Object in the Drums track, then press Shift and select
the Bass 1 MIDI sequence.

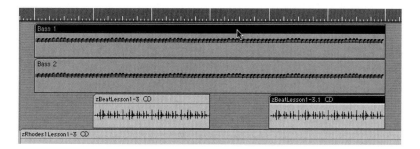

Both Objects are selected. You can continue to add Objects to the
selection by Shift-clicking more Objects.

Rubber-Band Selecting

Rubber-band selection refers to the process of dragging a selection range around one or more objects at the same time.

1   Click and hold in the empty area between the track column and the first Object in the Scratch track, and then drag up and to the right until the pointer is in the empty area between the Objects in the drum track.

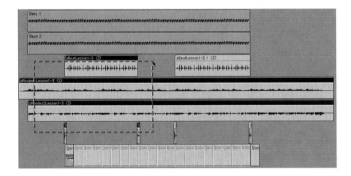

A rectangular outline is traced behind the pointer, and all Objects touched or enclosed by the rubber-band outline are selected.

2   Hold down the Shift key and drag a rubber band over *all* the Arrange area's Objects.

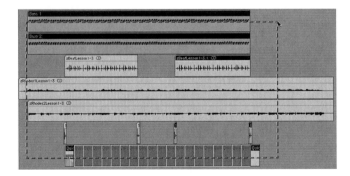

This reverses the selection! Holding down Shift while rubber-banding objects causes previously selected objects to be deselected, while unselected objects are added to the selection range.

3 From the Arrange window's local menus, choose Edit > Toggle Selection (Shift-T).

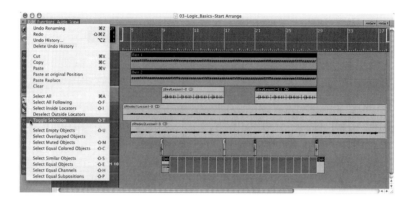

The selection range inverts, or toggles, so that all unselected objects are selected, and vice versa. The toggle selection command comes in handy if you have to select all but a few objects in the Arrange area, because it's often easier to first select the few objects, and then toggle the selection.

MORE INFO ▶ *You might have noticed that the Edit menu contains several different selection options. There are too many here to go over individually, but they all have specific functions that are immediately identifiable by their names. Pay particular attention to Select Inside Locators (Shift-I), which is a good way to select all the Objects that make up a particular verse or chorus, and Select Muted Objects (Shift-M), which offers a great way to select all muted Objects for deletion.*

4 Click the Arrange area's background to deselect all objects.

Working with Windows

Why is real estate such a good investment? Because land is the only thing they're not making more of. The same holds true for screen real estate, or the amount of space you have available on your computer monitor. While you can actually increase your screen real estate by using multiple monitors, if you're like most of us, you have only a single screen at your disposal, and this screen is capable of displaying only a limited number of windows at any one time. Juggling editing windows is a fact of life in Logic, so let's explore a few basic windows-management techniques.

Making Windows Active

The active window is the window that's ready to receive input from the mouse or keyboard—it's the one you are going to interact with.

> **NOTE ▶** The active window is not necessarily the top window. Logic uses floating windows to keep important windows on the surface at all times. The Transport window is an example of a floating window, and you'll learn about others a bit later in this section.

1 First choose Windows > Open Event List, then choose Windows > Open Score (Cmd-3).

The Event List opens on top of the Arrange window, and then the Score editor opens on top of the Event List. Your screen currently shows three windows, with the Score editor being the *active* window.

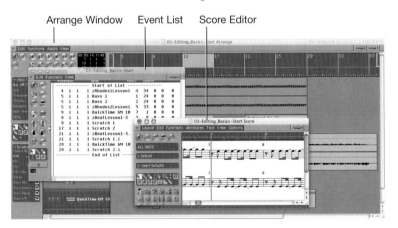

Arrange Window   Event List   Score Editor

2 Click anywhere in the Arrange window.

The Arrange window is brought to the surface and made active. But more important, the Arrange window is now hiding the Event List and Score editor! Without moving the Arrange window out of the way, you can't click the Event List or Score editor to make them active. Here's a trick to help you solve this problem:

3   Click and hold the Windows menu.

Near the bottom of the Windows menu there is a list of Logic's currently open windows. This is the *windows list*. Look closely at this windows list and you'll see a checkmark next to the Arrange window, indicating that the Arrange window is active.

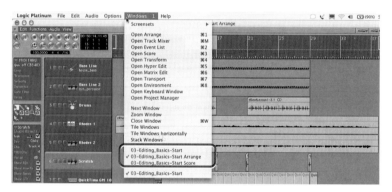

Of course, you don't need the windows list to show you which window is active—you can just look at the screen to see that. In fact, the windows list's primary function is to help you quickly locate windows, such as the Score editor, that are buried under other windows on your screen.

4   From the windows list, select 03-Editing_Basics-Start Score.

The Score editor jumps to your screen's surface and becomes the active window.

5   Use the trick you've just learned to make the Event List the active window.

6   Close the Event List, but leave the Score editor open for the next exercise.

Using Floating Windows

Floating windows always remain above other windows. In previous exercises you might have noticed that the Transport window is always visible. That's because it's a floating window, and as such it cannot be hidden behind other windows (however, a floating window *can* be covered by another floating window). Other examples of floating windows include Logic's software instruments and plug-in windows.

You can distinguish a floating window from a normal window by looking at its title bar. Normal windows have a taller title bar with rounded corners, while floating windows have a shorter title bar with square corners. Incidentally, floating windows are not unique to Logic. For example, Adobe Photoshop's palettes are floating windows, and Microsoft Word's toolbars are also floating windows—in fact, any window that can't be hidden under other windows is a floating window, regardless of the software program.

> **NOTE ▶** Another interesting fact about floating windows is that switching to a different application causes them to disappear, while the normal document windows remain visible.

While Logic is not unique in its use of floating windows, it does have one special feature not found in any other program: Logic lets you, the user, turn any window into a floating window. Any window at all! For example, if you're making important edits in the Matrix editor and you want to ensure that the window doesn't get lost behind others, hold down the Option key while you open the window.

Let's practice making floating windows and moving them around.

1   Press Option and choose Windows > Open Event List.

The Event List opens as a floating window. Note how the Event List's title bar is now shorter than normal, with square corners.

Floating Event List

2   Click the Score editor to make it the active window.

The Score editor becomes the active window, but it does not jump above the floating Event List!

3   Close the Score editor.

4   Now, hold down Option and once again choose Windows > Open Event List.

Floating Event List Number 2

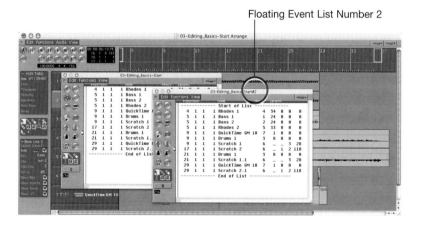

A second Event List opens as a floating window, and its title bar is labeled with #2 at the end to help you differentiate between it and the first floating Event List. This demonstrates an interesting Logic feature: You can have several versions of the same window open at the same time. You might ask yourself, "What's the use of that? Don't both windows just show exactly the same thing?" Right now, they do indeed show the same data, but this doesn't have to be the case, as you'll learn in the following exercise. But let's save that for a moment and continue exploring floating windows.

5   Click the first floating Event List, and drag it over the second, or newer, floating Event List.

Aha! The first floating Event List can be moved over the second one, showing that floating windows can be moved above other floating windows.

Before moving on, let's set up the screen so that it's prepared for the next exercise.

6   Position the SPL at 9 1 1 1.

7   Arrange the windows as shown in the following figure.

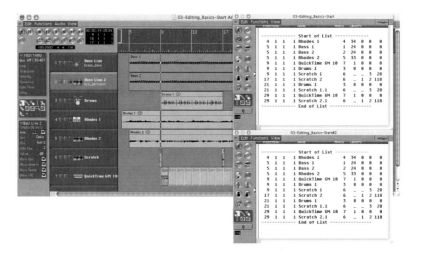

Linking Windows

In the top-left corner of most editing windows there is a button with a chain-link icon. This is called the Link button, and enabling it links Logic's editing windows together. There are two ways to link windows together; the first is called Link mode, and the second is called Content Link mode.

- In Link mode, the Link button is violet, and a window always displays whatever is selected in the currently active window.

- In Content Link mode, the Link button is yellow, and editors show the *contents* of any Object selected in the active window.

These may seem like esoteric features at first glance, but they are actually very useful. The best way to see the differences between these two modes is to try them out.

1   In the first floating Event List, make sure the Link button is violet. If it's gray or yellow, click it slowly until it's violet.

Link Button

If the Link button is gray (off), you need click only once. If it's yellow, you'll need to click twice.

2   In the second Event List, double-click the Link button.

The Link button turns yellow and displays a downward-pointing triangle, indicating that Content Link mode is enabled.

3   In the Arrange window, select the Bass 2 sequence.

The first Event List is in Link mode, which means it updates to show you whichever Object is selected in the Arrange window. The second Event List, however, is in Content Link mode, so it updates to show you the contents of the Object selected in the Arrange window. In other words, the first Event List is showing you that the Bass 2 sequence is selected, while the second Event List is showing you the individual note events *inside* the Bass 2 sequence.

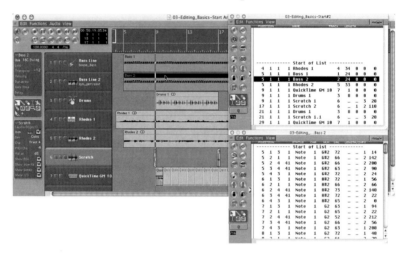

4   In the second Event List (the one in Content Link mode, with the yellow Link button), select any event.

The first Event List is linked to all other windows and shows whatever is selected in the active window. By clicking an event in the second Event List, you make it the active window. Consequently, the first Event List updates to show the same selected note.

5 In the second Event List, click the Link button to turn it off (gray).

The second Event List is no longer linked to other windows.

6 Back in the Arrange window, click the Rhodes 1 region.

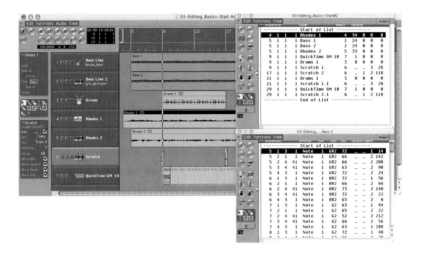

The second Event List no longer updates and instead remains just as it was.

7 Click a few more Objects in the Arrange area.

The first Event List is still in Link mode, so it updates to show whatever is selected in the Arrange window, but the second Event List remains unlinked, and its display does not change.

8 Close both floating Event Lists.

Using the Catch Function

In the Arrange window's top-left corner, the little walking man button enables Logic's Catch function. This button is called the Catch button, and when it's enabled, the Arrange area's visible section follows the SPL as the song plays.

> **NOTE ▶** Catch mode is available to all windows that show a progression of song events, such as the Matrix editor, Event List, and Score editor.

1   Using the Arrange window's telescopes, horizontally zoom in until bars 5 to 9 fill the Arrange area.

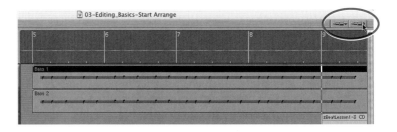

> **NOTE ▶** The song you're working on isn't very long. To see Catch mode in action, the Arrange area's Objects must stretch beyond the Arrange area's right edge, so you need to zoom in.

2   Ensure that the Arrange window's Catch button is blue, which means it's enabled. If the Catch button is not blue, click it to enable it.

Catch Button

3   Press the spacebar to play the song.

The SPL plays to the right edge of the Arrange area. When the SPL hits the right edge, the Arrange area jumps forward and the SPL commences playing from the left to right edges once more.

4   At the bottom of the Arrange window, grab the scroll bar and scroll so that bars 5 to 9 are once again centered in the Arrange area.

The song continues to play, but notice that the Catch function has been disabled, and the Catch button is now gray (off). This demonstrates an important point: If you manually change the displayed area of the song (by either moving the scroll bar along the Arrange window's bottom edge or using the Magnifying Glass tool), the Catch function is automatically disabled, so the newly selected display area does not disappear.

5   Your song should still be playing. With the Catch function remaining off, single-click the Bar Ruler's lower portion at bar 5.

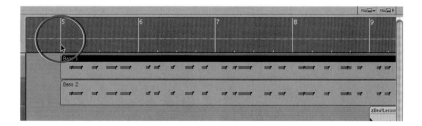

The SPL jumps back to bar 5 and the song starts playing from that point. But more important, the Catch function is turned back on. This is an example of Logic's *Autocatch function*. The Autocatch function enables Catch mode each time the Play or Pause buttons are clicked, or whenever a playback command is initiated. Typically, you will want to keep Autocatch on, but you can disable it by choosing Logic > Preferences > Global Preferences and clicking the "Enable Catch when sequencer starts" check box to remove the check mark.

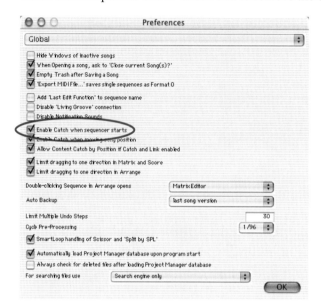

Using Scroll in Play

Scroll in Play works in a similar way as Catch mode, but instead of having the SPL play across the Arrange area's Objects, the Arrange area's Objects scroll past a stationary SPL.

1   From the Arrange window's local menus, choose View > Scroll in Play.

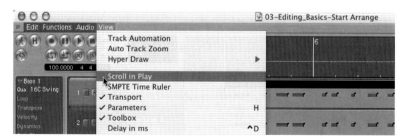

2   Play from the beginning of the song.

The SPL plays to the middle of the Arrange window, at which point it stops and the Arrange area's Objects start scrolling left past the SPL.

3   To turn Scroll in Play off, choose View > Scroll in Play once again.

Naming Objects

The toolbox has a special tool used for naming MIDI sequences, Audio regions, and other Objects—the Text tool.

1   From the Arrange window's toolbox, grab the Text tool.

2   Click the audio region in the Rhodes 1 track.

A text box opens.

3   Type *Rhodes 1,* and press Return.

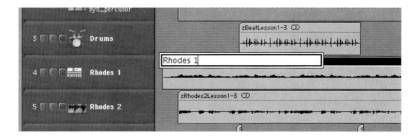

The audio region is named Rhodes 1.

In the above example, you gave an audio region the same name as the track it's in. Logic provides an even easier way to accomplish this:

4   In the Track column, select the Rhodes 2 track.

5   From the Arrange window's local menus, choose View > Tracknames To Objects (Option-Shift-N).

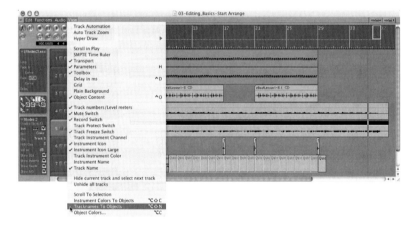

The Rhodes 2 track's name is applied to its audio region.

You can also use the Text tool to name several Objects at the same time.

6   Using the Text tool, rubber-band select both audio regions in the Drums track.

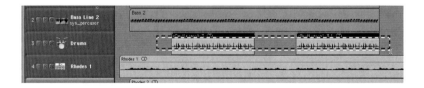

7 With the Text tool, click the first audio region, name it *Drums 1*, and press Return.

The first region is given the name Drums 1, while the second is given the name Drums 2—Logic has automatically recognized the number at the end of the name and incremented it in the following audio region. This works with as many Objects as are sequentially selected.

If you don't want selected Objects to be given sequentially numbered names, use the following trick:

8 With the Text tool, click the first audio region, name it *Drums 1 (Space)*, and press Return (that's a spacebar space—you don't need to type the word *Space*).

Both of the selected audio regions are named exactly the same thing— Drums 1!

Hiding Tracks

Logic projects can get large, and it's common to have dozens of MIDI and audio tracks populating the Arrange window. With so many tracks competing for valuable screen real estate, you will sometimes want to hide certain tracks temporarily to get them out of the way. You'll still hear the hidden tracks, but they won't be visible in the Arrange window.

> **NOTE** ▶ Hiding tracks is a feature new to Logic 6, so users of older versions do not have access to this function.

1   In the Arrange window's upper-left corner, select the global HideView button.

The global HideView button turns from gray to green (aqua-green). In the Track column, an individual Hide button appears beside each track's name.

2   Select the Hide buttons on the Rhodes 1 and Rhodes 2 tracks.

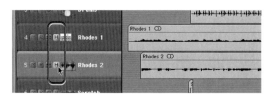

As you select these Hide buttons, they turn green to match the color of the global HideView button, but the tracks are not yet hidden.

3   In the Arrange window's upper-left corner, click the Global HideView button one more time.

The Rhodes 1 and Rhodes 2 tracks disappear, and the global HideView button turns orange. This orange color is important to note, because this is your visual clue that some Arrange window tracks are hidden.

The global HideView button is orange, indicating that tracks are hidden

MORE INFO ► *The global HideView button has three different color states:*
- *Gray—No tracks are hidden.*
- *Green—Setup mode; displays Hide buttons for all tracks.*
- *Orange—One or more tracks are hidden.*

To unhide tracks (show them again), just reverse the process.

4   Click the global HideView button once again.

The hidden tracks reappear.

5   Deselect the Rhodes 1 and Rhodes 2 tracks' Hide buttons.

6   Click the global HideView button one last time to turn off Logic's Hide function.

Using Key Commands

While the mouse remains your primary source of interaction with Logic, key commands provide an alternative way for you to control the program. Key commands give you access to most of Logic's functions directly from the keyboard, which saves you having to search through Logic's menus and look for the function you're after. Becoming familiar with Logic's key commands—and using them—will save you time as you arrange your songs. In fact, there are some key command functions that just plain aren't available from Logic's menus—if you don't know these key commands, you can't use the functions! (You'll learn several of these secret key commands over the course of this book's lessons.)

> **TIP ▶** To become a true Logic commander, a hand on the keyboard is just as important as a hand on the mouse. By default, Logic comes pre-configured with several key commands, many of which you've already seen and used. A word of advice: As you work through this book, pay attention to all discussed key commands, and be sure to try them out.

Restoring the Default Key Commands

To make sure you are working from the same page as this book's steps, it's a good idea to restore Logic's default key command set before continuing any further. This is particularly true if you've upgraded to Logic 6 from an older version of the program, because installing Logic 6 may automatically load the older version's key commands, and several of these have changed in Logic 6. For example, in previous versions, Cmd-2 opened the Event List, whereas now it opens the Track Mixer. Pressing C used to enable Cycle mode, but this key command has now been changed to slash (/).

> **NOTE ▶** Key commands are saved with your Logic preferences and are available to all songs.

1   Choose Logic Platinum > Preferences > Key Commands (Option-K).

The Key Commands window opens, and you are presented with a large list of key commands, along with their functions.

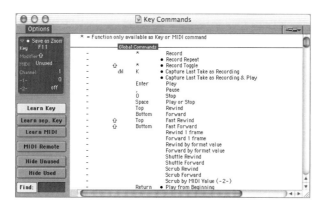

NOTE ▶ The Key Commands window breaks Logic's key commands into several different sections. Global key commands (the ones that affect all of Logic's editing windows) are listed first, with subsequent sections listing key commands unique to each different type of editing window.

2   From the Key Commands window's Options menu, choose Initialize > all Key Commands.

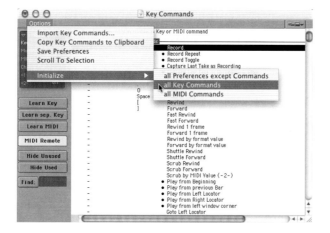

Logic 6's default key command set is loaded, and you can now be sure your key commands match the ones used in this book.

Changing Key Commands

Logic lets you assign any function you want to any key or combination of keys. If you don't like Logic's default key commands, feel free to change them. But keep in mind that this book uses Logic's default key command set, so if you change any of these commands, you may experience some differences between this book's steps and their expected results.

Bearing this warning in mind, let's go ahead and assign some new key commands—the important word here is *new*, because we are not changing any of the default commands. Instead, the following exercise adds a few new key commands to the recall zoom setting functions, which are currently unassigned.

> **NOTE ▶** The functions whose names are preceded by a bullet (·) are available only by using key commands.

1   In the bottom-left corner of the Key Commands window, click the Find button.

    The Key Commands window's Find function is enabled. The Find function lets you search through the key commands to quickly locate the command you are interested in. Use this function to find unknown commands, or to search for commands you wish to change or reassign to different key combinations.

2   In the text box next to the word Find, type *zoom* and press Return.

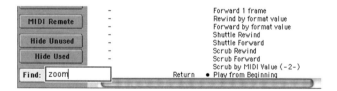

    The Key Commands window changes to list only key commands that have the word *Zoom* in their function name.

3 Click the function that says Recall Zoom 1.

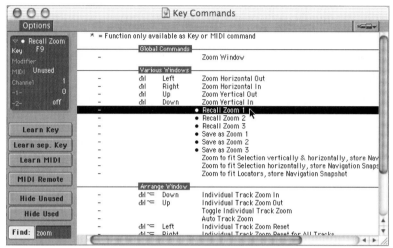

The Recall Zoom 1 function currently has no key command assigned.

4 Click the Learn Key button.

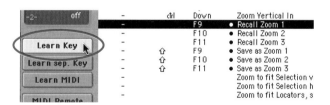

5 Press the F9 function key to assign that key to the Recall Zoom 1 function.

F9 appears to the left of the Recall Zoom 1 function, alerting you that the key command has been assigned and is now ready for use.

6 Repeat steps 4 to 6 to assign the following key commands:

- Recall Zoom 2: F10

- Recall Zoom 3: F11

- Save as Zoom 1: Shift-F9

- Save as Zoom 2: Shift-F10

- Save as Zoom 3: Shift-F11

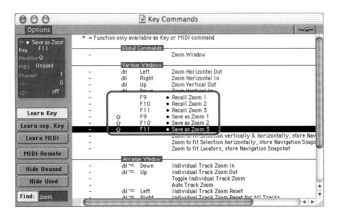

7 Click the Key Commands window's Learn Key button to turn it off.

8 Close the Key Command window.

9 In the Arrange window, use the telescopes to zoom out until the Arrange area's Objects are quite small.

10 Press Shift-F9.

You have just stored this zoom value as the Zoom 1 preset.

11 Use the telescopes to zoom in on the Arrange area's Objects, and press Shift-F10.

This new zoom value is saved to Zoom Preset 2.

12 Zoom in until the Arrange area's Objects fill the Arrange window, and press Shift-F11.

13 Press the F9, F10, and F11 keys to experiment with your new zoom presets.

> **TIP** ▸ For quick reference, print out your key commands! In the Key Commands window, click the Hide Unused button to show only those key commands that have been assigned. Then, in the Key Commands local menu select Option > Copy Key Commands to Clipboard. After doing this, start up any text-editing software, and select the paste command in that software. You should now be able to use your text editor's Print command to print a list of your key commands.

What You've Learned

- You can use the telescopes in an editing window's top-right corner to zoom in and out on objects in the window's display area.

- Rubber-banding lets you drag a selection range around multiple adjacent objects. All objects enclosed or touched by the rubber band are selected.

- Floating windows, such as Logic's Transport window, always sit above normal windows and can be covered only by another floating window.

- Linked windows update to display edits made in the active window.

- Content Link mode causes editors to show the contents of the Object selected in the active window.

- The little walking man button in the top-left corner of an editing window enables Logic's Catch mode. With this button enabled, the window's display area follows the SPL as the song plays.

- To disable Catch mode, move the scroll bar at the bottom of the editing window.

- Key commands give you access to most of Logic's functions directly from the keyboard. You create them using the Key Commands window (choose Logic Platinum > Preferences > Key Commands [Option-K] to open the Key Commands window).

4

Start	04-MIDI_Enviro-Start
Complete	04-MIDI_Enviro-Finished
Bonus File	MIDIDeviceChart.pdf
Time	Approximately 1 to 1.5 hours, depending on the number of MIDI devices in your studio
Goals	Learn MIDI signal flow into and out of Logic
	Connect Logic's sequencer to your computer's MIDI ports
	Create and configure MIDI Instrument Objects
	Gain comfort and confidence in working with Logic's Environment
	Create a personalized Logic Environment that represents the MIDI devices in your recording studio

Setting Up the MIDI Environment

At the moment Logic is configured to use the default workspace. You can start making music right away, using this workspace as the basis for your composition, but chances are the default workspace does not reflect the setup of your studio. The default workspace is only configured to support one General MIDI (GM) synthesizer—a very basic setup, indeed. Fortunately, Logic's Environment is extremely customizable, and you can tailor it to exactly reflect the instruments and MIDI devices you use on a daily basis. Are you excited? You should be. You're about to configure Logic in a way that will match your studio and enhance your creativity.

Getting Started in Logic's Environment Window

Take a moment to look at the studio around you. What do you see? At the very least you must have a MIDI controller (a keyboard or other device that produces MIDI signals) or you will find it difficult to interact with Logic. You may also have other synthesizers, a sampler, and even a few software instruments like Propellerhead Software's Reason or Bitheadz's Unity Session. These instruments are your cherished toys, and they are all part of your music production environment.

You can easily look around your studio and see these MIDI devices, but Logic does not have the benefit of eyes—for Logic to "see" your studio, virtual copies of each MIDI device, called Objects, must exist inside a special Logic window called the Environment.

Opening the Environment Window

The Environment window is an essential piece of the Logic puzzle, so let's open it now and take a look around.

1   Open the file named **04-MIDI_Enviro-Start**.

    The Arrange window opens on your screen. It's currently empty except for a single MIDI Click track.

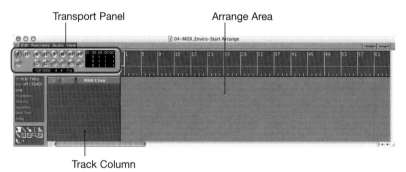

Transport Panel   Arrange Area

Track Column

2   In the Transport panel (top-left corner of the Arrange window), click the Metronome button, then click the Transport's Play button.

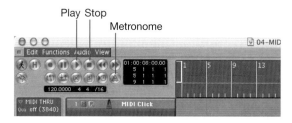

You will hear a clicking sound. This is Logic's metronome clicking in time to the song's tempo.

NOTE ▶ If you can't hear the Click track, check to make sure your computer is making sound. The easiest way to do this is to press the volume up and volume down keys at the top of your keyboard to create a system beep (on PowerBooks, these are usually the F4 and F5 keys). If your computer is not producing sound, you must fix this before continuing.

3   Position the pointer over the MIDI Click track's name, and double-click.

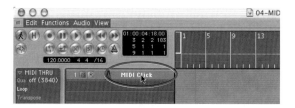

Logic's Environment window opens, and an Object named MIDI
Click is selected. This is a Metronome Object, and it's responsible for
sending out that clicking sound.

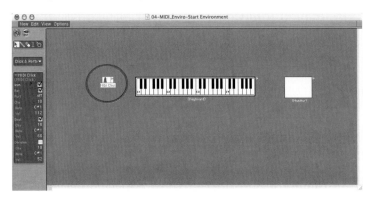

Exploring the Environment Window

Now that you have the Environment window open, let's take a look at
what's in it.

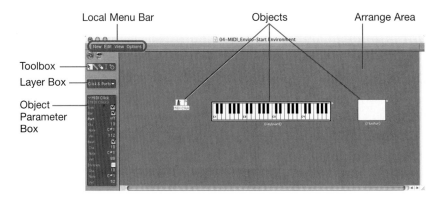

Objects Dictionary.com defines an object as *the purpose, aim, or goal of a
specific action or effort*. The Environment's goal is to create connections
between Logic and your studio's other MIDI devices, and each connection
is represented by an Object. For example, the Instrument Object connects
Logic to a synthesizer, while an Audio Object connects Logic to your com-
puter's hardware audio interface, such as an Emagic EMI 2|6 sound card.

The Environment Toolbox The toolbox is the cornerstone of many Logic windows, and it's no different in the Environment. The tools in this box are used to select, create, erase, and name Objects.

The Layer Box The Environment can hold many different types of Objects, so to keep them all organized and easy to find, Logic lets you divide the Environment into layers that group similar Objects and instruments together.

The Object Parameter Box The behavior of each Environment Object is controlled by setting its parameters. These parameters are found in the Object Parameter box, which is a context-sensitive display that updates to show you the unique settings of any selected Object.

This box is not as straightforward as the other two. For starters, the Object Parameter box has a bit of an identity problem. The Logic manual sometimes calls it the Instrument Parameter box, but the Object Parameter box displays the properties of any selected Environment Object—it doesn't have to be an instrument. For the sake of consistency, this book will always call it the Object Parameter box.

To make things slightly more confusing, the Object Parameter box also has two homes. It lives along the left edge of both the Environment and Arrange windows. Don't let these dual locations fool you, because it's the same box in both windows, and changing the parameters in one box changes the parameters in the other.

Cabling MIDI Objects Together

Your Environment window currently holds three objects; a Metronome, a Keyboard, and a Monitor Object. These are all examples of MIDI Objects used to control the flow of MIDI signals. In the top-right corner of each MIDI Object you'll find a small triangle, called the Object's *output*. This output is used to pass the Object's MIDI signals to other Environment Objects, through a cable.

In this exercise, you will cable the MIDI Click Metronome Object to the Keyboard, and then the Monitor, creating a MIDI signal path that lets you see the MIDI data being produced by the Metronome.

1   Click and hold the triangle on the right side of the MIDI Click Object, and drag a cable to the Keyboard Object.

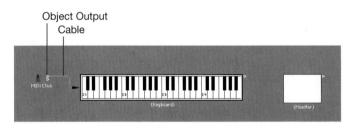

Dragging a cable between the MIDI Metronome and the Keyboard connects these two Objects together. A quick look at the Keyboard shows the MIDI Click is now triggering the Keyboard's C#1 key.

NOTE ▸ Logic should still be playing and producing a MIDI click sound. If you stopped playback after the last exercise, press the space-bar to start playback once again.

2   Drag a cable from the Keyboard's output to the Monitor Object.

The Monitor Object keeps a list of all MIDI events that enter it. As you've just seen, the MIDI Click is playing the note C#1. These note events are now passing through the Keyboard and into the Monitor Object, which shows a progressing series of C#1 note events.

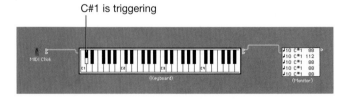

Because the MIDI Click generates note events, it can also be used to trigger synthesizers.

3   From the Environment's local menu bar, choose New > Internal > Apple QuickTime.

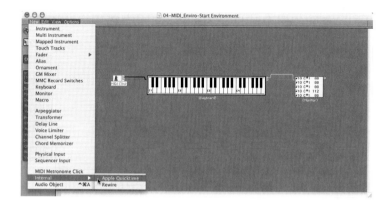

A QuickTime Synth Object appears to the left of the MIDI Click.

MORE INFO ▶ *Apple's QuickTime contains a built-in General MIDI (GM) synthesizer. The Object you've just created is used to trigger that QuickTime synthesizer. The QuickTime Synth provides a convenient way to start making sounds, but it isn't often used for serious music applications because its audio output is actually outside the Logic program, so you can't bounce its sound as part of your song (bouncing is covered in Lesson 16, "Working with Surround Sound").*

4   Drag a cable from the second arrow on the MIDI Click, and drop it onto the QuickTime Synth Object.

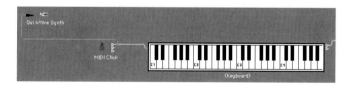

The QuickTime Synth taps out a rim shot in time with the metronome.

5 Select the MIDI Click Object.

6 From the Environment's local menu bar, choose Edit > Clear Cables Only (Ctrl-Delete).

The Clear Cables Only command breaks the selected Object's links to other Environment Objects, so all cables leading from the MIDI Click disappear.

NOTE ▶ You can also delete cables by using the Eraser tool, or by dragging a cable back onto the instrument it came from.

7 Press the spacebar to stop playback and halt the clicking sound.

Activating Logic's Sequencer

Logic's Environment is a *virtual representation* of the physical environment in your recording studio. It's the gatekeeper connecting Logic to the outside world, because all data entering or leaving Logic must pass through the Environment. While Logic's Environment does contain some MIDI signal processors that change MIDI data as Logic plays (the Arpeggiator, for example), the Environment primarily listens for incoming MIDI information and also sends MIDI information back out to your synthesizers and samplers.

The Environment you're working in is currently not set up to receive MIDI data. It's missing two important Environment Objects, a Physical Input and a Sequencer Input.

The Physical Input Object This Object listens to all of your computer's MIDI input ports. If it hears a MIDI signal, the Physical Input grabs that signal and brings it into Logic's Environment.

The Sequencer Input Object This Object transfers MIDI signals from the Environment to Logic's sequencer. From the sequencer, MIDI signals are directed to the track currently selected in Logic's Arrange window, which allows you to record MIDI sequences or trigger MIDI devices.

Let's create these two Objects and use them to activate the sequencer.

NOTE ▶ Logic comes preconfigured to correctly receive MIDI signals, but for the purpose of this exercise the MIDI input path has been intentionally broken to give you a chance to explore how MIDI passes into Logic from the outside world.

1 From the Environment's local menus, choose New > Physical Input.

A Physical Input Object appears.

NOTE ▶ Your newly created Objects may not appear in the same places as the Objects in the following figures. That's OK. The position of an Object in the Environment makes little difference to its functionality, and you're free to place your Objects anywhere within the Environment window.

2 Drag a cable from the Physical Input's SUM output (arrow) and drop it on the QuickTime Synth.

Play the controller keyboard connected to your computer. MIDI is now passing from the Physical Input straight to the QuickTime Synth, and you hear the sound of a piano. Great! You have just verified that MIDI signals are coming into the Environment through the Physical Input. However, getting MIDI into the Environment is just half the battle; next you need to pass that MIDI into Logic's sequencer.

MORE INFO ▸ *The Physical Input's SUM output collects the MIDI signals from all your computer's MIDI ports and combines them. The numbers under SUM correspond to the individual MIDI input channels available to your system.*

3   From the Environment's local menus, choose New > Sequencer Input.

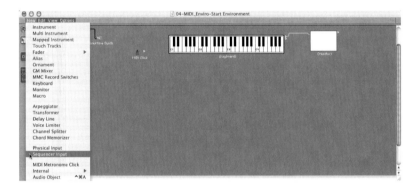

A Sequencer Input Object appears.

4   Drag a cable from the Physical Input's SUM arrow and drop it onto
the Sequencer Input.

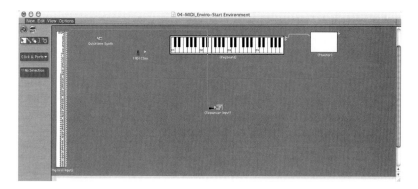

This breaks the connection between the Physical Input and the
QuickTime Synth Object, and instead connects the Physical Input to
the Sequencer Input. With this cable in place you've just connected
Logic's sequencer to the outside world, and Logic can now record
MIDI data.

5   Play your keyboard.

Do you hear anything? No. Logic makes no noise, so how do you
really know that MIDI data is coming in? The easiest way to find out
is to create a quick visual test using the Environment's Keyboard and
Monitor Objects.

6   From the Physical Input's SUM arrow, drag a cable to the Keyboard
Object.

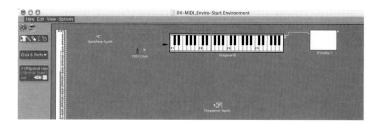

This breaks the connection between the Physical Input and the Sequencer Input, but only temporarily.

NOTE ▶ The Keyboard Object should still be connected to the Monitor Object. If it isn't, connect it now.

7 Drag a cable from the Monitor to the Sequencer Input.

MIDI events are now coming in through the Physical Input, which sends them down the cable to the Keyboard, Monitor, and finally the Sequencer Input.

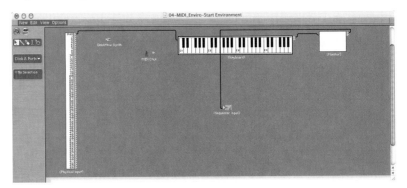

8 Play your controller keyboard.

The keys on the Environment's Keyboard play, and the Monitor updates a list of incoming MIDI events (in this case, notes). But do you hear anything yet? No, you don't, because Logic currently has no instruments to play. Let's change that.

Playing an Instrument

With the Sequencer Input connected to the Physical Input, MIDI signals are now passing from the outside world into Logic. Using the Arrange window, you can redirect those incoming MIDI signals to any MIDI device connected to your computer, including the QuickTime Synth.

1   Close the Environment window (Cmd-W).

The Arrange window is now the only one open.

2   In the Arrange window, click and hold the track named MIDI Click on the left side of its name.

A hierarchical menu called the Instrument List appears. This list is used to assign Environment Objects to tracks.

3   Choose Click & Ports > QuickTime Synth.

The track's name changes from MIDI Click to QuickTime Synth.

4   Play your controller keyboard.

You hear QuickTime's piano. Great news!

This experiment demonstrates an important point: Arrange window tracks always play through Objects in the Environment. But more on that later. We're not yet done with the Environment. There's lots more to learn, so open the Environment back up and get ready to dive in.

5   To open the Environment window once again, press the 8 key.

TIP ▶ Don't forget that Screenset 8 is the Environment window! To jump between the Arrange window (Screenset 1) and the Environment (Screenset 8), just press the 1 and 8 keys on your keyboard.

Working with Layers

The Environment is capable of holding many different Objects. To keep them all properly organized, Logic's Environment provides layers. How you organize your Environment layers is up to you—any Object can be placed on any layer. But as a general rule of thumb, Objects of the same type are usually placed on the same layer. For example, so far in this lesson you've been working in the Click & Ports layer. This layer holds a Metronome Object that clicks, and Input Objects connecting Logic's sequencer to your computer's MIDI input ports: Click & Ports!

Earlier in this lesson you created a QuickTime Synth Object on the Click & Ports layer. Remember that old *Sesame Street* song, "One of these things is not like the others …"? The QuickTime Synth Object is happy to live in the Click & Ports layer, but it's not a MIDI click or port! It's an instrument, so it makes a bit more sense to put the QuickTime Synth on a different layer.

1   Click and hold the Layer box, and choose **Create!**

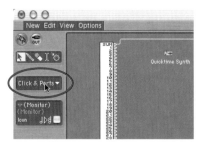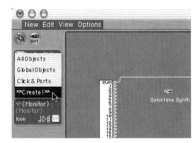

NOTE ▶ You can also create Environment layers by choosing Options > Layer > Insert (from the Environment's local menu bar). If you create too many layers, you can delete the unnecessary ones by choosing Options > Layer > Delete.

A new, unnamed layer is created. Unnamed layers don't tell you much about the Objects they hold. In a moment you will transfer the QuickTime Synth Object to this layer, so give the layer an appropriate name.

2 Double-click the Layer box.

A text input field appears. Type *QuickTime Synth,* and press Return.

3 Click and hold the Layer box, and reselect the Click & Ports layer.

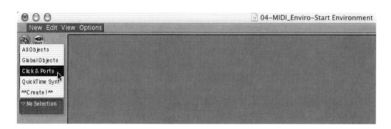

4 In the Click & Ports layer, select the QuickTime Synth Object.

5 Hold down the Option key, then from the Layer box select the QuickTime Synth layer.

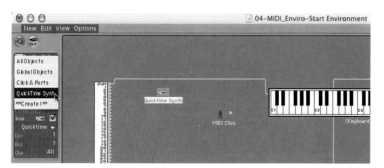

The QuickTime Synth layer appears, and the QuickTime Synth Object automatically jumps to its new home.

NOTE ▶ You can also cut (Cmd-X) and paste (Cmd-V) Objects between Environment layers.

6   Select the Click & Ports layer.

Notice that the QuickTime Synth Object is now gone from the Click & Ports layer!

Creating a Standard Instrument

Synthesizers have come a long way in the 20 years since MIDI became standard on all keyboards. In the early days of computer music, most synthesizers were *mono-timbral*, which means they could only send and receive MIDI data over a single MIDI channel. By today's standards these early synths were MIDI-challenged, to say the least! But even today some digital-effects units only use a single MIDI channel, so to simplify using these MIDI devices in your songs, Logic provides the Standard Instrument Object.

The Standard Instrument transmits MIDI data over just one channel, which makes it perfect for connecting to an external, mono-timbral MIDI device such as a Lexicon Alex reverb, so this lesson shows you how to set up this reverb in Logic. If you have an external, mono-timbral MIDI device, follow this section's steps by substituting your device for the Lexicon Alex reverb used here. Even if you don't have a mono-timbral

MIDI device at hand, you should still work through this exercise, because it covers MIDI ports and Object icons, which are important parameters common to all Logic instruments. (When you're finished with this exercise, just delete the newly created Standard Instrument Object.)

1   Create a new Environment layer and name it *MIDI Instruments*.

By the end of the lesson, this layer will hold Instrument Objects that point to all of your studio's MIDI devices. Begin the process now by creating a Standard Instrument:

2   From the Environment's local menu, select New > Instrument.

A new Standard Instrument is created.

3   In the Object Parameter box, click the instrument's name to open a text entry box, and type the name of the MIDI device this Instrument Object represents.

Setting an Instrument's MIDI Port and Channel

The Instrument Object's Port setting connects it directly to one of your computer's MIDI ports. All MIDI ports are available, including *virtual* MIDI ports for some software instruments (such as Bitheadz's Unity Session).

> **NOTE ▶** By now, your studio's MIDI devices should be connected to your computer. If not, take a moment to connect them. Pay particular attention to which of your computer's MIDI ports you plug each device into, because you'll need to know this to correctly set up your instruments inside Logic.

1   From the Object Parameter box's Port setting, click and hold the menu option All, and select the MIDI-in port connecting this Standard Instrument to its MIDI device.

MIDI data flows through MIDI ports in *channels*, and up to 16 separate MIDI channels can pass through each port at the same time. However, mono-timbral MIDI devices can only receive data on one MIDI channel at a time, so you must set the Standard Instrument Object's MIDI channel to match the MIDI channel of the device it represents.

2   From the Object Parameter box's MIDI Channel setting (represented by the term Cha), double-click the number 1 and enter the MIDI channel that your mono-timbral MIDI device is set to receive on.

NOTE ▶ You can also click and drag the MIDI Channel setting to quickly increase or decrease its value.

Selecting an Object Icon

An Object icon provides a visual reminder of an Object's purpose. Logic 6 contains new, high-resolution instrument icons that look great and help you tell at a glance exactly which instrument is which (this Object icon also shows up in the Arrange window's Track column after you assign the Object to a track). You don't have to select an instrument icon for every Object you create, but doing so makes your workspace a little nicer—and more personalized! It takes very little extra time, so why not do it?

▶   In the Object Parameter box, click the Instrument icon and select a graphic to represent your instrument.

 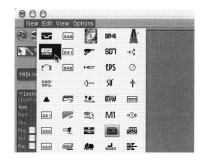

Creating a Multi Instrument

Multi Instrument Objects are designed to represent *multi-timbral* MIDI devices: devices that send and receive MIDI signals over many channels at once. All modern synthesizers and samplers can do this, so unless you collect vintage synthesizers, this is the Instrument Object you'll use most while working with Logic.

To demonstrate how a Multi Instrument works, this exercise sets up a Novation Supernova II, but feel free to use any multi-timbral synthesizer connected to your computer, including hardware synthesizers, or software synthesizers like Bitheadz's Unity Sessions.

1 From the Environment's local menus, choose New > Multi Instrument.

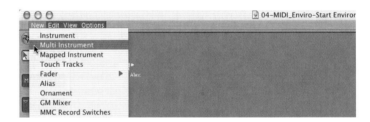

A new Multi Instrument is created.

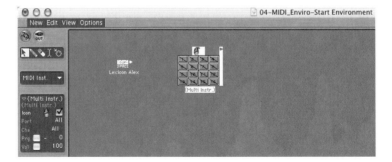

2   From the Environment's toolbox, select the Text tool.

3   On the Multi Instrument Object, click the Multi Instrument's name
and type the name of the MIDI device this Object will transmit MIDI
signals to; press Return.

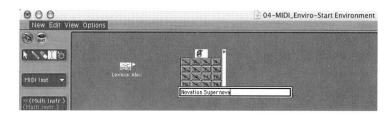

4   In the Object Parameter box, click and hold the word All (located
directly to the right of the word Port), and select the MIDI port that
this Multi Instrument will transmit MIDI data through.

   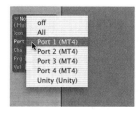

5   In the Object Parameter box, click the Instrument icon and select a graphic to represent your instrument.

A dialog appears asking if you'd like to change the icon for all subchannels.

6   You will explore subchannels in the next exercise, so for now click Change.

Logic assigns the selected icon to the Multi Instrument, and also to all of its subchannels.

Activating Subchannels

Multi-timbral instruments can use several different MIDI channels at the same time. To give you access to those multiple channels, the Multi Instrument provides 16 small buttons. These buttons represent subchannels within the Multi Instrument, with button 1 equal to MIDI channel 1, button 2 equal to MIDI channel 2, and so on.

1   In the Object Parameter box, you'll notice the instrument's Channel parameter (Cha) is currently set to All. Leave this setting untouched.

With the Channel parameter set to All, this Multi Instrument will transmit on all 16 MIDI channels—but in a very particular way: Subchannel 1 (the 1 button on the Multi Instrument) transmits through MIDI channel 1 of the instrument's port, subchannel 2 transmits through MIDI channel 2 of the instrument's port, and so on.

2   From the toolbox, grab the Arrow tool and click subchannel buttons until you've enabled all the MIDI channels over which your multi-timbral MIDI device is able to receive MIDI signals.

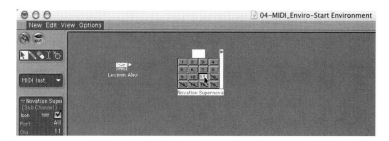

Clicking a subchannel removes the strike through it and enables it. You can now select this subchannel from the Arrange window's Instrument List and assign it to a track.

Using Instruments

Multi Instruments are rather complex, so to help you hit the ground running, this exercise walks you through setting up and playing a Multi Instrument, and then finishes by showing you how to use *programs* to select synthesizer sounds.

If you don't have an external synthesizer, don't worry—the QuickTime Synth you created earlier is a multi-timbral MIDI device! Even though the QuickTime Synth is software on your computer, it works just like any other multi-timbral synthesizer and provides a good example of how to use Multi Instruments. Work through this exercise using the QuickTime Synth, and then apply what you've learned to setting up Multi Instruments for your other multi-timbral MIDI devices.

TIP Lesson 10 depends on the QuickTime Synth being set up correctly, so don't skip this exercise!

Setting Up a Multi Instrument

1 In the Environment, select the QuickTime Synth layer.

2 Create a new Multi Instrument, and name it *QuickTime GM*.

3 Enable subchannels 1–16 (by clicking the appropriate buttons on the Multi Instrument's surface).

4 From the Output arrow in the Multi Instrument's top-left corner, drag a cable to the QuickTime Synth Object.

This arrow represents the Multi Instrument's MIDI output. Dragging a cable from this output to another Environment Object creates a MIDI signal path, so all MIDI data passing through the Multi Instrument will now go directly to the QuickTime Synth Object.

5   Logic asks if you want to remove the Port setting. Select Remove.

You want this Multi Instrument to send MIDI data to the QuickTime Synth only. Clicking Remove turns the Multi Instrument's Port setting off, and MIDI data will now only transmit through the cable to the QuickTime Synth Object.

6   Select the QuickTime GM Multi Instrument.

In the Instrument Parameter box, the QuickTime GM Multi Instrument's Port setting is now off, which means it sends no MIDI data to any of your computer's MIDI ports. Instead, all MIDI data is transferred through the cable to the QuickTime Synth Object.

The Multi Instrument's port setting is now off

This Multi Instrument is now set to play the QuickTime Synth only. But first, you must assign the Multi Instrument to one of the Arrange window's tracks, using the Instrument List.

Playing an Instrument

Arrange window tracks and Environment Objects are two hands that play
together to make sound. In previous exercises you've seen there's a direct
relationship between Arrange window tracks and Environment Objects,
because double-clicking a track's name in the Arrange window pops open
the Environment and automatically selects an Object. This selected Object
is called the track's *Output Object*, and you assign it to the track using the
Arrange window's Instrument List.

The Instrument List   The Instrument List is a hierarchical menu that determines which Environment Object a track plays through. It operates via
several levels: The first level displays your Environment's layers, the second
level lists the type of Objects on each layer, and the third level displays
each Object's channel(s).

1   Press the 1 key to make the Arrange window the active window.

2   Click and hold the left side of the QuickTime Synth track's name to
open the Arrange window's Instrument List.

3 From the hierarchical menu that appears, choose QuickTime Synth > QuickTime GM > 1 (Grand Piano).

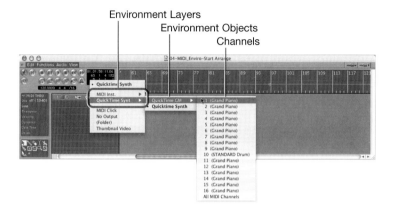

The Instrument List's Objects level shows the QuickTime Synth Object along with the QuickTime GM Multi Instrument. Notice that the QuickTime Synth Object is highlighted in bold letters, which indicates that it's the currently selected Object. From now on you will use the QuickTime GM Multi Instrument to target specific channels in the QuickTime Synth. To avoid clutter and make things easy to find, you will want to remove the QuickTime Synth from the Instrument List.

4 Press the 8 key to open the Environment.

5 Select the QuickTime Synth Object.

6   In the Object Parameter box, deselect the QuickTime Synth's Icon
check box.

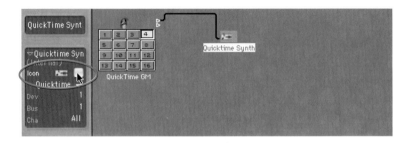

The Arrange window's Instrument List only shows Objects with this
check box ticked. By deselecting the Icon check box, you tell Logic to
remove the QuickTime Synth from the Instrument List.

NOTE ▶ On a Multi Instrument, the slash through each subchannel
is similar to the check box beside the Object icon. Enabling a subchannel makes it available for selection in the Instrument List, while
disabling a subchannel removes it from the Instrument List.

7   Open the Arrange window (press the 1 key).

8   Click and hold the left side of the QuickTime Synth track name and
check out the Instrument List.

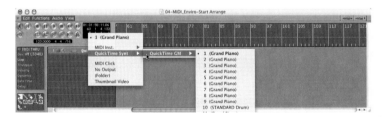

The QuickTime Synth Object is no longer displayed on the
Instrument List's Objects level.

9   From the Instrument List, choose QuickTime Synth > QuickTime GM > 1 (Grand Piano).

10   Play your controller keyboard.

The QuickTime Synth still sounds like a piano—exactly the same as before! To change this you can select a different instrument sound using the Object Parameter box's Program setting.

Using Programs to Select Sounds

Programs are sounds on your synthesizer. One of the most creativity-draining parts of making music is reaching over to select programs on hardware synthesizers, or switching between windows to control your software instruments. Logic is designed to enhance your creativity by making music production easy, and it happily lets you select synthesizer programs from right inside its workspace (no need to take your eyes off the screen).

Effectively using Instrument programs turns your studio into an extension of Logic itself, because selected programs are saved into your song. Session after session, just turn your MIDI devices on, open your song, and Logic automatically sets up your synthesizers by telling them which programs to play.

1   In the Object Parameter box on the left edge of the Arrange window, check the Prg (Program) check box.

   NOTE ▶ If you can't see the Object Parameter box, drag the bottom of the Arrange window down.

Program selection is now enabled.

2   To the right of the Prg check box, click and hold the number 0.

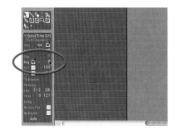

The program list appears.

3   Choose program 49 (Slow Strings).

4   Play your controller keyboard.

You now hear a string patch. Choose a few more programs and try out their sounds.

To make sure that programs are recalled and properly loaded into your synthesizer when the song is opened, you need to make one final setting.

5   Choose File > Song Settings > MIDI Options.

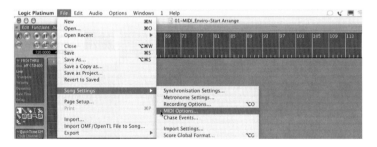

The Song Settings dialog opens.

6   Select "Send Used Instr. MIDI Settings after loading," and to ensure that your synthesizers play the patches at the correct volume, also select the "Send All Fader Values after loading" check box.

Now, when you open the song, Logic automatically loads the correct programs into your synthesizers and sets their volume and pan positions to the same levels as when you last saved and closed the song. This sets up your synths to play the proper patches, so that your songs sound the same, session after session after session.

Customizing the Program List

Logic's default program list represents the GM sound set. The QuickTime Synth also uses the GM sound set, and Logic's default program names conveniently match the QuickTime Synth's sounds. That's great for the QuickTime Synth, but the reality is that most synthesizers don't conform to the GM sound set. To make the names in the program list match the names of your synth's programs, you must modify the program list.

> **MORE INFO ▶** *Some synthesizer manufacturers have a download section on their Web sites where you can find Logic projects containing pre-configured instruments. When customizing your program lists, these files save you from having to type program names by hand.*

1 At the top of the Arrange window's Object Parameter box, click the Object's name.

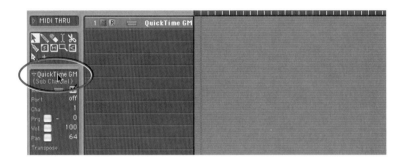

A window opens showing the programs in the GM sound set. The program currently used is selected.

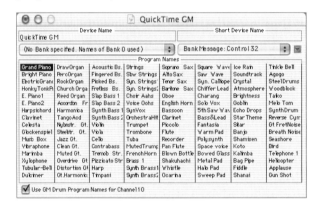

NOTE ▶ You can also open this window from the Environment window by double-clicking the small Instrument icon at the top of a Multi Instrument Object.

2 Double-click a program name.

A text box appears over the program's name.

3   Type a new program name into the text box.

4   Work through the program list until you've changed all programs to the names used by your synthesizer.

5   If your synthesizer has more than one bank of sounds, choose Bank 1 from the Bank selection menu.

Logic asks if you'd like to initialize the new bank.

6   Choose Initialize.

NOTE ▶ Initialize new banks only when absolutely necessary, as each new bank adds to your project file's size.

7   Follow steps 2 to 4 to enter the program names for this new bank.

8   To select the new bank, choose it by number from the Object Parameter box's Bank menu, which currently looks like a hyphen (-) beside the Prg check box.

Finishing Your MIDI Environment

To finish setting up your MIDI Environment, create Standard or Multi Instrument Objects to represent every MIDI device in your studio. If your studio is small and has only a few MIDI devices, you can probably remember which MIDI port and channel(s) each device is connected to. But if your studio is more complex, using many MIDI devices connected to several different MIDI ports, you'll benefit from compiling a studio inventory.

MIDI Device Chart

MIDI Device	Port		MIDI Channels															
			1	2	3	4	5	6	7	8	9	10	12	11	13	14	15	16
Novation Supernova	MT4 1	In	X	X	X	X	X	X	X	X								
		Out	X	X	X	X	X	X	X	X								
Yamaha A5000	MT4 1	In									X	X	X	X	X	X	X	X
		Out																
Sequential Multi-Trak	MT4 2	In	X															
		Out																
Lexicon Alex	MT4 3	In	X															
		Out																
BBE Sonic Maximizer	MT4 3	In		X														
		Out																
Unity Session	Internal	In	X	X	X	X	X	X	X	X	X	X	X	X	X	X	X	X
		Out																
		In																
		Out																
		In																
		Out																
		In																
		Out																
		In																
		Out																

MIDI DEVICE CHART. Here's a sample of a MIDI device chart filled in to reflect the instruments in an example project studio.

A studio inventory is simply a chart that lists each of your MIDI devices, the MIDI ports that connect each device to your computer, and the MIDI channel(s) they are set to receive/transmit on. You can find a studio inventory chart in PDF format inside the Lesson 4 > Extras folder on this book's companion CD-ROM.

1   Open and print the PDF file named **MIDIDeviceChart.pdf**.

2   Fill out the chart.

3   Refer to this studio inventory while creating Instrument Objects for each MIDI device in your studio.

Depending on the complexity of your MIDI setup, this may take some time. But you only need to do it once. In the next exercise you will save this custom Environment as your personal Autoload song, and it will serve as a template from which you'll begin all new Logic compositions.

About the Autoload Song

Over the course of this lesson, you've filled Logic's Environment with Instrument Objects that reflect the MIDI devices in your studio. You've created MIDI Input Objects to channel MIDI signals into Logic and Instrument Objects to send MIDI signals back out to your MIDI devices, and you've arranged all of the Environment's Objects on their own layers, which makes them easier to find when needed. Only one step remains, and that's saving the "song" you've built as your own personal Autoload song. Each time you start Logic or create a new project, this Autoload song will automatically open on your screen, providing you with a blank workspace perfectly configured to get you making music.

1   Press 1 to open Screenset 1, and make sure the Arrange window is the only window open on your screen.

You'll want to start new songs from the Arrange window, so it's best to save the Autoload song with only the Arrange window open. This ensures that the Arrange window is the first one to appear onscreen each time you open Logic or create a new song by choosing File > New (Cmd-N).

2   Choose File > Save As.

The Save As dialog opens.

NOTE ▸ Make sure you choose File > Save As! Choosing File > Save simply saves the file you're currently working on to its current place on your hard disk. But the Autoload file needs to be saved in a very particular place on your hard disk, and only the Save As dialog will let you do that.

3   Type *Autoload* into the Save As field.

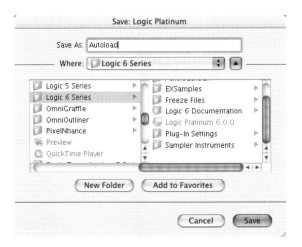

This is an important step. The file you save *must* be called exactly Autoload, or Logic will not recognize it as the Autoload song.

4 Navigate to the folder that contains the Logic Audio application.

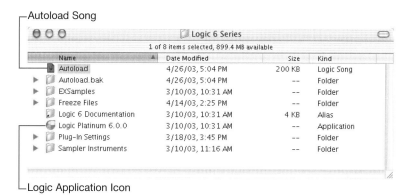

For Logic to recognize the Autoload song, it must be located in Logic's root folder, at the same level as the Logic Audio application icon. If the Autoload song is moved out of Logic's root folder, new projects will use the default workspace, so make sure you save your Autoload song in the right place.

NOTE ▶ By default, the Logic installer places the Logic Audio application in the System Drive > Applications > Logic 6 Series folder on your hard disk. If you installed Logic in a different location, find it now.

5 Click Save.

What You've Learned

- To get MIDI data into Logic, the Environment must have a Physical Input cabled to a Sequencer Input.

- To make things easier to find, Logic's Environment is organized into layers holding similar Objects.

- Standard Instrument Objects point to mono-timbral MIDI devices that use only one MIDI channel.

- Multi Instrument Objects point to multi-timbral MIDI devices that use up to 16 different MIDI channels. The boxes on top of the Multi Instrument represent each of the 16 available channels.

- By using the Instrument Object's Program parameter to select instrument sounds, you ensure that the correct synthesizer programs are saved with your song and then properly recalled every time the song is opened.

- The Autoload song contains customized Instrument Objects that reflect the setup of your personal studio.

- For Logic to recognize the Autoload song, it must be saved in the same folder as the Logic application icon (inside the Logic 6 Series folder on your hard disk).

5

Start	05-Audio_Enviro-Start
Complete	05-Audio_Enviro-Finished
Time	Approximately 40 minutes
Goals	Configure Logic to work with audio
	Learn how audio enters and exits Logic through channels
	Create Audio Objects in a customized Environment Audio layer
	Explore the basics of the channel view
	Learn how to use Logic's software instruments

Lesson 5
Setting Up the Audio Environment

In Lesson 4 you learned that Objects form the connections between Logic and the rest of your studio. For example, MIDI signals enter and exit Logic through Instrument Objects in Logic's Environment. Audio is handled much the same way, and before Logic will record or play sound, you must populate the Environment with Audio Objects that connect Logic to your computer's audio interface.

Configuring Audio Hardware and Drivers

To get sound into and out of your computer, you must have an *audio interface.* An audio interface is a device that converts digital audio from your computer to analog waves that speakers can broadcast; or, in the other direction, an audio interface converts analog waves into digital audio you can save and manipulate on your computer. Either way, an audio interface has only one purpose: It converts sound between the digital and analog domains.

> **MORE INFO** ▶ *The audio interface that comes with your computer is sufficient for using Logic, but it offers only two eighth-inch inputs (PowerBooks do not have inputs) and two eighth-inch outputs. These are connections usually reserved for attaching a set of headphones to your computer or for basic recording purposes. They do not offer professional sound quality. To make your recordings really shine, you need a professional audio interface such as Emagic's EMI 2|6.*

To communicate with its audio interface, a computer needs a small software application called a *driver.* All audio interfaces have their own special drivers, and in most cases you'll have to install that driver before Logic will recognize it. But once that driver's installed, there's very little else you need to do. Logic will automatically recognize your audio interface along with all available inputs and outputs.

However, situations might arise where Logic unexpectedly uses the wrong audio interface. For example, if Logic starts playing from the speaker on your computer, it's using your computer's *built-in audio controller* instead of your audio interface. Fortunately, this situation is easy to fix—just select your audio interface's driver from Logic's Audio Hardware & Drivers Preferences pane.

NOTE ▶ In OS X, Logic uses the system's Core Audio architecture to communicate with your audio interface(s). Core Audio represents a massive step forward for audio on the Macintosh. Finally, several applications can stably share a single audio interface at the same time. For example, you can now play a Logic arrangement, preview a video in QuickTime, and audition audio loops in iTunes—all at the same time! (Try doing that in OS 9.)

Selecting an Audio Driver

1 Open the Autoload song you saved at the end of the last lesson.

   NOTE ▶ If you don't have this file, you can follow along using the file named **05-Audio_Environment-Start**.

2 Choose Audio > Audio Hardware & Drivers

The Audio Driver Preferences window opens. Core Audio is automatically selected, and Logic will choose either the built-in audio driver or your audio interface from the Driver menu.

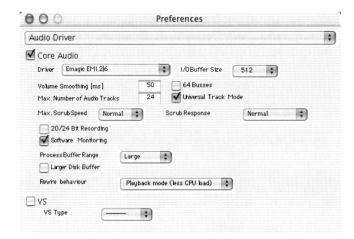

If you have more than one audio interface attached to your system, you can choose a different one than that which Logic has automatically selected.

NOTE ▶ In OS 9 several driver choices will now be presented to you. Select the driver that works with your audio interface.

3   From the Driver menu, choose the audio interface you want to use.

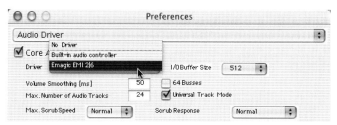

If you selected a different audio interface than the one Logic automatically chose, you will be presented with a new dialog that asks you to
reboot Logic.

4   Select Try (Re)Launch.

You do not actually need to reboot Logic, because the audio interfaces
switch in the background while Logic remains open.

Increasing Available Audio Tracks

By default, Logic gives you 24 audio track channels. If you need more than
24 audio tracks, you can increase this number using the Max. Number of
Audio Tracks setting in the Audio Hardware & Driver Preferences window.

1   If you closed the Audio Driver Preferences window, reopen it now by
choosing Audio > Audio Hardware & Drivers.

The Audio Driver Preferences window opens. Close to the top there's a
preference that says Max. Number of Audio Tracks.

2 Set this number to the number of audio tracks you'd like to enable.

> **NOTE ▸** Logic Audio users can enable up to 48 tracks. Logic Gold users have access to 64 tracks, while Logic Platinum 6 users can enable up to 128 stereo audio tracks!

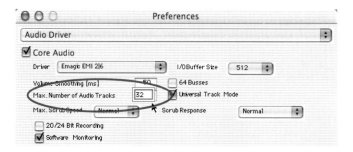

3 Click OK to close the Preferences window.

Exploring the Audio Configuration Window

A *channel* is a path used to transport a signal. Lesson 4 demonstrated how MIDI channels transport MIDI signals between your studio's MIDI devices and Logic. Audio channels are similar, but instead of sending MIDI messages to a synthesizer, audio channels transport sound to and from your audio interface's outputs and inputs.

Audio channels can also be used to move audio around inside your computer. Busses, which transmit audio from Object to Object inside Logic, are channels. Audio tracks are also channels, but a very special type that reads and records audio files on your hard disks. To see an overview of the audio channels available on your system, check out the Audio Configuration window.

1   Select Audio > Audio Configuration.

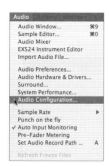

The Audio Configuration window opens.

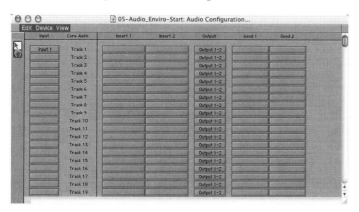

2   Scroll down the Audio Configuration window to see a list of your system's available audio channels.

In the preceding figure, the channels for the system (in this case, a system using the Emagic EMI 2|6 audio interface) are listed in the column under the Core Audio heading. If you are using a different audio interface, your Audio Configuration window may list a different configuration of audio channels.

3   Using the descriptions that follow as a reference, check out the types of channels available for your system. Then, close the Audio Configuration window.

The types of channels that may appear for your system include the following:

Inputs Input channels represent the physical audio inputs of your audio interface.

Tracks Track channels record audio to your computer's hard disks and also play recorded audio files back.

Instruments Using any of Logic's software instruments, Instrument channels transform MIDI information into audio signals that are transmitted to your audio interface's outputs.

> **NOTE** ▶ KlopfGeist (German for "knocking ghost") is inserted on Instrument channel 64. Logic automatically assigns Instrument channel 64 to the Metronome Object, which means KlopfGeist is the synthesizer that makes the metronome's clicking sound. If you remove KlopfGeist from Instrument channel 64, your metronome won't make a sound! For this reason, using or modifying Instrument channel 64 is not recommended.

Bus Bus channels move sound from channel to channel inside Logic. For example, you can send sound from several different channels into the same bus, then insert a real-time effect (such as a reverb) on the bus. This lets you use a single reverb on several tracks at the same time.

Aux Aux channels are similar to inputs but can also receive signals from busses, making them perfect for creating submixes.

Outputs Output channels represent the physical outputs of your audio interface.

Stereo Inputs and Outputs Stereo Input and Output channels are stereo versions of the standard inputs and outputs.

Master The Master channel is a global volume control for all output channels.

Using Audio Objects

The channels listed in the Audio Configuration window are always available and ready for use—but first you have to assign them to Audio Objects. Audio Objects connect Logic to your audio interface, and their primary function is to show Logic where to send audio signals.

Creating and Populating an Audio Layer

In Lesson 4 you created a couple of new Environment layers to hold MIDI Instrument Objects. Now, it's time to make a new Environment layer for Audio Objects and create your first one.

1   Press 8 to open the Environment window.

The Environment window opens and displays the layer that was on screen the last time you used the Environment.

2   From the Environment's Layer box, choose **Create!**.

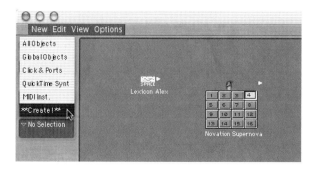

A new, unnamed layer is created.

3   In the Layer box, double-click the word "(unnamed)" to open a text box, then name the layer *Audio*.

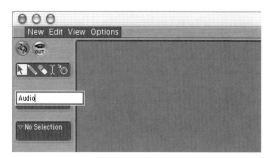

4   From the Environment's local menu, choose New > Audio Object.

TIP ▶ You can (and should!) assign a key command to create new Audio Objects! Check out the Environment Window section of the Key Commands window. Cmd-Ctrl-A (A for "Audio Object") is a good choice for this key command.

A new, unnamed Audio Object appears in the Environment's Audio layer. This Object currently looks like a little rectangular icon.

5   Double-click the new Audio Object icon.

The Object expands into a channel strip! This is called the *channel view*, and it looks just like a channel strip on a standard hardware mixing console. The channel view provides an interface used to control and manipulate a channel's sound by boosting or attenuating (lowering) the volume, changing a sound's pan position, and inserting digital signal processing (DSP) effects.

NOTE ▶ Audio Objects can be reduced to their smaller size by double-clicking the upper-left corner of an Object that is in channel view.

Taking In the Channel View

Let's take a moment to check out the channel view and find out what it lets you do.

The Channel View Areas We'll start with five different areas included in the channel view.

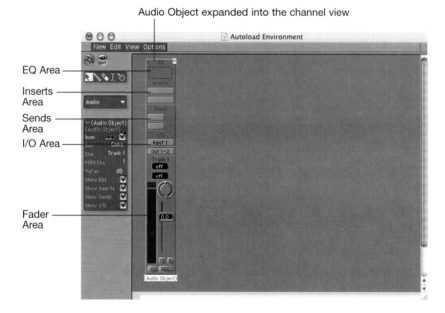

Audio Object expanded into the channel view

EQ Area

Inserts Area

Sends Area

I/O Area

Fader Area

The EQ Area The EQ area opens to reveal an eight-band equalizer with spectrum analyzer. With the exception of a Master channel, each channel may have its very own dedicated EQ used to boost or attenuate specific frequency ranges in the channel's sound.

The Inserts Area The Inserts area assigns DSP effects such as dynamic range compression and delay to a channel's sound.

The Sends Area The Sends area sends the channel's sound to a system bus, which transports the sound to a different channel in Logic.

The I/O Area The I/O area sets the channel's input and output path. Depending on the type of channel assigned to the Audio Object, the input can be an audio interface input, a bus, or one of Logic's software instruments.

The Fader Area The Fader area sets the channel's volume and pan position and also has Mute and Solo buttons. The Mute button turns off the channel's sound, while the Solo button turns off the sound of all channels other than the one being soloed (you will also hear other channels that have the Solo button enabled).

The Audio Object Parameters Now, let's zoom in on the box to the left of the channel view that shows the settings for the Audio Object parameters. These parameter values govern the channel each Audio Object uses, the scale used by the Object's fader, and the areas displayed in the Object's channel view.

Channel Parameter
   Device Parameter
      Object Parameter Box

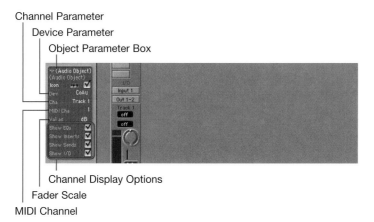

      Channel Display Options
   Fader Scale
MIDI Channel

Dev (Audio Driver) The *Dev* parameter selects a driver and, in turn, an audio interface for the audio channel to use. Unless you changed this driver in the exercise at the beginning of this lesson, this parameter will say CoAu, which is short for Core Audio.

Cha (Audio Channel) *Cha* sets the Audio Object's channel. By default, new Objects are assigned to the first unused Track channel, but you can use this setting to assign the Object to any channel that Logic has available.

MIDI Cha (MIDI Channel) *MIDI Cha* determines which MIDI channel the Object receives controller information from. Controller information is used to automate channel plug-ins and mix parameters, such as volume or pan.

Val as (Fader Scale) *Val as* changes the scale of the Object's fader between decibels (dB) or numbers (0–127).

Channel Display Options *Channel Display options* enable and disable the selected channel's EQ, Insert, Send, or I/O area.

Exploring Audio Object Parameters

The above section provided an overview of the parameters available to each Audio Object. Now, let's put the theory to practice.

1 To the right of the Cha (Channel) parameter, click and hold the term Track 1.

A hierarchical menu opens to display a list of available channels. This list matches the channels shown in the Audio Configuration window. Is this starting to look familiar?

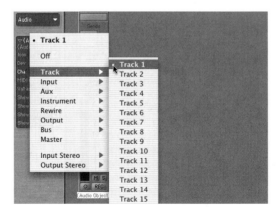

NOTE ▶ Items in bold lettering indicate that the channel is currently assigned to an Audio Object in the Environment. In the current example, only Track 1 is assigned to an Audio Object, so only Track 1 is bold.

2   Leave the Cha parameter set to Track 1.

The Audio Object is currently named *(Audio Object)*. That doesn't tell you very much about its function, and in fact, it's best to give all Objects descriptive names that indicate the type of channel the Audio Object represents, such as *electric guitar* or *lead vocal.*

TIP ▶ Bracketed names are names provided by Logic. If you see a bracketed name, it's a good idea to change it to something more descriptive of the Object's purpose, particularly if you plan to use the option Use Audio Object Name for File Name in the Set Record Path dialog.

3   At the top of the Object Parameter box, click the words *(Audio Object)*, and name the Audio Object *Track 1.*

4   Deselect the EQ, Insert, Send, and I/O check boxes.

On the Object's channel view, the corresponding areas are hidden.

5   Reselect the EQ, Insert, Send, and I/O check boxes.

Converting Channels to Stereo

Audio Objects are created as mono Objects, but you can convert them to stereo, and back again, by clicking the Stereo/Mono button in the Audio Object's bottom-left corner.

1   Click the Stereo/Mono button (the one with a single circle on it).

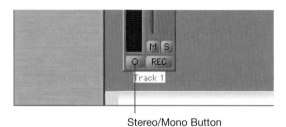

Stereo/Mono Button

The button changes to show two linked circles, and the channel is converted to stereo.

2   Click and hold the Stereo/Mono button.

A menu appears that lets you convert the channel to mono, stereo, or even the left or right channels of a stereo signal.

3   Choose Stereo.

Using Logic's Audio Instruments

Software synthesizers (soft-synths) have come of age, and Logic's soft-synths are some of the best around. In the olden days (circa 2001!) soft-synths sounded thin and were far less aurally impressive than today's breed of software instruments. Emagic has created an arsenal of great-sounding software instruments that are designed exclusively for Logic users. They all have huge, lush sound, and when you need a floor-shaking bass stab or an ethereal pad to add depth to your arrangement, these built-in instruments are just the ticket.

All versions of Logic come with the following three software instruments, and you can enable the other instruments by purchasing a user license (visit Emagic's Web site, www.emagic.de, for more details).

ES E The ES E is a pad synth that is great for adding atmospheric sounds to trip hop, techno, and even video sound tracks.

ES M If you're looking for a bass sound to punch through your mix, the ES M should be your starting point. The sounds in this synth are very deep techno, jungle, and R&B.

ES P This is a polyphonic synthesizer designed for chords, sweeps, and heavier synth stabs. A touch of your controller keyboard's modulation wheel will often change the ES P's sounds dramatically.

> **NOTE ▶** The trial version of Logic that comes with this book provides you with time-limited demos of every Emagic instrument, so make sure you try them all out (pay particular attention to the extremely useful EXS24 sampler and superb-sounding ES2 soft-synth).

EXS 24 SAMPLER

Let's try creating an ES M synth in your Audio Layer and see how it sounds.

1   In the Environment's Audio layer, create a new Audio Object.

2 Click and hold the new Object's Channel parameter (in the Object Parameter box), and choose Instrument > Instrument 1.

 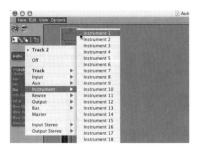

The Audio Object is assigned to Audio Instrument 1.

3 Double-click the Audio Object to expand it into the channel view, and name the new Object *Audio Inst. 1.*

4 Click and hold the I/O area's Input box, and choose Mono > ES M.

 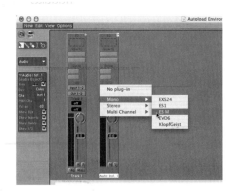

NOTE ▶ Your instrument list might look different from the one pictured. The figure above shows all of Logic's mono software instruments. To activate these extra software instruments, you will have to purchase a key from Emagic.

The ES M synth is assigned as the input for Audio Instrument 1.

5 On the Audio Instrument 1 channel, double-click the I/O area's Input
box (on ES M).

The ES M synth opens on your screen.

NOTE ▶ The Audio Preferences window has an option in its Display
area labeled "Open plug-in window on insertion." With this option
enabled, software instruments pop open immediately when assigned
to a track, which saves you from having to double-click the input box.

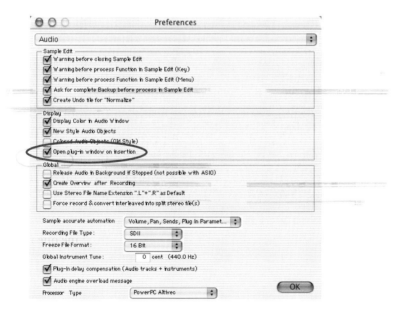

6   Press 1 to open the Arrange window.

The Arrange window currently has just one track. To hear the ES M, use the instrument list to assign this track to the new Audio instrument.

7   Click and hold the left edge of the track name to open the instrument list, and choose Audio > Audio Instrument > Audio Inst. 1.

8   Play your controller keyboard.

That's the ES M you're hearing!

Choosing Instrument Presets

Each Logic instrument has dozens of preset sounds, and because all Logic instruments are fully programmable, you can use the presets as launch points for quickly designing your own unique sounds. Let's explore the presets available for the ES M synth you just created.

1   Press 8 to open the Environment.

In the last exercise you left the ES M open in screenset 8, so you'll need to reopen that screenset to see the ES M.

2 On the ES M synth, click the Settings menu (beside the Bypass button) and choose factory 2 > house_bass.

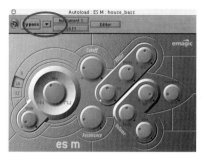

The Settings menu looks like a small, downward-pointing triangle, but don't let its size fool you—this menu hides large functions because the instrument presets are all stored here.

3 Play your controller keyboard.

4 Continue exploring the instrument's presets to see what they sound like, and make a mental note of each one—later, if you ever need these sounds, you'll know exactly where to find them.

Changing Presets with Key Commands

Choosing presets from the instrument's Settings menu slows you down when trying to find that perfect sound. To make selecting presets faster, you can set up key commands that let you cycle through presets by pressing keys on your computer's keyboard. Follow this exercise's steps to make Option-N choose the next instrument preset, and Option-B choose the previous preset.

1 Choose Logic > Preferences > Key Commands (Option-K).

The Key Commands window opens.

2 Scroll to the bottom of the Global Commands section, until the Next Plug-In Setting and Previous Plug-In Setting commands are visible.

3 Select the Next Plug-In Setting command.

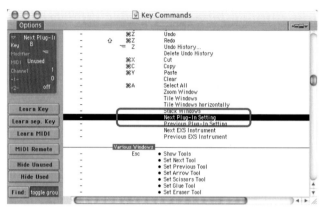

4 On the Key Commands window's left side, click Learn Key.

5 Press Option-N.

Option-N is now assigned to the Next Plug-In Setting command. As long as an audio instrument is open on your screen, you can now jump to the next preset sound by pressing Option-N (think "option-next") on the keyboard.

6   Directly below the Next Plug-In Setting command, select the Previous Plug-In Setting command and press Option-B.

Option-B is just like Option-N but instead jumps back one preset (think "option-back").

7   Close the Key Commands window.

8   Play your controller keyboard, and press Option-N or Option-B to cycle through the instrument presets.

Saving Your Finished Autoload Song

Some Logic users preconfigure their Autoload song with several Audio Objects, making many tracks and instruments available to each new song. However, each Audio Object takes up a small amount of system resources, so save CPU power for more important things (like DSP effects!) by creating only as many Audio Objects as your project requires, as you need them.

Creating Audio Objects is simple and quick. To help you practice this important technique, you are going to clear your Autoload Environment of all Audio Objects. Throughout the rest of this book's lessons, whenever you need an Audio Object, you'll just create one!

MORE INFO ▶ *As you become more comfortable with Logic, you may decide to save a few more Audio Objects into your Autoload song—this is up to you and is fully dependent on how you make music. For example, you might often use the Emagic EXS24 sampler. In this situation it makes sense to populate your Autoload song with some Audio Instrument Objects set up with the EXS24. Now, a few EXS24s will be available every time you start a new song, letting you jump right in and make music.*

1   Press 8 to open the Environment.

2   Rubber-band select both the Track 1 and Audio Inst. 1 Objects, and press Delete.

3   Press 1 to open the Arrange window.

4   Save your Autoload song (Cmd-S).

    NOTE ▶ If you started this lesson with the included Start file, and not your own Autoload song from Lesson 4, you'll need to use the Save As option to save your Autoload song in the Logic 6 Series folder on your hard disk (see the end of Lesson 4 for details).

Locking the Autoload Song

Cmd-S! This key command saves your song, and good habits dictate that you should Cmd-S often while working with Logic. OS X is incredibly stable when compared with OS 9—but crashes do happen (particularly when USB audio interfaces are accidentally unplugged). To avoid the sadness of seeing creativity disappear into a frozen or crashed program, you are well advised to make Cmd-S your friend, and then visit her often.

However, Cmd-S is no friend to your Autoload song, and it's easy to accidentally Cmd-S unwanted changes into this very important file. To protect your Autoload song, lock it.

1   In your computer's Finder, locate and select your Autoload song.

 If you've added the Logic application icon to the Dock, Ctrl-click the application icon and select Show in Finder, and the Logic 6 Series folder will jump open on your screen. Inside you'll find your Autoload song.

2   Choose File > Get Info (Cmd-I).

An Info window opens.

3   Select the Locked check box.

Your Autoload song is now locked and cannot be changed or saved over (if you look closely at the song file, you'll see a little lock attached to its bottom-left corner). If you need to change your Autoload song, you'll have to unlock the song file by deselecting this check box.

What You've Learned

- Audio drivers tell Logic how to communicate with your system's audio interfaces, and you select your audio driver from Logic's Audio Driver Preferences window (Audio > Audio Hardware & Drivers).

- The Audio Configuration window lists all the audio channels available to Logic.

- To access an audio channel, you must first assign it to an Audio Object.

- Audio Objects provide the graphic interface for audio channels and look like the channel strips on any hardware mixing console.

- Audio Objects should be kept on their own Audio layer in the Environment. This makes them easy to locate when needed.

- Logic's built-in synthesizers are called *audio instruments,* and they provide you with instant access to a vast library of sounds (called *presets*) that you can use in your songs.

- Each Audio Object takes up a small amount of system resources, so to save your CPU for more important things (like DSP effects), create only as many Audio Objects as your song needs.

6

Media	Bass Line.mid
	8 Bar Beat
	Rhodes 1 (100 BPM)
	Rhodes 2 (100 BPM)
Start	06-Prerecorded_Media-Start
Complete	06-Prerecorded_Media-Finished
Bonus File	Herbie Hancock Keys
Time	Approximately 30 minutes
Goals	Learn how to import MIDI and audio files
	Set up an Audio Monitor channel to use for previewing files listed in the Audio window
	Examine and update waveform overviews that graphically represent your audio files
	Move audio files from the Audio window to Arrange window tracks

Lesson 6
Using Prerecorded Media

Samples. Samples. Samples! These days there's a huge wealth of audio sample collections available (either in stores or via direct download from the Internet), and it's becoming increasingly common to create songs by combining prerecorded files into an arrangement. Prerecorded media includes MIDI and audio files stored on your computer's hard disks, and unless you're a musical purist focused on creating all of your song's sounds by hand, you'll find drum loops, recorded vocals, and MIDI sequences commonly forming the base for your work in Logic.

Importing MIDI Files

MIDI files are easy to import into Logic—you simply drag them from the Finder and drop them onto any Arrange window track. Let's use that technique to import a bass line for the arrangement you're going to create.

1   Open your Autoload song.

   NOTE ▶ If you haven't worked through Lesson 4 and Lesson 5 to create your Autoload song, open the file named **06-Prerecorded_Media-Start**.

2   Use the Finder to locate the file named **Bass Line.mid**.

   NOTE ▶ The **Bass Line.mid** file is located in the Logic Course Media folder, which you should already have copied from this book's companion CD-ROM to your hard disk.

3   From the Finder, drag the **Bass Line.mid** file over the No Output track, and drop it at bar 5. (If your Arrange window doesn't have a No Output track, just drop the MIDI file on any available track.)

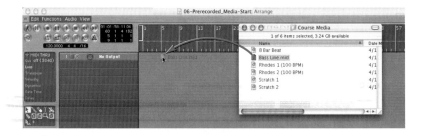

The MIDI file will drop at the pointer's position to create a MIDI sequence, so before you release the mouse button make sure the pointer is at bar 5 of the No Output track. (If you drop the MIDI file at a different bar, grab it and drag it to bar 5.)

TIP ▶ If you're using a lot of MIDI sequences in your arrangement, it's a good idea to start your songs at bar 5 instead of bar 1. This provides you with four extra bars at the beginning of your arrangement, which can be used to hold control change, program change, and even sysex information that automatically sets up your synthesizers to play the correct sounds. When it comes time to bounce the song, cut off the extra space at the arrangement's beginning by adjusting the Song Start marker (see Lesson 12, "Sweetening the Mix").

4   Depending on how your version of Logic is configured, you might see a dialog that says, "New SMPTE Frame rate recognized! Use it?" SMPTE is used to measure time in video, but you are not using video in this project, so if you get this dialog, click Cancel to dismiss it.

Right now the MIDI sequence looks like a little beam, or a tiny black rectangle with one corner snipped, in the Arrange area. If you zoom in on the track, you'll be able to see MIDI notes right on the beam, which helps you identify what kind of content the track contains.

5   Use the Arrange window's telescopes to zoom in on the track.

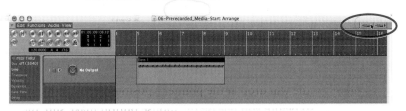

As you increase the track's height, notes become visible on the MIDI sequence's surface. Zoom in until you can comfortably see the notes.

Assigning an Instrument to the Sequence's Track

The imported MIDI file is called **Bass Line.mid**, and as you might expect, this MIDI file will form your song's bass line. Logic 6 comes with a great bass synthesizer called the ES M, which you learned how to use in Lesson 5. This file is designed for the ES M's house_bass preset, so set up the ES M now.

1 Press 8 to open the Environment, and navigate to the Audio layer.

2 Create a new Audio Object, name it *Bass Line,* and assign its channel to Instrument > Instrument 1.

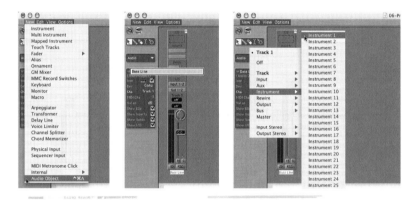

NOTE ▶ Don't forget to double-click the Audio Object to expand it into the channel view!

TIP ▶ Look closely at the New > Audio Object option in the figure above, and you'll see that the custom keyboard command Ctrl-Cmd-A has been assigned to it. This command forms a handy little triangle (like the letter A, for Audio Object) in the bottom-left corner of your screen. You'll be creating a lot of Audio Objects as you work with Logic, so when you have a spare moment, open the Key Commands window and set up this custom key command.

3 Click and hold the Bass Line Object's Input, and choose Mono > ES M.

 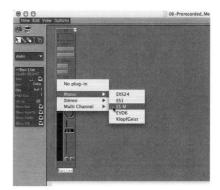

4 If the ES M doesn't automatically open, open it by double-clicking the
Instrument Object's Input (on ES M).

5 Use the ES M's Presets menu to assign the house_bass preset, then
close the ES M.

6 Press 1 to open the Arrange window.

7 Click and hold the left side of the No Output track's name, and choose Audio > Audio Instrument > Bass Line.

8 From the Arrange window's Object Parameter box, choose an icon (such as the bass) to reflect the content of the track.

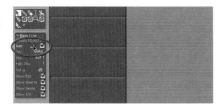 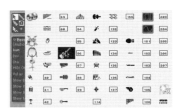

9 Play the song and listen to the bass line.

Importing Audio: The Arrange Window

Importing audio files directly into the Arrange window is just as easy as importing MIDI files—simply drag them straight in from the Finder. However, there is a bit of a catch. Before you can drag in an audio file, you must have an audio track preconfigured and waiting to accept it. In the following steps, you'll create an audio track and add an audio file to it.

[handwritten: "Preconfigured" audio track required]

> **NOTE** ▸ Logic will accept audio files in AIFF (Audio Interchange File Format), SDII (Sound Designer II), or WAV (Windows Wave) formats—and depending on your sound card's capabilities, Logic supports all major bit depths and sampling rates (from 16 bit, 44.1 kHz straight through to 24 bit, 192 kHz).

1 Press 8 to open the Environment.

2 Create a new Audio Object, name it *Drums,* and assign its channel to Track 1.

3 If the Audio Object is mono, click its Stereo/Mono button to make it a stereo channel.

4 Press 1 to open the Arrange window.

5 Double-click the empty track below the Bass Line.

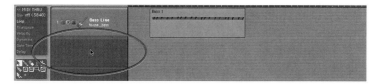

Logic creates a new track and automatically assigns it to the Bass Line Audio Object. This is not the correct Object, so you'll need to use the instrument list to assign the Drums Object to this track.

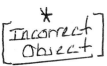
[Incorrect Object] (handwritten annotation)

NOTE ▶ When you create a new track, Logic automatically assigns it to the same Object as the last track selected in the Arrange window.

⑥ Click and hold the left side of the new Bass Line track's name, and choose Audio > Audio Track > Drums.

⑦ From the Arrange window's Object Parameter box, choose an icon graphic to reflect the content of the track (try the drum set).

⑧ Use the Finder to locate the file named **8 Bar Beat**.

[Emagic SAMPLE CD]
— and —
[EXS24 SAMPLER]

NOTE ▸ This file is located in the Logic Course Media folder. The **8 Bar Beat** drum loop is from the Emagic Extreme HipHop sample CD, which is a great collection of down-tempo break beats and other hip-hop samples configured for use with Logic's EXS24 software sampler.

⑨ Drag the **8 Bar Beat** into the Arrange window, and drop it at bar 5 of the Drums track.

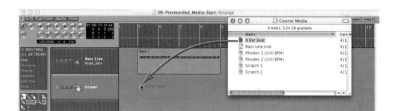

Logic adds the **8 Bar Beat** to your song. If the **8 Bar Beat** doesn't land quite where you intended, just grab it and drag it to bar 5.

I IMPORT AUDIO
FILE TO PRE-EXISTING
AUDIO TRACK

TIP ▸ To quickly import an audio file into a pre-existing audio track in the Arrange window, grab the Pencil tool, hold Shift, and click in the audio track. An Open dialog appears. Use the Open dialog to locate and open an audio file, which is then added to your arrangement at the exact position in the Arrange area that you clicked with the Pencil tool.

Importing Audio: The Audio Window

The Audio window serves as a library that lists all of your song's audio files and also displays information about each file, including its sampling rate, bit depth, file size, and location on your hard disk. The Audio window can hold files that aren't currently used in the song's arrangement, and importing audio files into the Audio window provides one major benefit over dragging them directly into the Arrange window: You don't need to have a track ready and waiting to accept the file. If you're adding many audio files to your project at one time, using the Audio window can speed up the import process dramatically.

> **NOTE** ▶ Most software applications on the Macintosh have an Import option under the File menu, and Logic is no exception. You might assume that this Import option is the way to import audio files into Logic—but it's not! The File > Import option allows you to import MIDI song files from sequencing applications other than Logic, such as Steinberg's Cubase.

Let's use the Audio window to import an audio file that will later form the melody for your arrangement.

1   Choose Audio > Audio Window (Cmd-9).

The Audio window opens.

The **8 Bar Beat** audio file you imported directly into the Arrange window is already part of your song, and as such it's automatically listed in the Audio window.

2   Click the triangle to the left of the audio file's name to reveal its waveform overview.

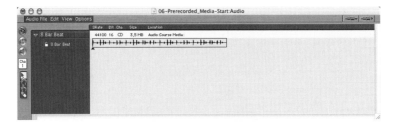

This waveform overview is actually a region. When you add an audio file to your song, Logic automatically creates a region that points to the audio file on your hard disk. As you edit in Logic, it's actually this region, and not the audio file itself, that gets trimmed, cut, and so on. More on that in Lesson 8. For now, let's continue on and add a few more audio files to the song.

3   From the Audio window's local menus, choose Audio File > Add Audio File (Ctrl-F).

An Open dialog appears.

4   In the Open dialog, navigate to this book's Course Media folder, and
    select the file named **Rhodes 1 (100 BPM)**, but don't click Open just
    yet, because there are a few things in this Open dialog worth paying
    attention to.

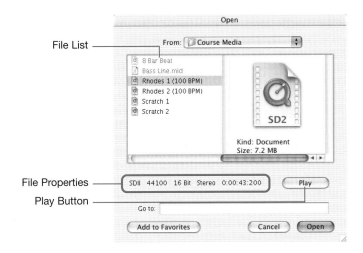

First, notice that the **8 Bar Beat** audio file is grayed out, indicating it's
already used in your song and can't be re-added (the **Bass Line.mid**
file is also grayed out because you can't import MIDI files into the
Audio window). Next, check out the **Rhodes 1 (100 BPM)**'s file properties, all prominently displayed across the Open dialog's lower third.

> **NOTE** ▶ Logic can import and work with AIFF, SDII, or WAV files
> without having to convert them. Now, in Logic 6, you can add MP3
> files to your song, though Logic will need to convert the files to an
> editable format, such as SDII, before they will appear in your project.

Beside the bit-depth and sampling-rate information there's a Play
button you can click to audition the audio file before adding it to
your project.

5 Click the Play button and listen to **Rhodes 1 (100 BPM)**.

The Play button turns into a Stop button, and the file will loop until you click the Stop or Open button.

MORE INFO ▶ *The* **Rhodes 1 (100 BPM)** *and* **Rhodes 2 (100 BPM)** *audio files were played by Herbie Hancock and recorded using the Emagic EVP88, an award-winning Rhodes emulator. This lesson's Extras folder contains the original MIDI sequences used for these audio files. Feel free to unlock the EVP88 demo that came with this book and listen to these files as Hancock himself recorded them.*

6 Click the Open button.

The Open dialog closes and the file appears in the Audio window.

7 Click the small triangle to the left of the audio file.

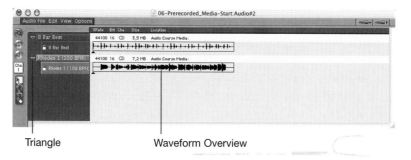

Triangle   Waveform Overview

You can also import audio files by dragging them from the Finder into the Audio window.

8 In the Finder, open the Course Media folder and position it next to the Audio window.

9 Select the **Rhodes 2 (100 BPM)** file and drag it into the Audio window.

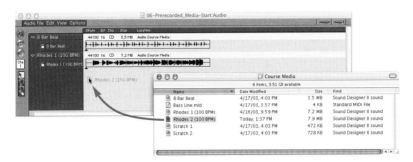

TIP You can select multiple files in the Finder and drag them all into the Audio window at once.

Monitoring Audio Files

The Audio window allows you to monitor, or audition, audio files to see what they sound like before adding them to your arrangement. Let's try monitoring **Rhodes 1 (100 BPM)**.

1 Click and hold the pointer over a file's waveform.

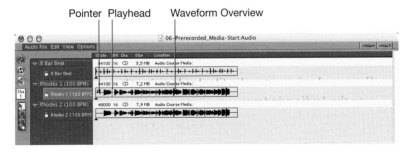

The pointer turns into a speaker, and the file begins playing from the pointer's position.

2   On the left side of the Audio window, click the Cycle button and then the Speaker button.

The Cycle mode is enabled, and the selected file begins to play. Because you've enabled the Cycle mode, the audio file loops, ensuring that Logic continues to make sound as you experiment with the following steps.

3   Press Cmd-8 to open the Environment window, and select the Audio layer.

Notice that the Drums Object's level meter is active, indicating that sound is passing through it. This sound is coming from the file you are monitoring in the Audio window.

Leave the audio file looping as you work through the next exercise.

Setting the Monitor Channel

By default, all audio files are monitored through the Track 1 audio channel. On the left edge of the Audio window there's a box that says Cha 1. This box sets the audio channel that Logic uses for monitoring.

Track 1 is not a good channel to use for monitoring. For starters, Track 1 will almost always be assigned to an Arrange window track, and if you apply DSP effects to Track 1, all previewed audio will play back through those effects! For this reason it's a much better idea to create a channel that's dedicated to monitoring audio, and nothing else.

1   In the Environment's Audio layer, create a new Audio Object, name it
    Audio Monitor, and double-click to expand it into the channel view.

2   Using the Object Parameter box's Cha setting, assign the Audio
    Monitor's channel to Track 24.

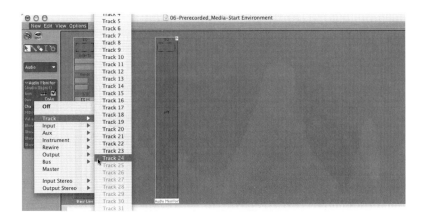

You don't have to use Track 24, but selecting a Track channel far down
the list makes it unlikely you'll ever accidentally assign this Audio
Object to an Arrange window track. If you'd prefer to use a different
Track channel, feel free to do so (but make sure you remember which
one you chose).

3   Click the channel's Stereo/Mono button to make it a Stereo Object.

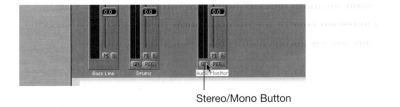

Stereo/Mono Button

This is an important step! If you leave the Object in mono, monitoring stereo files causes them to sound like mono files.

NOTE ▶ It sometimes happens that clicking the Stereo/Mono button stops the audio file monitoring. Should this occur, switch back to the Audio window and click the Speaker button to start the preview again.

4   To get the Audio Monitor Object out of the way, move it to the Environment's right side. Your Environment's Audio layer now looks like this:

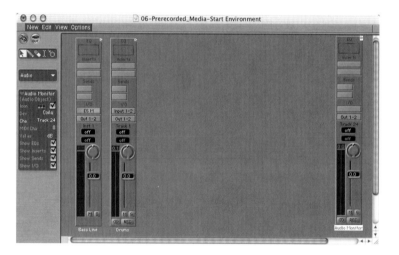

The Audio window should still be open on your screen. If not, open it now.

5   Double-click the Audio window's Channel box and type in *24*. (If you used a different track, enter that track's number.)

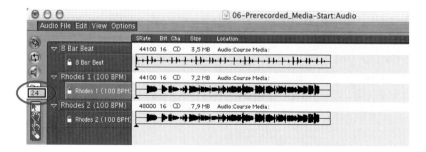

In the Environment, the level meters on your Audio Monitor channel are now active, indicating audio is now being monitored through this Object instead of the Drums Object.

6   Close the Environment so only the Audio and Arrange windows are open.

7   In the Audio window, click the Speaker button to stop monitoring the audio file.

> **TIP** ▶ To ensure that a proper Monitor channel is available to all your songs, open the Autoload song and follow this exercise's steps to create an Audio Monitor Object; then resave your Autoload song.

Updating Waveform Overviews

In addition to pure audio data, audio files also contain information used to graphically display the file inside Logic, and this information is called the *waveform overview*. From time to time you'll encounter files that don't contain a waveform overview, or that have a waveform overview that does not match the sound of the audio file. Logic can still use these files, but until you update the waveform overview, you will not be able to accurately edit them.

How can you tell if the waveform overview is incorrect? There's really only one way: listen to the audio file and watch the overview. If the sound doesn't seem to match up, you've got a problem. For example, in the Audio window the Rhodes 1 (100 BPM) and Rhodes 2 (100 BPM) waveforms look exactly the same, but if you monitor these files you'll notice they sound different. Rhodes 1 (100 BPM) uses an incorrect waveform overview! This problem has implications far beyond the Audio window alone, because this waveform is used in the Arrange window as well as the Sample editor, so you'll need to fix this overview before you use the file.

1   In the Audio window, select the **Rhodes 1 (100 BPM)** audio file (click the filename shown as selected in the figure that follows, not the region name with the lock next to it) and click the Speaker button.

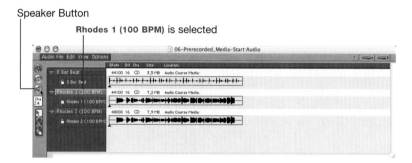

Speaker Button

Rhodes 1 (100 BPM) is selected

Watch the play line as it passes along the file. You'll hear sound before the play line reaches the beginning of the waveform.

2   Choose Audio File > Refresh Overview(s)

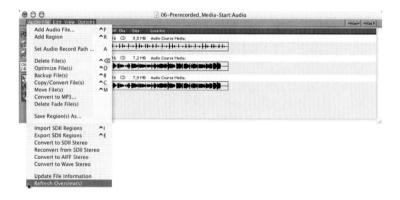

A small progress window opens to keep track as Logic refreshes the file's waveform overview.

TIP ▶ To stop the waveform overview calculation, double-click the waveform overview progress dialog.

When the progress bar hits the right edge, Logic is finished refreshing the waveform overview.

Refreshed Waveform Overview

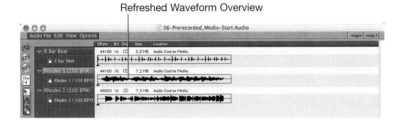

3   Click the Speaker button to play **Rhodes 1 (100 BPM)**. The waveform now closely resembles its sound.

Adding Audio Files to Tracks

To move imported audio files from the Audio window into the Arrange window, you simply drag them from the Audio window and drop them onto any available track. Let's do this now to add **Rhodes 1 (100 BPM)** to your arrangement.

1 Press 8 to open the Environment window.

In a few steps you'll add **Rhodes 1 (100 BPM)** to the Arrange window, but first you need to create a new Audio Object and Arrange window track for **Rhodes 1 (100 BPM)** to play through.

2 Create a new Audio Object, name it *Rhodes 1,* and assign its channel to Track 2.

3 If the Audio Object is mono, click its Stereo/Mono button to make it a stereo channel.

4 Press 1 to open the Arrange window, then select the Drums track by clicking its name in the Track column.

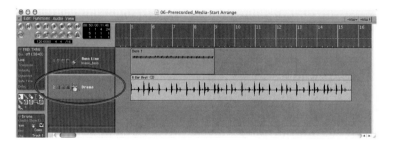

5 From the Arrange window's local menus, choose Functions > Track > Create with next instrument (Ctrl-Shift-Return).

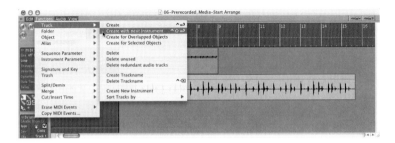

Logic creates a new track and automatically assigns it to the Rhodes Object!

NOTE ▶ Because the Drums track is selected (which plays through the Track 1 Audio Object), the next instrument in the list is the Rhodes 1 Object (Track 2 Object). "Create with next instrument" is a handy function that saves you from having to create a track and hand-assign its Output Object, so remember this function!

To drag a file from the Audio window to the Arrange window, you need to be able to see both windows at once. Both windows are currently open on your screen, but the Arrange window is probably on top of the Audio window. Logic has a command that quickly fixes this problem …

6 Choose Windows > Tile Windows horizontally.

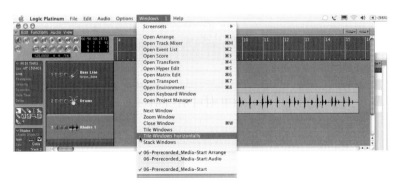

The Arrange and Audio windows tile with the Arrange window above the Audio window.

NOTE ▶ When using the "Tile Windows horizontally" command, the top-left corner of the active window is always placed in the top-left corner of the screen.

7   Select **Rhodes 1 (100 BPM)**, drag it into the Arrange window, and drop it at bar 5 of the Rhodes 1 track.

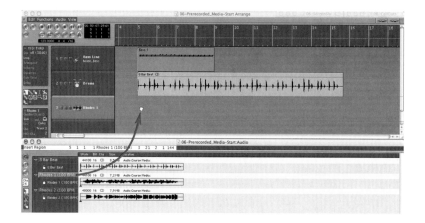

Rhodes 1 (100 BPM) is added to the Rhodes 1 track.

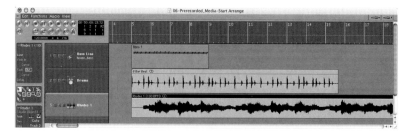

8 In the Arrange window's Object Parameter box, click and hold the Icon setting, and choose an icon to represent the Rhodes track.

 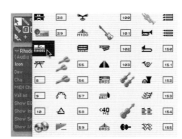

TIP ▶ With the Arrange and Audio windows tiled horizontally on your screen, it's very easy to add audio files to tracks. Make this layout accessible with a keystroke by assigning it to a screenset.

9 Close the Audio window.

10 Play the song.

You'll notice right away that everything's out of sync. The Bass Line clashes with the Audio loops, and everything sounds like a general mess. And that's how it should be! The files you've imported are raw files, all recorded in different studios, at different bpm rates, by different artists. The next step in making a song is cleaning up the timing of your source files to make everything sound pretty. You'll learn how to do this in the next lesson, so soldier on.

Saving Your Song

This is the first time you've saved the project. Keep in mind that this book is a start-to-finish tutorial that results in a finished song, so each lesson builds upon the previous one. Consequently, you should save this song using a name you can remember, because you're going to need it for Lesson 7.

Just in case something goes awry along the way, you should save the song after (and during!) each exercise, using a different name each time. For example, you could name this saved file *LogicLesson6*, the song for the next lesson *LogicLesson7*, and so on. The name you choose is up to you; just make sure you remember what it is and where you put it.

▶ Choose File > Save As, and save your song.

> **TIP** ▶ You should always save incremental versions of your songs by adding a number to the file each time you save it (MySong1, MySong2, MySong3, etc.). Project files do occasionally become corrupt; if you haven't saved incremental versions, you have nothing to go back to when something goes wrong. But more practically, from time to time you might go off on musical tangents that a few hours later don't sound as musical as expected—in other words, it's pretty easy to turn a great track into something you're no longer happy with. If you haven't saved incremental versions of your song, you can't easily return to that great mix from a few hours earlier.

What You've Learned   *CHAPTER 6 SUMMARY*

✓ To import a MIDI file into Logic, drag it in from the Finder and drop it on an Arrange window track.

✓ To quickly import audio files you can either open the Audio window and choose Audio File > Add Audio, or simply drag the file(s) from the Finder straight into the Arrange or Audio windows.

✓ The Monitor channel is used to audition audio files listed in the Audio window. By default Logic uses Track 1 as the Monitor Channel, though you can change this to any currently available Track channel.

✓ A waveform overview is the graphic representation of the audio file.

✓ To add an audio file to your arrangement, drag it out of the Audio window and drop it onto any Arrange window audio track.

7

Start	07-Setting_Tempo-Start
Complete	07-Setting_Tempo-Finished
Time	Approximately 30 minutes
Goals	Learn how to set a song's tempo
	Program tempo changes into a song
	Set a song's tempo to match the tempo of an audio loop
	Time-compress an audio loop to perfectly match a song's tempo
	Choose time-compression algorithms that preserve the sound of the original audio file

Lesson 7
Setting the Tempo

Ever since our ancestors learned to beat sticks on logs to make rhythms, music has had tempo. Tempo gives music its pace and is in part responsible for the way the music feels. Songs using a fast tempo, such as jungle, samba, or hard house, have a certain sense of urgency (and fun!) not found in music of a slower tempo like jazz, trip-hop, or deep house. Working with tempo is a big part of creating a song's mood, so Logic provides several methods for setting the tempo and changing it as your song plays.

Setting the Bpm

Tempo is measured in beats per minute (bpm). Sometimes you'll set the tempo based on the style of music or mood you're trying to create, while other times you'll choose a bpm that matches the tempo of samples or drum loops you intend to use. In any case, Logic's metronome clicks along to the bpm you set for your song, and Arrange window audio regions snap to a grid with its timing determined by the song's tempo, so setting the tempo is one of the first things you'll do when creating a new song.

1   Open the song file you saved at the end of Lesson 6.

> **NOTE** ▶ If you don't have a finished song file from Lesson 6, open **07-Setting_Tempo-Start**.

This song's sequences and regions all use different tempos. If you play the song now, it sounds like a massive train wreck! This will soon change, but to keep it easier on the ears, you'll want to mute the audio tracks for few minutes.

2   In the Track column, click the Mute button on both the Drums and Rhodes 1 tracks (but no others).

Mute Buttons

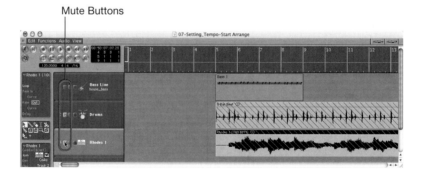

Mute buttons are labeled with an *M,* and every Arrange window track has one. This button temporarily disconnects the track from its Output Object, so the track makes no sound.

NOTE ▶ In the Arrange area, Logic can display muted tracks with a diagonal-line texture to show you at a glance which Objects are making sound and which are not. If the Mute buttons are enabled, but your tracks are not textured, choose Logic > Preferences > Display Preferences > Muted Objects are textured.

As you experiment with tempos, it helps to make your song play continuously by engaging the Cycle mode. (The Cycle mode is covered in Lesson 2, "Using the Transport.")

3   In the Transport area, click the Cycle button to enable the Cycle mode.

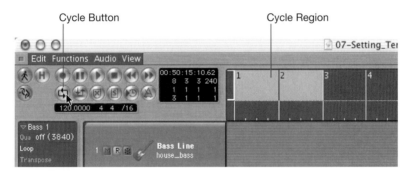

Cycle Button   Cycle Region

Unless you altered the cycle region in a past lesson, it's currently set around bars 1 and 2. (It's OK if your cycle region is different—you'll set it correctly in the next step.)

4   In the Arrange area, select the Bass 1 sequence and choose Object > Set Locators by Objects.

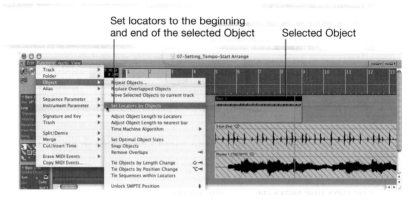

The cycle region jumps to sandwich the selected MIDI sequence.

NOTE ▶ Set Locators by Objects is a fast way to set a cycle region that loops around regions or sequences in the Arrange area, and in many cases it is easier and more accurate than the alternate method of dragging the cycle region into the Bar Ruler. Using the Key Commands window you can assign the Set Locators by Objects function to a key command (try Ctrl-L).

5   Play the song.

A quick glance at the Transport's Tempo area shows that the song plays at 120 bpm. In the last lesson you imported two Rhodes Audio files, and you probably noticed that the filenames say these audio loops are 100 bpm. To match your song to the tempo of these loops, you'll need to change its tempo to 100 bpm. But before you do so, let's take a moment to experiment with bpm settings and see how they affect the sound of the bass line MIDI sequence.

Tempo Area

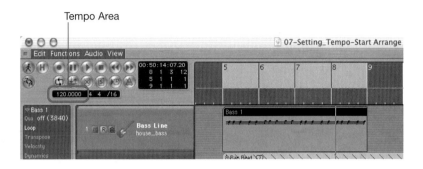

6   In the Transport, double-click the Tempo area, type in *60,* and press Return.

The bass line plays back at half speed.

NOTE ▸ Did you notice that changing the song's tempo caused its audio regions in the Arrange window to become shorter? This shortening affects only the way Logic *displays* audio regions, because these regions still take the same amount of time to play. However, at 60 bpm the song chugs along at half the speed it did at 120 bpm, which means it takes twice as long to play four bars. To reconcile the constant speed of the audio regions against the changing tempo of the song, Logic must shorten the display size of its audio regions.

7   Click and hold the Transport's Tempo area (on the numbers before the decimal point) and drag up until the tempo reaches 100.

The song changes tempo in real time, which can make it a lot easier to find that perfect bpm.

NOTE ▸ Dragging the Tempo before the decimal point adjusts the bpm in whole beats, while dragging behind the decimal adjusts the bpm in partial beats.

8   Press the spacebar to stop playback.

Programming Tempo Changes

While most songs play at a constant tempo, some music depends on tempo changes to move the listener through different moods or to create evolving ambiences (for example, in classical or jazz pieces, or movie sound tracks). Logic provides two editors to control tempo changes, the Tempo List and Tempo Graphic editors.

Tempo List Editor The Tempo List editor resembles the Event List editor, but instead of showing note events, it displays tempo changes.

Tempo Graphic Editor The Tempo Graphic editor creates a smooth transition between tempos.

Using the Tempo List Editor

Let's use the Tempo List editor to change the tempo of our arrangement at bar 7.

1   Make sure the playback is stopped, then click the lower third of the Bar Ruler precisely at 7 1 1 1 to place the song position line (SPL) at the beginning of bar 7.

Click the Bar Ruler at bar 7

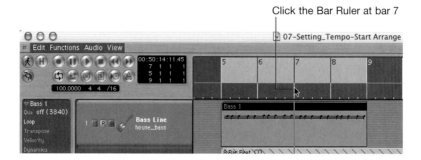

2 Choose Options > Tempo > Tempo List Editor (Option-T).

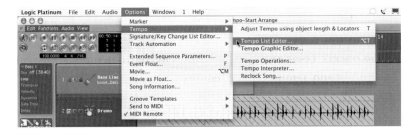

The Tempo List editor opens.

The Tempo List editor contains a list of your song's tempo changes. Right now there's only one event in the list, reflecting the tempo you set in the exercise above.

TIP ▶ You can also open the Tempo List editor by clicking and holding the Transport's Sync button and choosing Open Tempo List from the pop-up menu.

Sync Button

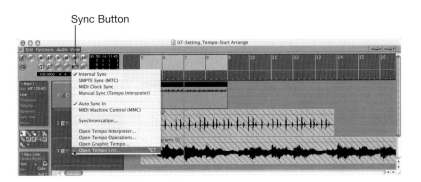

3 On the Tempo List editor's left edge, click the Create button.

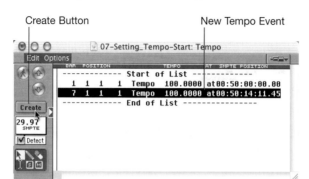

A new tempo event is created in the Tempo List editor, at the SPL's current position of 7 1 1 1.

NOTE ▶ The Tempo List editor has a small box on its left edge that says 29.97 SMPTE. If you're using Logic to spot sound to video, this box sets the frame rate you will use. By default, this box is set to 25 frames per second, reflecting the frame rate used in PAL video (the standard used in Germany, where Logic is made). Set this box to reflect the frame rate for your area.

4 On the new tempo event, double-click the tempo value, enter *60,* and press Return.

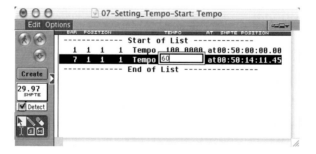

You've just added a new tempo event. As the song plays, at bar 7 its tempo will now change from 100 bpm to 60 bpm.

5 Close the Tempo List editor, and play the cycle region.

Listen for the tempo change at bar 7, and watch the Transport's Tempo area to observe the change.

Using the Tempo Graphic Editor

The Tempo List editor creates a sudden change from one tempo to another. If you need a gradual shift in speed, use the Tempo Graphic editor to create a tempo ramp that moves subtly from one rate (measured in bpm) to the next, over time.

Let's use the Tempo Graphic editor to create a gradual tempo change from bar 5 to bar 7 of our arrangement.

1 From the main menu bar select Options > Tempo > Tempo Graphic Editor.

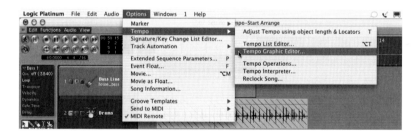

TIP You can also open the Tempo Graphic editor by clicking and holding the Transport's Sync button and choosing Open Graphic Tempo from the pop-up menu.

The Tempo Graphic editor opens. This editor provides a Bar Ruler across the top and a bpm scale along the left edge of the display area.

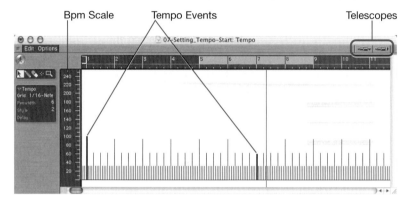

The events at bar 1 and bar 7 visually indicate your song's tempo changes.

2   If your tempo events are hard to see, use the telescopes in the window's top-right corner to zoom in on the action until your Tempo Graphic editor looks like the one in the figure above. (This also makes it much easier to draw in tempo events, which you'll do in the next steps.)

NOTE ▶ The Tempo Graphic editor's grid is currently set to sixteenth notes. To choose a finer degree of resolution for your tempo changes, alter this editor's grid setting, located in the Tempo box along its left edge.

3 From the toolbox, select the Pencil. At bar 5, click at around 100 bpm (reference the bpm scale) and then drag the pointer from bar 5 down to the tempo value at bar 7.

Info Line displays tempo at pencil tip

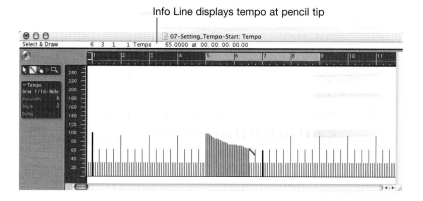

Logic now creates a ramp of tempo change events. The Info Line at the top of the window numerically displays tempo values as you drag through them.

4 Play the cycle region and listen to the tempo as it slowly changes.

Unless you have a surgeon's hands, the line of tempo events you've created is jagged, to say the least. To create a straight tempo ramp, you'll need to use the Crosshair tool.

5 From the toolbox, grab the Crosshair tool.

6 At bar 5, click and drag up or down to set the tempo of the first event at 100 (watch the Info Line as you set this tempo), then release the mouse and move the pointer to bar 7, tempo 60.

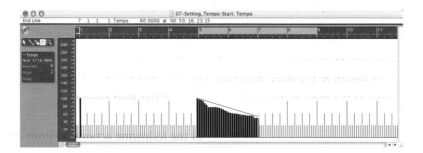

A line stretches out behind the Crosshair tool.

7 When the Crosshair tool is in the correct position, click the mouse one final time to finish creating your tempo ramp.

The tempo ramp is now straight as an arrow. However, you don't actually need this changing tempo in your final song, so let's erase these tempo events.

8 From the toolbox, select the Eraser tool, then click and drag across all of the tempo events except for the one at 1 1 1 1.

Logic deletes all tempo events except for the first one, and you're right back where you started.

9 Close the Tempo Graphic editor.

Adjusting Tempos to Objects

These days more than ever, music is based on sample loops. For example, it's common practice to start a song by selecting a good drum loop, around which you build a track. Unfortunately, you won't always know the bpm of the loop you're using, and that makes it hard to set your song's tempo. Thankfully, Logic provides an automatic way to set bpm based on the length of an audio region, and it's called the "Adjust Tempo using object length & Locators" function. Let's use that function to make the tempo of the song match the tempo of the 8 Bar Beat region.

1 You will want to hear the results of the following actions, so unmute all of the Arrange window's tracks.

2 Select the 8 Bar Beat region.

3 In the Bar Ruler's top half, drag from 5 1 1 1 to 13 1 1 1 to create a cycle region that's eight bars long (5 + 8 bars = 13).

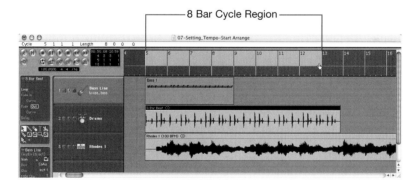

This step is very important, because Logic uses the length of the cycle region to determine how long the audio region should be, then sets the song's tempo accordingly.

4 Compare the 8 Bar Beat region with the 8 Bar cycle region. They are both eight bars long, but in the Arrange window there's a big difference between the two.

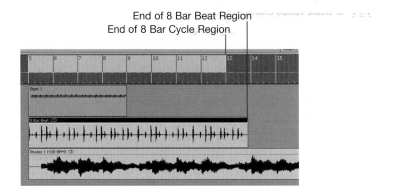

5 Choose Options > Tempo > Adjust Tempo using object length & Locators (T).

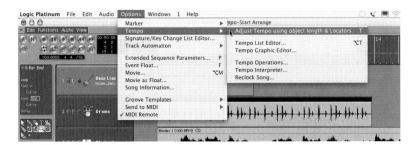

6 Logic asks if you want to change the tempo globally, or create a tempo change for the cycle region only. Select Globally.

NOTE ▶ Choosing Globally adjusts the tempo of the entire song to the new value. Choosing Create changes the tempo only for the specified cycle region.

Logic changes the song's tempo so that eight bars exactly match the length of the 8 Bar Beat region. Notice that the Transport's Tempo area now reads 90 bpm (which is exactly the bpm of the 8 Bar Beat region, by the way).

Song tempo is 90 bpm

End of 8 Bar Beat and end of cycle region now match

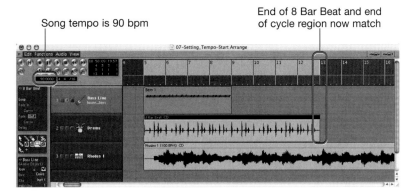

NOTE ▶ Logic can have tempos set to an accuracy of 1/10,000 of a beat per minute!

Adjusting Objects to Tempos

In the previous exercise you discovered that the 8 Bar Beat region's tempo was 90 bpm, but your song needs to be 100 bpm. To resolve this difference in tempos, you must use a process called *time-compression* to change the 8 Bar Beat region to match your song's tempo.

In the old days of audio design, this was a time-consuming task that took a bit of trial and error using the Time and Pitch Machine, located in the Sample editor's Digital Factory™. But with Logic 6, this task is now easily and quickly accomplished right in the Arrange window using Logic 6's new Adjust Object Length to Locators function.

[handwritten margin note: SAMPLE EDITOR → DIGITAL FACTORY → TIME & PITCH MACHINE]

NOTE ▶ When you perform this function, Logic automatically creates a new audio file and adds it to the Audio window. (The original audio file will remain unaltered in the Audio window, just in case you need it later.)

1 Use the Transport's Tempo area to set the song's tempo back to 100 bpm.

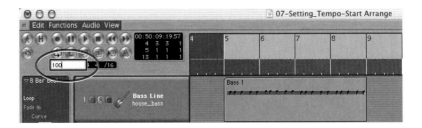

The 8 Bar Beat region is once again longer than the 8 Bar cycle region.

2 Make sure the 8 Bar Beat region is still selected, then choose
Functions > Object > Adjust Object Length to Locators.

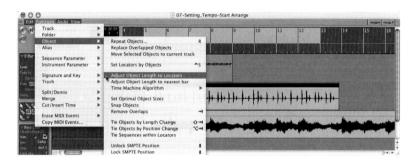

While Logic processes your sound file, watch the Info Line to keep
track of the progress.

Info Line displays samples to process

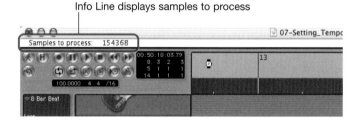

NOTE ► This is a processor-intensive function. If the spinning beach
ball is onscreen for a long time, don't worry—Logic is just thinking.
Depending on the speed of your processor, this function can take anywhere from 30 seconds to several minutes.

As Logic processes the audio region, it creates a brand-new audio file and saves it beside the original audio file on your hard disks. This new file is named exactly the same as the original, except that it has a *.1* extension added to its name.

Original Audio File

Name	Date Modified	Size	Kind
8 Bar Beat	4/17/03, 4:03 PM	3.5 MB	Sound Designer II sound
8 Bar Beat.1	Today, 2:37 AM	3.2 MB	Sound Designer II sound
Bass Line.mid	4/17/03, 3:57 PM	4 KB	Standard MIDI File
Rhodes 1 (100 BPM)	5/2/03, 5:30 PM	7.2 MB	Sound Designer II sound
Rhodes 2 (100 BPM)	5/2/03, 1:37 PM	7.9 MB	Sound Designer II sound
Scratch 1	4/17/03, 4:03 PM	472 KB	Sound Designer II sound
Scratch 2	4/17/03, 4:03 PM	728 KB	Sound Designer II sound

Course Media — 7 items, 3.5 GB available

Processed Audio File

In the Media folder there is now a file called 8 Bar Beat.1

This new audio file is automatically listed in your song's Audio window …

Original Audio File

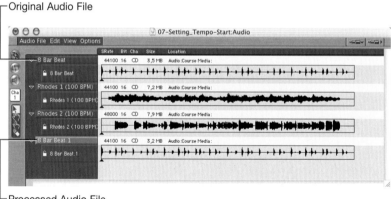

Processed Audio File

… and it also replaces the original region in the Arrange window.

8 Bar Beat.1 is the new audio region

NOTE ▶ The original 8 Bar Beat audio file is left unaltered, so if you need it back at some later point in time, you can grab it from the Audio window.

3   Play the cycle region again.

At 100 bpm the 8 Bar Beat is now a perfect loop, and all of the Objects in the Arrange window play in time with each other. (Well, almost; the Rhodes 1 region comes in a bar late, but you'll fix that problem in the next lesson, so keep reading!)

TIP ▶ Adjusting Objects to tempos relies on the region being a perfect loop. You may need to use the Sample window to trim your audio regions to the correct length before performing this function. (Trimming regions in the Sample editor is covered in the next lesson.)

Choosing a Time-Compression Algorithm

Now that you've seen Logic time-compress a file (a process that physically alters the length of an audio file without changing its pitch), it's time to consider whether you want to keep using the default time-compression algorithm or choose a different one. Logic's default time-compression algorithm is very good at maintaining the sound of the original file, but in some situations it might introduce *artifacts*, or slight changes, into the file's sound. To help you avoid this problem, Logic 6 includes several new algorithms used for time and pitch modifications. Each of these algorithms is designed for a certain type of audio material, so selecting the correct algorithm will help you avoid introducing unwanted artifacts into your audio file. The available algorithms include

- *Version 5:* This is the tried and trusted algorithm used in Logic 5.

- *Any material:* A universal algorithm that produces acceptable results for almost any type of audio material. This is the best default algorithm choice.

- *Monophonic:* Best used on mono vocal, brass, woodwind, or other mono audio regions.

- *Pads:* Audio regions with a lot of harmonic content (such as choirs, strings sections, or synth swells) should use this setting.

- *Rhythmic:* Steady rhythmic instrumental recordings (including synth stabs, rhythmic pianos, or guitar loops) benefit from this algorithm.

- *Beats:* Perfectly maintains the timing of percussive material and should be used with drum loops.

To choose an algorithm to be used the next time Logic performs time compression, first determine what type of audio your region contains, then do the following:

1   Choose Functions > Object > Time Machine Algorithm, and select an algorithm.

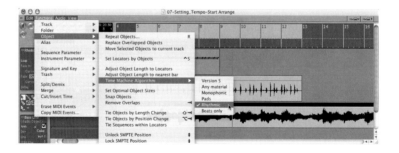

2   Save your song.

What You've Learned ✱ CHAPTER 7 SUMMARY ✱

✓ The Transport contains a Tempo area used to set the song's bpm (beats per minute).

✓ The Tempo List and Tempo Graphic editors let you program tempo changes into your song.

✓ The "Adjust Tempo using object length & Locators" function sets the song's tempo to match the tempo of an audio loop, and it's a great function to use if you don't know the bpm of an audio file.

✓ If you have an audio loop that plays at a different tempo from your song's, Logic 6's Adjust Object Length to Locators function will automatically resize the loop to match the tempo of your song, without changing the sound or pitch of the audio file.

8

Start	08-Audio_Files-Start
Complete	08-Audio_Files-Finished
Time	Approximately 55 minutes
Goals	Learn how to edit audio regions in the Arrange window, Audio window, and Sample editor
	Set anchors that govern how a region snaps to the Arrange window's quantization grid
	Explore Logic's Digital Factory™
	Learn how to convert the sampling rate of an audio file

Working with Regions

The audio that you arrange and edit in Logic is stored as digital files on your computer's hard disk. While arranging your song, you can take a few seconds of one audio file, fade it into a second audio file, and then layer a couple of minutes of a third audio file over the top of that. But all of this mixing, editing, and arranging does not change the original audio files! That's because when you bring the audio into Logic, the program automatically creates a pointer to the audio file, called a *region*. Back in the Arrange window, when you trim or shorten a region, you tell Logic, "I only want to use this portion of the audio file," but Logic does not actually shorten or change the source audio file in any way.

For this reason, Logic is classified as a *nondestructive* audio editor, in much the same way as a video program like Apple's Final Cut Pro is a nondestructive video editor. In Final Cut Pro, you take separate pieces of video footage, trim some here, mix others in there, add a few effects such as blurs or color correction, and then render out a finished video stream. The source video, however, is never touched or altered. Logic does the exact same thing, but with sound instead of moving pictures. And this is an important concept to understand, because it means that even if you mangle your regions to an unlistenable state, the source audio files themselves always remain safe on your hard disk, ready to be used again. With that in mind, let's go mangle … er, edit some audio regions!

Editing Regions in the Arrange Window

Audio regions exist in two different places, the Arrange window and the Audio window. Despite this dual locality, the regions themselves are the same in both places. For example, if you trim the length of a region in the Arrange window, back in the Audio window the region also becomes shorter. Let's start experimenting with region edits by trimming the 8 Bar Beat.1 region in the Arrange window. But first, open the Audio window. With both windows onscreen at the same time, you can graphically see how changing a region in the Arrange window affects the same region in the Audio window.

1 Open the song file you saved at the end of Lesson 7.

   NOTE ▶ If you don't have a song saved from the previous lesson, open the file named **08-Audio_Files-Start**.

2 Press 9 to open screenset 9, which contains the Audio window.

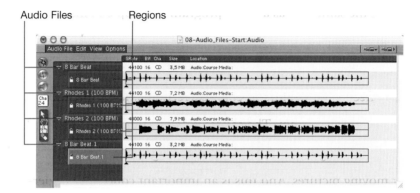

In the Audio window, audio files are represented by thin horizontal bars with a triangle at the left edge. Each bar is labeled with the file's name, and to its right there is an information area displaying the file's sampling rate, bit depth, stereo/mono status, file size, and location on your hard disk(s). If you click the triangle, it points down, and the file's audio regions are displayed.

As soon as an audio file is added to your song, Logic creates a default region that is the same length as the file. Although you can't make an audio region longer than the file it points to, you *can* trim a region to be as short as needed—all the way down to a single sample. With that in mind, it's time to open up the Arrange window and see what trimming regions is all about.

3 Choose Windows > Open Arrange (Cmd-1).

The Arrange window opens onscreen above the Audio window.

4 Choose Windows > Tile Windows horizontally.

The windows tile with the Arrange window on top and the Audio window on the bottom.

TIP ▶ If your windows tile in the reverse order, it's because the Audio window was active when you tiled the windows. Logic places the top-right corner of the active window in the top-right corner of the screen. To switch the order of your windows, click the Arrange window to make it active, then once again choose Windows > Tile Windows horizontally.

Look closely at these windows and you'll see that the 8 Bar Beat.1 region is found in both—it's the same one in both windows, so changing the region in one window also changes it in the other.

5   To make the following region edits easier, use the telescopes in both the Arrange and Audio windows to zoom in until you can clearly see all object waveforms.

TIP ▶ To zoom both horizontally and vertically at the same time, hold down the Command key while clicking the telescopes.

6   In the Arrange window, select the Arrow tool.

7   Click and hold the bottom-left corner of the 8 Bar Beat.1 region and
drag it to bar 7 (and do be careful to drag the bottom corner, because
if you grab higher up, you'll end up moving the whole region instead
of just trimming it).

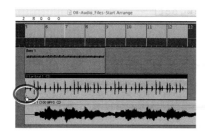 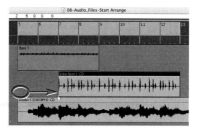

TIP ▸ As you drag a region's edge, it snaps (or jumps) along a scale
that is determined by the Arrange window's horizontal zoom value:
The more zoomed in you are, the finer the resolution of these snaps.
To make the edge drag smoothly, hold the Control key while dragging.

The Arrow tool turns into the Region Edit (Finger) tool, and the
region gets smaller—not only in the Arrange window, but in the
Audio window as well!

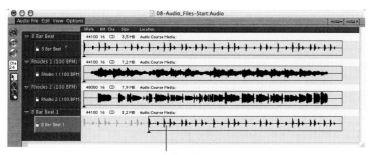

8 Bar Beat.1 region in the Audio
window is automatically trimmed

8 Click and hold the bottom-right corner of the 8 Bar Beat.1 region and drag it to bar 9.

Once again, check out the 8 Bar Beat region in the Audio window. It's no longer eight bars at all, because you've edited its boundaries in the Arrange window so that it now represents just two bars of the original eight-bar file! Behind the region you can still see the entire source audio file, but parts outside the region are grayed out to graphically show you which section of the audio file the region points to, and which part it does not.

Region is now two bars long

And that's really all there is to trimming regions in the Arrange window. Simple, isn't it?

NOTE ▶ In Logic 6, you can now make sample accurate edits to regions in the Arrange window. This is a great feature; however, to make such edits you'll need to use the telescopes to zoom way in on the region. Zooming in that close can sometimes be troublesome because it takes your attention away from the big picture of your arrangement, which is what the Arrange window is all about. If you need to make sample accurate edits to audio regions, use the Sample editor, as described in the last half of this lesson.

Editing Regions in the Audio Window

Editing regions in the Arrange window is a good technique if the audio file is already a part of your arrangement. However, if the audio file is very long and you only need to add a small section of it to your song, you'll appreciate the Audio window's ability to make rough edits to a region before adding the region to your arrangement. The key words here are *rough edits*—edits in the Audio window are only accurate to within *256 samples*. That's far from sample-accurate!

But sample-accurate editing (making edits that are precise down to the exact sample) is not the purpose of the Audio window—it's there to help you manage your song's audio and provide an overview of the regions used in the arrangement. And it does a great job of this. For example, looking at the Audio window you can see that both the Rhodes audio files start and end with what looks to be silence. You have no need to play this silence in your song, and in fact, you shouldn't play it! There might be line noise or other unwanted sounds in this seemingly silent part of the file. At any rate, this is not a part of the file you are interested in.

For this sort of quick-and-dirty edit, the Audio window really shines because you don't need to be too exact when trimming the silence off these files. If there's a little left over, it's not that big of a concern, so let's use the Audio window to edit these silent sections out of the Rhodes 1 (100 BPM) region. For now, don't worry about the Rhodes 2 (100 BPM) region—you'll edit that one later in this lesson, using the Sample editor.

1 From the Audio window's toolbox, grab the Region Edit tool (the hand with extended index finger).

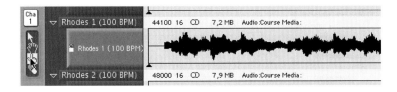

NOTE ▶ In the last exercise you used the Arrow tool to edit region boundaries in the Arrange window. You probably noticed that as you made these edits, the arrow turned into a finger shape. This, of course, is the Region Edit tool, and by temporarily changing pointer icons Logic is acknowledging that you're editing the region's boundaries.

2 Drag the *left* edge of the Rhodes 1 region toward the right, until you've eliminated the silence at the beginning of this region.

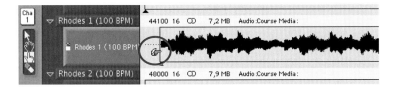

As you drag, the Region Edit tool turns into a right-pointing finger and the region's beginning is moved into the audio file. In the Arrange window, the Rhodes 1 region is also changed to reflect this edit and the silence at its beginning is removed.

3 From the Audio window's toolbox, grab the Arrow tool.

The Region Edit tool is specially designed for altering regions, but nonetheless all of its editing features are also available to the Arrow tool. In fact, you may never use the Region Edit tool as you edit, because the Arrow tool saves you from having to grab the Region Edit tool each time you want to alter a region boundary.

4   Drag the *right* edge of the Rhodes 1 region toward the left until you've
eliminated the silence at its end.

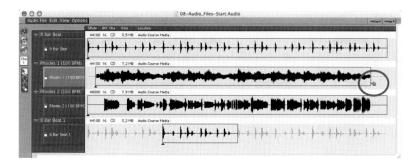

As you drag, the arrow turns into a left-pointing finger and the
region's end is moved earlier in the audio file. Once again, this edit is
also reflected in the Arrange window.

Searching for the Zero Crossing

All edits to region boundaries should ensure that the boundary intersects
the waveform precisely where the waveform crosses zero. If you fail to
make an appropriate edit, you will hear unwanted pops and clicks in your
song (it's sort of like trying to shove a doorstop under a door, big end
first—there's going to be some noise!). The following figure shows an
extreme close-up of an audio file with a region boundary that does not
cross the waveform at zero:

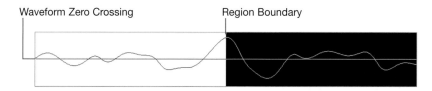

This inappropriate edit will result in a slight clicking or popping sound
when the region begins playing. To avoid this unwanted noise, you must
ensure that your region boundaries cross the waveform at zero, as shown
in the next figure:

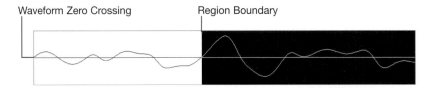

Fortunately, Logic has an option that will automatically find the closest zero crossing to your edit, so you don't need to zoom in on every edit you make. Let's turn this option on to make future edits sound better.

▶ From the Audio window's local menus, choose Edit > Search Zero Crossings.

Now whenever you move a region boundary, Logic automatically moves the edit to the closest zero crossing. If the file is stereo, Logic looks for the nearest point where both the left and right channels cross zero and places the region boundary there.

Setting the Region's Anchor

Every region has an Anchor that serves as a temporal reference point, or the point Logic uses to snap the region to the Arrange window's timing grid. The resolution of this timing grid changes depending on the Arrange window's zoom level, but at all resolutions the timing grid's function is the same—it's there to ensure that the region's Anchor always snaps to a bar or beat position (or division and tick, if you're zoomed in close enough), which in turn lets you confidently move audio regions around the Arrange window, safe in the knowledge that no matter where you move a region, it will always play in rhythm with the other objects in your song.

In the Audio window, the Anchor is represented by a small triangle under the region. When a region is created, an Anchor is automatically placed at its start boundary, but you're free to place the Anchor anywhere you'd like within the region. For regions like 8 Bar Beat.1, it's fine to have the Anchor right at the region's beginning, because the region starts on the downbeat of a drum loop. But regions like Rhodes 1 (100 BPM) present a bit more of a challenge. This region does not begin on a downbeat, but rather begins with two upbeats that form an intro into the downbeat at the beginning of the main section. To make this region line up correctly with other Arrange window Objects, adjust the Anchor so that it falls on the region's first downbeat.

1 Play your song and listen carefully to the Rhodes 1 (100 BPM) region.

You'll quickly notice it's not playing in time with the bass line or drums. Let's fix this discrepancy by correctly setting the Rhodes 1 (100 BPM) region's Anchor.

2 Stop the playback.

3 In the Audio window, select the Rhodes 1 (100 BPM) region and click the Speaker button.

Click the Speaker button to audition the selected region

The Rhodes 1 (100 BPM) region is selected

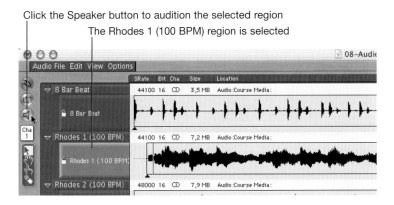

The region plays. Notice how the region begins with two upbeats that form a lead-in.

4   Grab the arrow under the Rhodes 1 (100 BPM) region and move it to
the first downbeat after the lead-in.

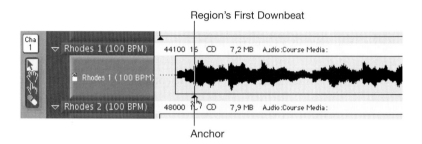

In the Arrange window, the Rhodes 1 (100 BPM) region shifts slightly
to the left and now begins before the other Arrange area Objects.

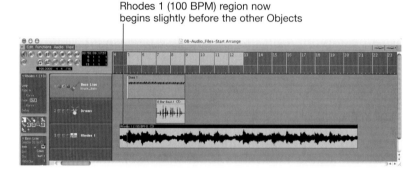

NOTE ▶ When you move a region in the Arrange window, the
Info Line displays the position of the region's Anchor, not the region's
left edge.

5   Play your song from the beginning of bar 4.

The Rhodes 1 (100 BPM) region is now more or less in time with the
Arrange area's other Objects. (If it isn't, readjust the Anchor until you
get it close.) However, it might still sound slightly off. This is because
the Audio window's region edits are accurate only to within 256 samples, so it's very difficult to align the Anchor exactly to the region's
downbeat. To make this type of exact edit, you need the Sample editor.

Using the Sample Editor

The Sample editor is the place for making precision edits to audio regions. It's called the Sample editor for a reason—using this editing window you can zoom in until individual samples are visible. Because the Sample editor gives you such exact control, it's classified as a sample-accurate editor, and when it comes time to edit region boundaries and anchors, no other window provides the same level of precise control.

But before getting into the nitty-gritty of editing regions in the Sample editor, let's take a moment to explore this window.

Navigating the Sample Editor

Because you will often be zoomed closely in on the waveform, navigating the Sample editor becomes a major concern. You could use the scroll bar at the bottom of the window to zip around the file, but when you're zoomed in close, this becomes a difficult and time-consuming process. Fortunately, Logic provides a few great techniques for navigating in this window.

1   In either the Audio or Arrange window, double-click the Rhodes 1 region.

The Sample editor opens. As you can see, the Sample editor already gives you a much closer view of the audio file's waveform than either of the other windows. Right now you are zoomed in on the very beginning of the Rhodes 1 (100 BPM) region.

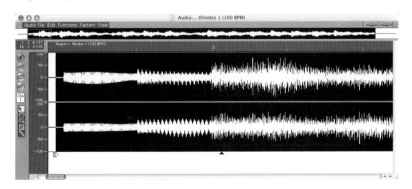

Along the top of the Sample editor there's a waveform overview that shows the entire audio file the region points to. At the front of this overview there is a dotted box that shows you the area of the waveform currently shown in the Sample editor's main display area. To quickly jump to other points along the audio file, click the waveform overview.

2   In the waveform overview at the top of the Sample editor, click somewhere close to the middle (this is just for practice, so it doesn't matter exactly where you click).

Dotted box moves to clicked area
of waveform overview

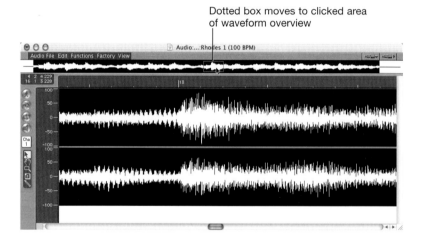

The Sample editor's display area updates to show the portion of the waveform outlined by the dotted box.

Of course, you often won't be able to tell by sight alone which part of the waveform you need to jump to, and in this situation it helps to hear the waveform before moving the dotted box.

3   Click and hold the pointer above the waveform overview.

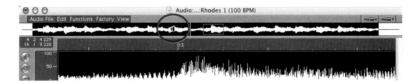

The pointer turns into a speaker, and Logic plays the waveform from the pointer's position.

In the Sample editor's main display area, regions are defined by the start and end playback indicators. The start playback indicator looks like a right-pointing arrow with an *S* on it, while the end playback indicator is a left-pointing arrow labeled with an *E*. Somewhere between those icons you'll find the region's Anchor, which looks like an upward-pointing triangle (just the same as in the Audio window). When you're zoomed in close on a waveform, these three things are a bit hard to find. You can click the waveform overview to get close, but the following key commands are much more precise:

4   Press the right arrow key on your computer keyboard.

The Sample editor jumps to display the end playback indicator.

5   Press the down arrow key.

The Sample editor jumps to display the Anchor.

6   Press the left arrow key.

The Sample editor jumps to the start playback indicator.

Remember these three key commands! Using the arrow keys provides a convenient way for you to quickly jump between region playback indicators and the Anchor without having to zoom out and find the part you're looking for.

Auditioning a Subsection of a Region

These days editing audio is becoming a very visual process, and you can quite safely edit region boundaries and anchors just by looking at the waveform. Even still, it's nice to hear what you're doing, so auditioning the portion of the waveform around your edit is an important part of this process. The Sample editor has a Speaker button designed for just this purpose.

The Speaker button plays only the portion of the wave that is selected in the Sample editor. When you first open the Sample editor, the entire region is selected by default and is consequently highlighted in black. It's important to note that this black highlight simply denotes a selection, and not the region itself. If you want to audition a smaller part of the waveform, such as the area surrounding the region's Anchor, you'll need to change this selected area as demonstrated in the following steps.

1   Press the down arrow key to center the Anchor in the Sample editor, then click and drag out a selection from the beginning of the waveform to a point after the Anchor.

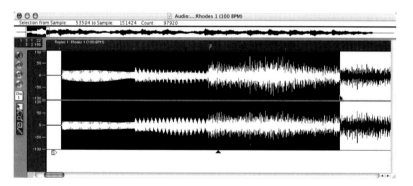

This selected area straddles the Anchor.

2   On the Sample editor's left edge, click the Speaker button.

The selection plays, and then stops.

3   Above the Speaker button, click the Cycle button, and then press the spacebar.

Playback begins again, and the selection loops.

4   Press the spacebar to stop playback.

You can also use the Sample editor's Solo tool to scrub the audio file in forward or reverse.

5   From the Sample editor's toolbox, grab the Solo tool (the square with an *S* on it).

Solo Tool

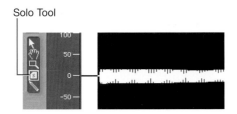

6   Click and drag the Solo tool along the waveform in the Sample editor's display area.

The sound scrubs back and forth, following the Solo tool.

MORE INFO ▶ *The Sample editor monitors sound through the same channel as the Audio window. Just as in the Audio window, there's a Channel box on the left edge of the Sample editor that you can use to change this monitoring channel. For more information on monitoring audio, see Lesson 6.*

Editing the Region's Boundaries and Anchor

Because the Sample editor displays a much more detailed overview of the waveform than the Audio window, you can clearly see that your Anchor is not exactly where it should be. In the next steps you will tighten up the rough edits you've already made to the Rhodes 1 (100 BPM) region, by setting the region boundaries and Anchor precisely where they need to be.

1   Grab the Anchor and drag it to the beginning of the waveform's more erratic section, which visually signifies the beginning of the region's downbeat.

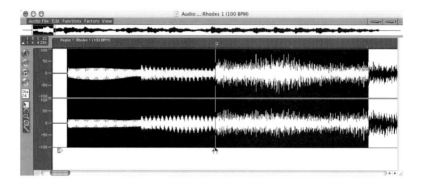

As you drag, a line stretches vertically across the Sample editor to show you the Anchor's new position in the region. It takes a little bit of practice and a trained ear to figure out exactly where the Anchor should go. In this example you need to drop it directly on the peak of the first spike after the more rounded waves at the region's beginning.

2   Use the Sample editor's telescopes to zoom in close on the beginning of the waveform; then grab the start playback indicator and drag the region's start boundary in until it just about touches the beginning of the waveform.

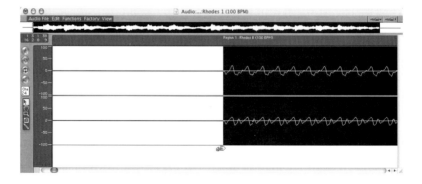

NOTE ▶ The Sample editor's Magnifying Glass tool provides a great way to zoom in on the waveform. The Magnifying Glass tool operates just the same as in any other window, so you can quickly revert to the pre-magnified display by double-clicking the waveform. Quick, and easy!

3 To jump to the region's end playback indicator, press the right arrow key.

The Sample editor's display area jumps to the end playback indicator at the far right side of the waveform.

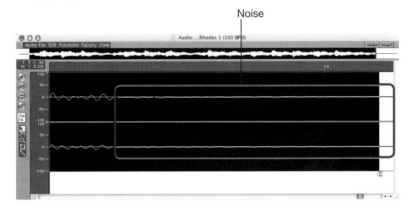

Here you have a bit of a problem. The waveform doesn't drop off to dead silence, and it appears there's a little bit of low-level noise left over in the recording. This noise needs to be trimmed off. But first things first—earlier in this lesson you learned that to avoid unwanted pops and clicks in your song, you must ensure that your region boundaries intersect the waveform at an exact zero crossing. With all this noise, it's difficult to determine where, exactly, a zero crossing is. Fortunately, the Sample editor has a Search Zero Crossings function, just like the Audio window.

4   Choose Edit > Search Zero Crossings to select it (if it's already selected with a checkmark, don't deselect it by accident).

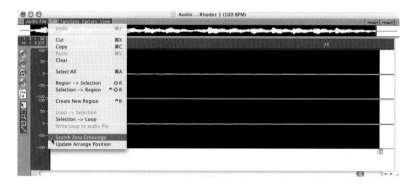

5   Grab the end playback indicator and drag the region's end boundary in until it just about touches the end of the waveform.

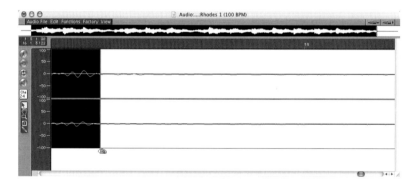

With the Search Zero Crossings function enabled, you can drop the end playback indicator anywhere near the end of the waveform— Logic will automatically find an appropriate zero crossing. Presto! You have a perfectly edited region!

6   Close the Sample editor.

Working with Sampling Rates

When audio comes in through your audio interface, analog-to-digital (A/D) converters sample the audio stream a certain number of times per second. The rate of this sampling process determines the digital audio file's *sampling rate*. CD-Audio uses a sampling rate of 44.1 kHz, which means the audio stream has been sampled 44,100 times per second. This is a lot of little samples, and consequently CD-Audio comes pretty close to representing the original audio waveform.

But the holy grail of digital audio is to perfectly copy an analog waveform. In pursuit of this perfect waveform, audio editors like Logic now let us record and edit audio at sampling rates of 48 kHz, 96 kHz, and even 192 kHz (audio hardware permitting). These sample rates provide significantly more samples per second than CD-Audio, which means these higher sampling rates come closer to representing a true analog waveform. Consequently, they sound better!

> **TIP** ▶ Using a higher sampling rate puts a greater strain on your computer. If your system's audio interface works with 96 or 192 kHz audio, you may want to edit at this sampling rate to preserve as much of the original analog signal as possible. However, unless you're using a cutting-edge Mac, at higher sampling rates you won't be able to use too many audio tracks and DSP effects before your computer's CPU maxes out. For this reason, 48 kHz is a common sampling rate that provides good quality without straining your computer.

Exploring Sampling Rates

All of this song's audio files use a sampling rate of 44.1 kHz, except **Rhodes 2 (100 BPM),** which has been recorded at 48 kHz. You can still use **Rhodes 2 (100 BPM)** in the song, but it will not sound correct unless you convert its sampling rate to 44.1 kHz (the sample rate used by the song). The following steps demonstrate why by showing you what happens if you add a 48 kHz file to a 44.1 kHz song.

1 In the Audio window, check out the sampling rate of your song's audio files.

All of the audio files use a sampling rate of 44.1 kHz except for **Rhodes 2 (100 BPM)**, which uses a sampling rate of 48 kHz.

2 Click the Options menu.

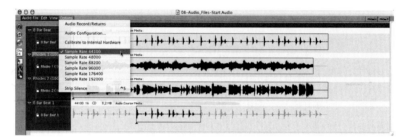

The Options menu has several sampling rates listed, and choosing one of these sets the sampling rate for your entire song (this setting is also available from Logic's main Audio menu at the top of your screen). Right now Sample Rate 44100 is selected, graphically demonstrating that your song is using a sampling rate of 44.1 kHz. This is correct, so don't change it. However, the **Rhodes 2 (100 BPM)** audio file uses a sampling rate of 48 kHz, so what happens if you add it to your arrangement? Well, why not try it out?

NOTE ▶ This book's lessons were created to play back on any Macintosh capable of running Logic 6, so to allow the greatest degree of compatibility the song uses a sampling rate of 44.1 kHz. This doesn't mean you should always use 44.1 kHz. In fact, 44.1 kHz is recommended only if your songs are going straight to audio CDs (or if the bulk of your project's samples are ripped from audio CDs and you don't want to convert a lot of audio files).

3   Press 8 to open the Environment.

Before you can add **Rhodes 2 (100 BPM)** to your arrangement, you must create an Audio Object for it to play through, and assign that Audio Object to a track in the Arrange window. Let's do that now.

4   Create a new Audio Object, name it Rhodes 2, and assign its channel to Track 3.

5   On the new Rhodes 2 Audio Object, click the Stereo/Mono button to make it a Stereo channel.

6   Press 9 to get back to the Audio window/Arrange window screenset.

7   In the Track column, select the Rhodes 1 track and choose Functions > Track > Create with next Instrument.

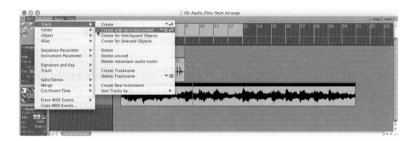

A new track is created and automatically assigned to the Rhodes 2 Audio Object.

8   From the Audio window, drag the Rhodes 2 (100 BPM) region onto the Arrange window's Rhodes 2 track, and drop it at bar 5.

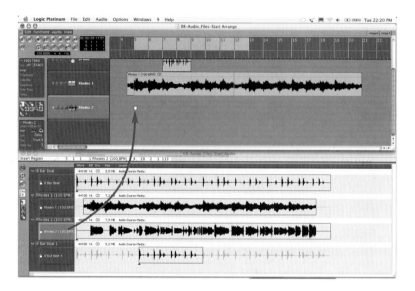

9   In either the Audio or Arrange window, double-click the Rhodes 2 (100 BPM) region, move its region start and end boundaries closer to the waveform, and most important of all, position the Anchor at the very start of the audible portion of the waveform.

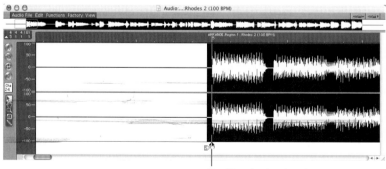

Position Anchor here!

Be judicious in your placement of the Anchor, because the timing of this region is entirely dependent upon positioning it correctly!

10 Click the Arrange window to make it active, and play the song.

Yikes! What's happening? It sounds terrible—but for good reason. The Rhodes 2 (100 BPM) region is playing back much slower than it should. Here's why: Your song uses a sampling rate of 44.1 kHz, but the audio file used for Rhodes 2 (100 BPM) is 48 kHz. To play this file in a 44.1 kHz song, Logic must slow it down so that only 44,100 samples play per second, instead of 48,000. This means the file is playing approximately 8 percent slower than it should. To fix this, you must change the file's sampling rate with the help of the Sample editor's Digital Factory.

Using the Digital Factory

The Digital Factory is a suite of digital signal processors designed to change audio regions in several ways. For example, you can use the Factory to time-compress or -expand an audio region, change its pitch, add groove or swing to a machinelike audio loop, or, for the purpose of this exercise, alter its sampling rate.

Protecting Your Source Files At the beginning of this lesson you learned that Logic is a nondestructive audio editor that does not change your source audio files in the course of editing. For the most part this is true, but as with all rules, there is a notable exception—enter the Digital Factory. Almost all Digital Factory functions are destructive, which means they permanently alter your source audio files. This can cause problems if you ever need to get those source files back or if they are used in another song. Fortunately, Logic has a preference setting that, when enabled, tells Logic to make a backup of the source file before destructively altering it in the Digital Factory. For safety's sake, make sure that preference is enabled by following these steps.

STEPS TO SECURE SOURCE FILES FROM DESTRUCTION IN DIGITAL FACTORY - CONT'D

1. Choose Audio > Audio Preferences.

NOTE ▶ You can also open the Preferences window by choosing Logic > Preferences > Audio Preferences, but opening it from the Audio menu is a bit more direct and thus faster.

The Audio Preferences window opens.

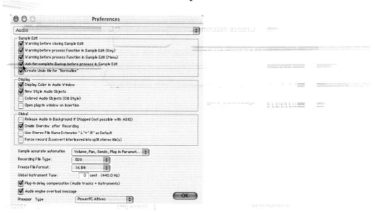

At the top of the Audio Preferences window is a section labeled Sample Edit. Make sure all these check boxes are selected, but pay particular attention to "Ask for complete Backup before process in Sample Edit." This preference tells Logic to ask if it should make a backup of an audio file before it alters it, which can save you a lot of grief if you accidentally change something you shouldn't have!

2. Select all the check boxes in the Sample Edit section and then click OK to close the Audio Preferences window.

Converting Sampling Rates

With the "Ask for complete Backup before process in Sample Edit" prefer-ence enabled, you can now confidently change the **Rhodes 2 (100 BPM)** file's sampling rate, safe in the knowledge that a backup file will be cre-ated, should anything happen to go awry.

1   Click the Sample editor to make it the active window.

The Sample editor still shows the Rhodes 2 (100 BPM) region, which is good, because this region points to the audio file you need to convert.

2   From the Sample editor's local menus, select Factory > Sample Rate Convert.

The Factory dialog opens.

On the right side is a Source [Hz] field displaying the file's current sampling rate (48,000 Hz, or 48 kHz), and a Destination [Hz] field displaying your song's sampling rate (44,100 Hz, or 44.1 kHz). This is all correct, so there's no need to change anything here.

3 Click the Convert button.

A dialog pops up to recommend converting the entire audio file and not just the region. This is good advice to follow.

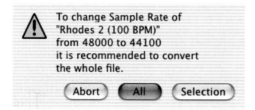

4 Click All.

Logic now processes the conversion, and the spinning beach ball appears on your screen. Depending on the speed of your computer, this beach ball will spin for between 30 seconds and several minutes. Logic is not hung, but rather is thinking, so be patient and wait for the beach ball to stop spinning.

Once Logic finishes processing the audio file, it asks if you'd like to create a backup of the original audio file. (Remember the preference you set in the last step? This is that preference in action.)

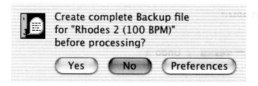

5   Click Yes.

Logic creates a new waveform overview …

… and then updates the Arrange window with the new, converted region. In the Arrange window, the Rhodes 2 (100 BPM) region now finishes at almost exactly the same time as the Rhodes 1 (100 BPM) region.

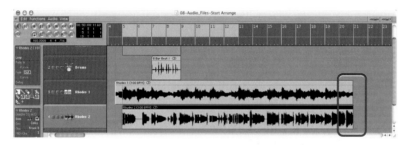

6   Close the Factory window; then close the Sample editor.

When you close the Sample editor, Logic asks if you'd like to make the last edit permanent.

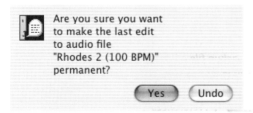

7 Click Yes.

This is a dialog that can cause concern, but don't worry. A few steps back, Logic created a backup of the original audio file, so you can safely click Yes, because even if you've made a mistake, Logic has already saved a backup of the **Rhodes 2 (100 BPM)** audio file in the same folder as the source file (in this case, your course Media folder).

Rhodes 2 (100 BPM) backup file

Name	Date Modified	Size	Kind
8 Bar Beat	4/17/03, 4:03 PM	3.5 MB	Sound Designer II sound
8 Bar Beat.1	5/4/03, 2:37 AM	3.2 MB	Sound Designer II sound
Bass Line.mid	4/17/03, 3:57 PM	4 KB	Standard MIDI File
Rhodes 1 (100 BPM)	5/5/03, 12:50 PM	7.2 MB	Sound Designer II sound
Rhodes 2 (100 BPM)	Today, 12:28 AM	7.3 MB	Sound Designer II sound
Rhodes 2 (100 BPM) dup	Today, 12:28 AM	7.9 MB	Sound Designer II sound
Scratch 1	4/17/03, 4:03 PM	472 KB	Sound Designer II sound
Scratch 2	4/17/03, 4:03 PM	728 KB	Sound Designer II sound

Course Media — 8 items, 3.45 GB available

8 Play your song.

Everything now sounds perfectly in time! Great news. You've accurately trimmed your song's audio regions, you've set their Anchors, and you're now ready to move on to Lesson 9, where you'll begin laying out these regions to create an actual song.

9 Save your song.

What You've Learned   *✐CHAPTER 8 SUMMARY ✱*

✓ Regions in the Arrange window are exactly the same as the corresponding regions in the Audio window, so editing a region in one of these windows automatically updates the region in the other window.

✓ A region's Anchor is used to snap the region to the Arrange window's timing grid.

✓ The Audio window makes region edits that are accurate to within 256 samples, while the Sample editor is capable of making sample-accurate region edits.

✓ To convert a file's sampling rate, use the Digital Factory.

✱ *DIGITAL FACTORY WARNING*

✓ Digital Factory functions (such as sampling-rate conversion) are destructive, which means they permanently alter your source audio files, so it's wise to make backups before using these functions.

9

Start	09-Arrangement-Start
Complete	09-Arrangement-Finished
Time	Approximately 45 minutes
Goals	Create an arrangement by organizing MIDI sequences and audio regions into a song
	Learn how to divide MIDI sequences and audio regions
	Move, copy, and delete Objects
	Experiment with Logic's Repeat Objects function
	Discover the advantages of looping repetitive Arrange window Objects
	Layer the bass line with a second instrument to make it sound thicker

Creating an Arrangement

Creating an arrangement is a process that involves dividing, copying, moving, repeating, and organizing MIDI sequences and audio regions in the Arrange window, to make a song. The Arrange window provides specialized tools for each of those actions, and in most cases the tools work with MIDI sequences and audio regions in exactly the same way. Where differences occur, they will be pointed out, but in general you can assume that the techniques you learn in this lesson will work equally well on both MIDI sequences and audio regions.

In earlier lessons you learned about Environment Objects, and you may be surprised to learn that MIDI sequences and audio regions are also considered Objects by Logic. Because there are so many similarities between the ways MIDI sequences and audio regions are edited, this lesson refers to both as *Objects*.

Dividing Objects

In the Arrange window, dividing Objects is the act of splitting one Object into two, and for this Logic provides the Scissors tool. This tool is one of the few that operate differently for MIDI sequences and audio regions, so you'll look at audio regions first, then move on to MIDI sequences.

Dividing Audio Regions

Dividing audio regions is a straight-ahead affair—just grab the Scissors tool and cut. However, there are a couple of things to keep in mind:

- Each time you divide an audio region, two new regions are created in both the Arrange window and the Audio window, which means a lot of dividing can quickly crowd your Audio window with new regions.

- Regions divide where you click the Scissors tool, and Logic pays no consideration to the waveform's zero crossing. As long as the divided regions remain side by side, this makes little difference, because the divided waveform lines up across the edit. But if you move or delete one of the regions (and let's face it, this is the reason for dividing it), you may experience clicks and pops around your divides. To fix these unwanted noises, you'll have to open the region in the Sample editor and move the region boundary to the nearest zero crossing (or else use fades, which are covered in Lesson 11, "Basic Mixing").

1   Open the song file you saved at the end of the previous lesson.

  NOTE ▶ If you didn't save your song, open the file named **09-Arrangement-Start**.

  Screenset 9 should still be open in the workspace (if not, press the 9 key to open screenset 9 now). This screenset has the Arrange window along the top and the Audio window along the bottom. This is a good layout for experimenting with dividing audio regions, because you can watch as Logic adds regions to the Audio window with each divide.

2 From the Arrange window's toolbox, grab the Scissors.

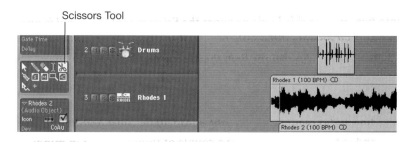

Scissors Tool

3 On the Rhodes 2 track, click and hold at bar 8, but don't release the mouse.

Indicator Line   Crosshair Pointer

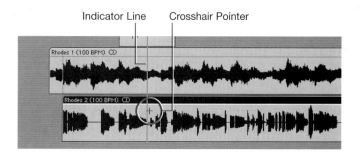

The Scissors tool turns into a crosshair, and an indicator line extends vertically down the Arrange area to show you the position of your divide. Across the top of the Arrange window the Info Line appears, showing the position of the indicator line, which in turn displays the position where the divide will occur if you release the mouse.

Function Being Performed

Position of Indicator Line   Info Line

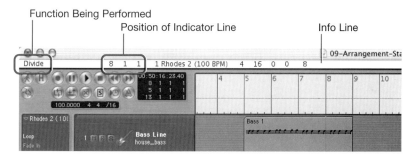

4 Drag the crosshair pointer along the Rhodes 2 Object.

As you drag, Logic enters the Scrub mode and plays a preview of the sound under the pointer, and the indicator line snaps along behind the crosshair pointer. The degree of this snapping is determined by the Arrange window's zoom setting, so using the telescopes to zoom in causes the indicator line to snap with a finer degree of resolution. This is an important thing to consider, because all Objects divide at the position of the indicator line, not at the position of the crosshair pointer.

TIP To temporarily disable snapping, hold down the Control key as you divide Objects. The indicator line will now precisely follow the pointer, enabling you to divide Objects between grid points.

5 Drag the pointer to 13 1 1 1 (the beginning of bar 13), and then release the mouse.

Divide region at start of bar 13

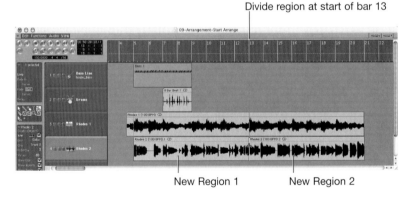

New Region 1   New Region 2

The Rhodes 2 Object divides at the start of bar 13, cutting the old region into two new ones.

In the Audio window, notice that two regions have been added to the **Rhodes 2 (100 BPM)** file. These regions represent the newly divided regions in the Arrange window. Logic also keeps the old region intact, so if you later decide this edit doesn't work, you can grab the old, intact region and drag it back into the Arrange window.

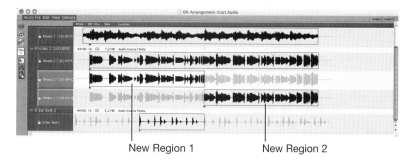

New Region 1   New Region 2

Dividing MIDI Sequences

For the most part, dividing MIDI sequences works exactly the same as dividing audio regions, but with one difference: It's possible for MIDI notes to overlap the point where you are dividing the sequence. When this happens, Logic asks if you'd like to Keep, Shorten, or Split the overlapping notes.

Keep Keep is the default action, and it leaves all the notes unaltered. The sequence is divided, but the new sequence on the left of the division will have a note, or notes, that extend beyond the end of the sequence. These notes will play in their entirety.

Shorten Truncates all overlapping notes at the point where the sequence is divided.

Split Divides the overlapping notes. Two notes are created with the same pitch and velocity; together, their lengths equal the total length of the original note.

Now that you know the theory, let's put it into action by dividing the bass line sequence. But before doing so, select the Bass 1 sequence and open up the Matrix editor so you can see the effect dividing a MIDI sequence has on the MIDI events it contains.

1   Select the Bass 1 MIDI Sequence and choose Windows > Open Matrix Edit (Cmd-6).

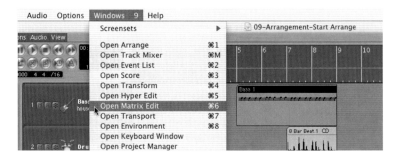

The Matrix editor opens. Notice that a single MIDI note crosses from bar 6 into bar 7. Let's now see what happens when you divide the Bass 1 sequence at bar 7.

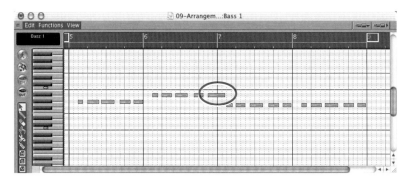

2   Position the Matrix editor and Arrange window so that you can see both.

3 In the Arrange window, grab the Scissors tool, then click the Bass 1 sequence at bar 7.

A dialog pops up to tell you that overlapping notes have been found! This means at least one MIDI note crosses the boundary between bar 6 and bar 7.

At this point you are presented with the three choices detailed above: Keep, Shorten, or Split. These choices are a result of that single note spanning the transition between bar 6 and bar 7—right where you're cutting the sequence!

4 Choose Shorten.

The sequence is divided in two, and the overlapping MIDI note is shortened to fit within the new sequence on the left, as you can see by taking a quick look at the Matrix editor.

Overlapping note is shortened

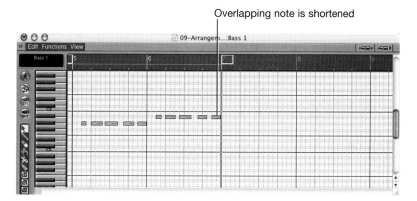

NOTE ▶ The decision to Keep, Shorten, or Split is based entirely on the MIDI sequence and the type of sound it triggers. If this were a long synth sweep, or a note triggering a long sample, you would instead choose to keep the note so that the synth swell or sample finished playing in its entirety.

5   Close the Matrix editor.

Dividing Objects by Locators

Dividing Objects by locators provides a quick way to create Objects that are the same size as a cycle region.

1   In the top portion of the Bar Ruler, drag from 5 1 1 1 to 13 1 1 1 to create an eight-bar cycle region.

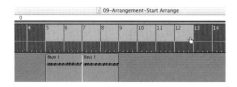

2   In the Track column, select the Rhodes 1 track.

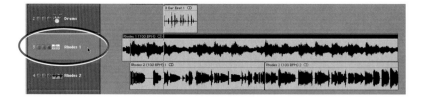

The Rhodes 1 Object is automatically selected.

3   Choose Functions > Split/Demix > Split Objects by Locators.

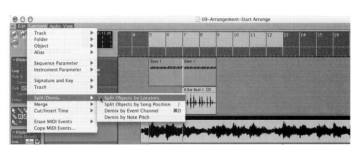

The Rhodes 1 (100 BPM) Object is divided into three regions.

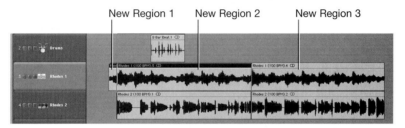

NOTE ▶ A cycle region does not actually have to be enabled to split Objects by locators—this function merely looks at the position of the left and right locators, and isn't concerned with whether or not Cycle mode is enabled. However, setting a cycle region is the fastest way to set the locators, so you'll often end up creating a cycle region before activating the Split Objects by Locators function.

Dividing Objects into Equal Sections

If you have a particularly long Object, you might need to divide it into several smaller Objects of equal size.

1   The Scissors tool should still be selected. If not, select it from the toolbox now.

2 Hold down the Option key, and click the second object in the Rhodes 1 track at 6 1 1 1.

Holding down the Option key tells Logic to cut the Object into multiple pieces, with the length of the new pieces determined by the length of the first segment. Consequently, Logic divides the Rhodes 1 (100 BPM) Object into eight one-bar regions.

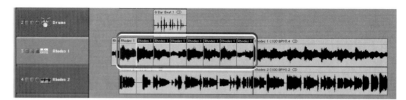

Moving and Copying Objects

Moving and copying Objects is a basic part of creating an arrangement, so take a moment to familiarize yourself with the following techniques.

1 From the Arrange window's toolbox grab the Selection tool, and then select the 8 Bar Beat.1 Object.

2 Drag the 8 Bar Beat.1 Object to 9 1 1 1.

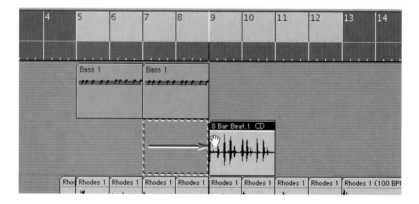

3 Next, hold down the Option key and drag the 8 Bar Beat.1 Object to 11 1 1 1.

A copy of the 8 Bar Beat region is created.

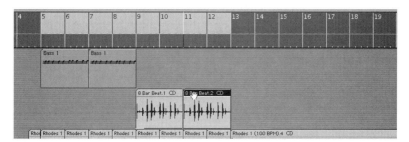

TIP ▶ Cut and paste is another great way to move Objects.

4 Rubber-band select the last Objects on the Rhodes 1 and Rhodes 2 tracks.

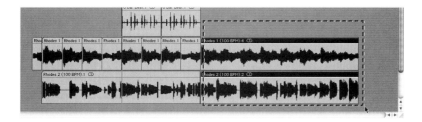

5 Press Cmd-X.

Logic cuts the Objects from the Arrange area and copies them to the Clipboard. Let's move these Objects a little ways down the Arrange area by pasting them back in at bar 29.

6 Use the Arrange window's telescopes to zoom out until the Bar Ruler displays at least 37 bars.

This gives you enough room to see the result of the following edits.

7 Click the Transport's Bar Position area and type in *29 1 1 1*, then
press Return.

NOTE ▶ You can also just click the Bar Ruler at measure 29 to move
the SPL, but this is an important edit, and with the Arrange window
zoomed out as much as it is, it's difficult to click exactly on 29 1 1 1.
In tight situations like this, positioning the SPL by entering a value
into the Transport's Bar Position area is much more accurate.

8 Press Cmd-V to paste the cut Objects from the Clipboard back into
the Arrange area.

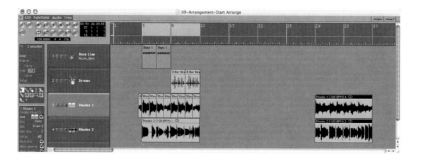

The cut Objects are pasted back in at bar 29 1 1 1, and a large gap is
left in the Arrange area. This is fine: You will fill this gap before the
end of the lesson.

Repeating Objects

Logic's Repeat Objects function provides a quick way to make multiple
copies of Objects in the Arrange window. The function can either copy
Objects and all the data they contain, or create aliases that link back to the
original Object.

Copies Each repeated Object is an exact duplicate of the original.

Aliases Each repeated Object is an alias that looks like the original but
contains no data. The repeated Objects simply reference the data contained in the original, so if you make a change to the original Object, the
change ripples through the repeated aliases. Aliases are immediately recog-
nizable by their italicized names and are particularly useful for repetitive
MIDI sequences. For example, in this song the bass line will repeat over
and over again. If you fill the arrangement with copies of the bass line
sequences but then decide you want to change the sequence in any way,
you'll have to alter every copied bass line sequence by hand. Aliases save
you this unnecessary labor because you just need to change the original
sequence, and each alias will be automatically updated!

Let's try out both ways of copying objects.

1   Select the first Object in the Rhodes 2 track.

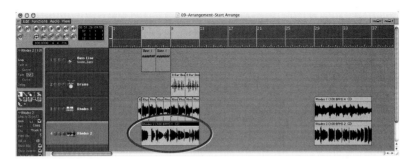

2   Choose Functions > Object > Repeat Objects.

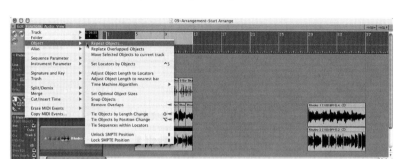

The Repeat Objects dialog appears.

3   In the gap between the Rhodes 2 track's Objects there are exactly 16 bars, which is just enough space for two copies of the first Rhodes 2 (100 BPM) region, so for the Repeat Objects dialog's Number of Copies setting, enter 2.

4   Leave the Adjustment setting set to Auto, and the "as" setting set to Copies.

The Adjustment menu determines where the repeated Objects begin. The Auto setting is usually the one you want because it automatically determines how the Objects should be copied by looking at the length of the Object. This Auto setting usually does a pretty good job, but the other settings found in the Adjustment pop-up menu are available if you need to quantize the start points for the repeated Objects. For example, if an Object is less than a bar in length, selecting Bar from the Adjustment menu ensures that all repeated Objects are quantized to the downbeat at the beginning of the next bar, instead of directly one after the other.

5 Click Do It.

Logic fills the empty space in the Rhodes 2 track with two copies of the selected Object.

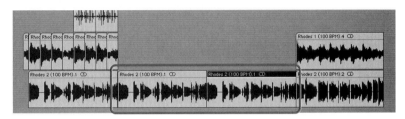

6 Rubber-band select both Objects on the Bass Line track.

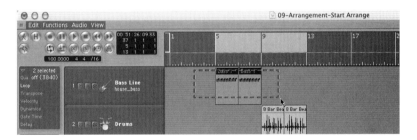

7 Choose Functions > Objects > Repeat Objects to open the Repeat Objects dialog.

The Repeat Objects dialog opens once again.

8 Change the Number of Copies setting to 5, leave the Adjustment setting at Auto, but change the "as" setting to Aliases, and then click Do It.

Logic creates a series of aliases of the original Bass Line Objects.

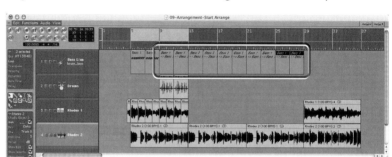

NOTE ▶ You can also create aliases of MIDI sequences by holding down the Shift key while copying (press Shift-Option while dragging the sequence).

Finding the Original of an Alias

In long arrangements it's easy to lose an alias's original Object. To guard against this, Logic provides a function that finds the original for you.

▶   Select the last alias in the Bass Line track, then choose Functions > Alias > Select Original.

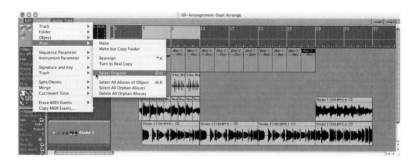

Logic selects the original Object.

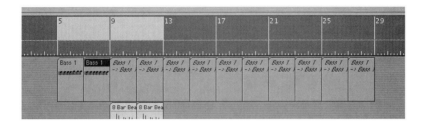

Converting Aliases to Editable Objects

If you need to make a change to an alias, convert it to an Object. The contents of the new Object will be exactly the same as the alias's original.

1   Select the last alias in the Bass Line track.

2   Choose Functions > Alias > Turn to Real Copy.

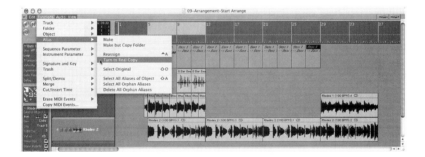

Logic turns the alias into an Object containing data you can edit.

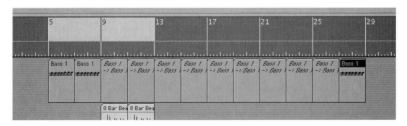

Looping Objects

Aliases are a great labor-saving technique, but if you're creating a repetitive sequence of the same Object, the Loop function also works well. Looping is set per Object, and when it is turned on, the Object is repeated until it either encounters another Object or hits the end of the song.

1   Select the Drums track's second Object (the one that begins at bar 11), and press the Delete key to erase it.

   You are about to loop the first Object in the Drums track, so the second Object is no longer needed.

2   Only one Object remains in the Drums track. Select it now.

3   In the Region Parameter box, click the empty space to the right of the word Loop.

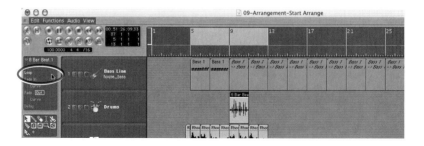

The word On appears, indicating that looping is on for the selected Object, and the selected Object loops for the length of your song.

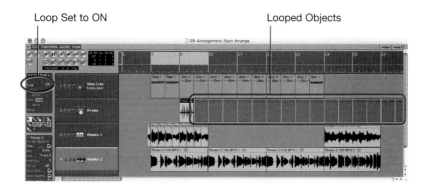

Loop Set to ON   Looped Objects

Looped Objects continue to loop until they hit another Object or the end of your song, so to stop the looped Objects, you need to create a new Object as a stopper.

4   Grab the Pencil tool.

5   Click the Pencil tool at 29 1 1 1 to create a new, empty Object.

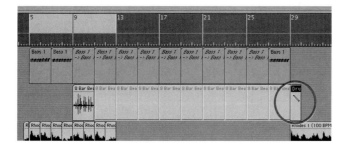

This stops the looping dead in its tracks!

The Loop function is attached to the region, so if you copy or move that region, the function sticks.

6 With the Pencil tool, create a new, empty Object in the Drums track at 17 1 1 1.

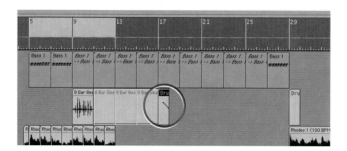

7 From the toolbox, choose the Arrow tool.

8 Hold down the Option key, then grab the 8 Bar Beat region and move it to 21 1 1 1.

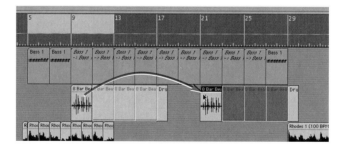

The copied Object retains the Loop function.

Merging Objects

Merging combines two or more Objects into a single Object. Logic provides a dedicated tool for merging—the Glue tool.

1   From the Arrange window's toolbox, select the Glue tool.

2   On the Rhodes 1 track, rubber-band select all Objects between 5 1 1 1 and 13 1 1 1.

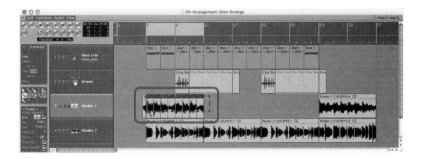

Eight regions are selected (make sure you don't select the small region before bar 5).

3   Click any of these regions with the Glue tool.

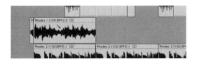

Logic merges the eight separate regions into one large one.

NOTE ▶ It doesn't matter which of the selected regions you click— the Glue tool merges all Objects selected in the Arrange window.

4 Using the Glue tool, click this newly merged Object to select it.

Directly following this Object there's a big hole in your arrangement. Fill this hole now by repeating the selected Object twice.

5 Choose Functions > Object > Repeat Objects to open the Repeat Objects dialog, enter *2* in the Number of Copies field, choose Copies from the "as" menu, and then click Do It.

The Object is repeated twice, filling the hole in the arrangement.

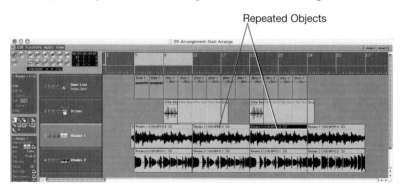

6 If you still have a cycle region enabled, click the Transport's Cycle button to turn it off (/).

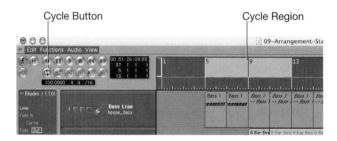

7   In the Track column, select the Bass Line track.

All of the Objects in the Bass Line track are selected.

8   Choose Functions > Merge > Objects per Tracks.

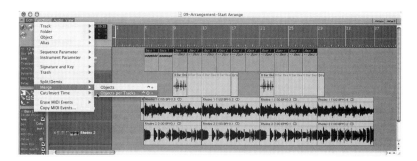

Logic merges all Objects in the Bass Line track into a single sequence.

Merged Object

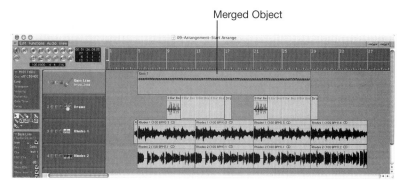

Layering Sounds

One great thing about MIDI sequences is that they are just a collection of MIDI notes, so you can use them to trigger any sound you want. Your bass line sequence is currently triggering the ES M's house_bass preset, which is a great-sounding program, but it could be a bit beefier. A quick way to add punch to this sound is to layer it with another instrument patch that uses the exact same MIDI sequence with a different sound.

Layering sounds provides a few other fun benefits. For example, you can apply different DSP plug-ins to each sound (a compressor on one and a delay on the other), or you can automate each sound separately to make an otherwise straight-ahead MIDI sequence really breathe and come to life. In Lesson 13, "Automating the Mix," you'll do exactly this by programming a filter sweep into the new bass layer you are going to add in the following steps. To prepare for this, let's choose a new sound that has a bit of bite, such as the ES P's syn_percusor preset.

1   Press 8 to open the Environment.

2   Create a new Audio Object, name it *Bass Line 2,* and assign its channel to Instrument 2.

  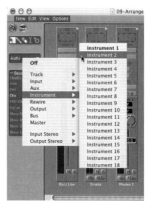

3 Click and hold this new Instrument Object's Input box, and choose
Stereo > Logic > ES P.

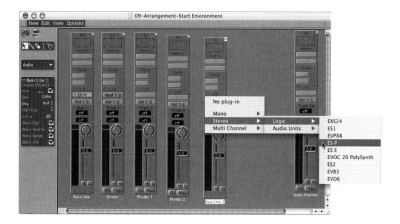

4 Open the ES P, and from its Settings menu choose factory 1 >
syn_percusor.

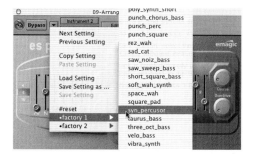

All that's left to do is create a new track to play this instrument, and
then copy the bass line sequence into the new track to create the layered sound.

5 Close the ES P.

6 Press 1 to open the Arrange window.

7 In the Track column, select the Bass Line track, and choose Functions > Track > Create with next Instrument.

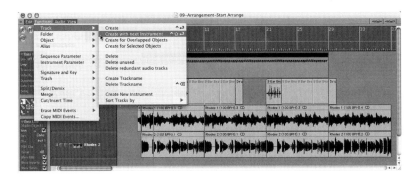

A new track is created directly under the Bass Line track, and it's automatically assigned to the Bass Line 2 Instrument Object you created in the Environment!

8 Hold down the Option key, grab the Bass 1 sequence, and drag it down to the Bass Line 2 track.

The bass line sequence is copied to the Bass Line 2 track.

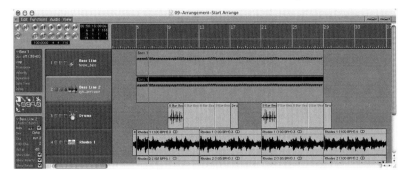

9 Play your song.

The bass line now sounds a bit thicker than it did before. Cool!

10 Save your song.

NOTE ▶ Feel free to experiment with other ES P presets until you find a sound you like. Don't forget that in Lesson 5 you assigned Option-N and Option-B to the Next Preset and Previous Preset commands, respectively, so with the ES P open on your screen, you can quickly cycle through its presets using these key commands.

What You've Learned *✶ CHAPTER 9 SUMMARY ✶*

- The Scissors tool is used to divide Objects.
- Dividing an audio region creates two new regions, both of which are added to the Audio window.
- Holding down the Option key as you divide an Object splits it into several new Objects, with the length of each new Object determined by the length of the first Object before the division.
- Repeating an Object is a quick way to fill a track with several copies of aliases.
- Aliases reference the data in the original Object. If you change the original Object, the change ripples through each alias.
- Looping an Object repeats it until it either encounters another Object in the same track or hits the end of the song.
- The Glue tool merges selected Objects together.

10

Media	Scratch 1
	Scratch 2
Start	10-MIDI_Editors-Start
Complete	10-MIDI_Editors-Finished
Time	Approximately 55 minutes
Goals	Use the Hyper Editor to create a hi-hat MIDI sequence that plays the QuickTime Synth's GM drum kit
	Edit note length, position in time, and velocity in the Matrix editor
	Learn how to filter and change events by making entries in the Event List editor
	Finish the arrangement by adding a record-scratch noise that acts as an intro and outro to the song's beat

Exploring the MIDI Editors

Logic has four editors designed specifically for editing MIDI data: the Hyper Editor and the Matrix, Event List, and Score editors. Each of these editors deals with MIDI information in a special way. The Hyper Editor is designed to display control-change data such as pan, modulation, and pitch-wheel changes. The Matrix editor uses a standard piano keyboard as a guide to edit note information such as position in time, length, and velocity. The Event List catalogs all MIDI events in order of occurrence and gives you access to MIDI events not available in the other editors. The Score editor lets classically trained musicians edit MIDI data as notes on a musical score. These MIDI editors all serve specific purposes, and understanding which editor to use—and when—is one secret to becoming a Logic master.

NOTE ▶ The Score editor depends upon an understanding of traditional music notation, but an understanding of traditional music notation is not a prerequisite to making music in Logic. Consequently, this lesson focuses on the other MIDI editors and does not cover the Score editor.

Exploring the Hyper Editor

Of all the MIDI editors, the Hyper Editor has the most limited capabilities. For example, this MIDI editor doesn't display note length or keyboard position. But that's not really its purpose—the Hyper Editor is designed to

- Add or edit control-change data, such as pan settings, velocities, or even program-change messages that tell your synthesizer which sounds to play

- Create drum sequences

Of the two, creating drum sequences is far more fun (and involved), so let's use the Hyper Editor to program a hi-hat line that plays the QuickTime Synth.

Opening the Hyper Editor

To open the Hyper Editor, a MIDI sequence must be selected in the Arrange area. If no MIDI sequence is selected, attempting to open the Hyper Editor results in this dialog:

Clicking anything other than Cancel in this dialog can get you into big trouble. Folders are an advanced topic not covered in this course, so you don't want to open one. And creating a new sequence replaces all the

data in the currently selected track. So, to prevent any encounters with
this tricky dialog, let's create a new MIDI track that plays the QuickTime
Synth. Once this new track is in place, you can safely use the Pencil tool to
create a new MIDI sequence and then open the Hyper Editor.

1   Open the song file you saved at the end of the previous lesson.

   NOTE ▶ If you didn't save your song at the end of the previous lesson, open the file named **10-MIDI_Editors-Start**.

2   In the Track column, double-click the empty track under Rhodes 2.

Logic creates a new track.

3   Click and hold the left side of the new track's name.

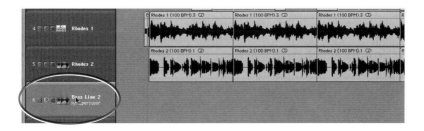

The Instrument List appears.

4 From the Instrument List, choose QuickTime Synth > QuickTime GM > 10 (STANDARD Drum).

With a QuickTime track in the Arrange window you're halfway to opening the Hyper Editor. All that remains is to create a MIDI sequence.

5 From the toolbox, grab the Pencil tool and click the QuickTime track at bar 9.

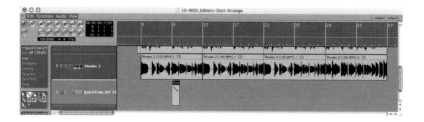

An empty, one-bar MIDI sequence is created.

6 Choose Windows > Open Hyper Edit (Cmd-5).

The Hyper Editor opens.

Working with Layers

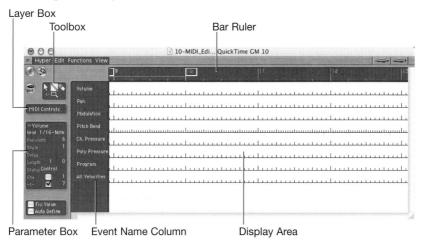

Layer Box

Toolbox

Bar Ruler

Parameter Box   Event Name Column   Display Area

The Hyper Editor's default display shows standard MIDI controls such as volume, pan, and program-change messages. These are all MIDI control-change messages, and a quick glance at the Hyper Editor's Layer box shows they belong to the MIDI Controls layer. This is a great layer for changing pan and program information, but to create a drum sequence, you need to switch to the GM Drum Kit layer.

1   Click and hold the Layer box.

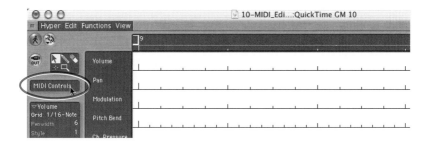

The Layer menu appears, showing two options: MIDI Controls and GM Drum Kit.

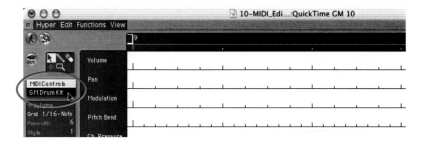

2   Choose GM Drum Kit.

In the GM Drum Kit layer, the Event Name column shows drum sounds.

The GM Drum Kit layer displays sounds
from the standard GM drum kit

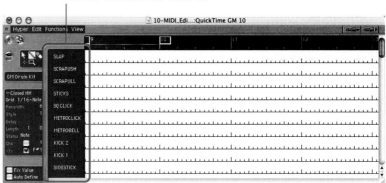

Great! Now let's add a hi-hat line.

Adding MIDI Events to the Hyper Editor

In the Hyper Editor, MIDI events are represented as vertical beams spaced horizontally along a grid. You can change the grid's resolution by selecting a new value from the Parameter box's Grid setting.

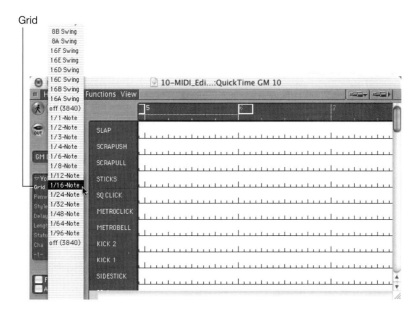

The Grid setting lists all the same values as Logic's standard Quantization menus, and indeed, the Grid setting is used to quantize the placement of events in the Hyper Editor by changing the spacing of the notched lines running across the Hyper Editor—its grid. For the purpose of creating a hi-hat line, the Hyper Editor's default ⅟16-Note setting is sufficient. Drum hits are short, and the ⅟16-Note setting provides perfect timing, so let's carry on and find the hi-hat.

1 Scroll down the Hyper Editor until you see Closed HH in the Event Name column.

2 Grab the Pencil tool, and click the Closed HH row at 9 1 1 1.

You hear a hi-hat sound, and a note event is created.

NOTE ▶ If you didn't hear a hi-hat sound, the MIDI-Out button in the Hyper Editor's top-left corner is not enabled. This button has a picture of a MIDI connector with the word *OUT* printed under it.

3 That new note event is pretty short and narrow, so use the Hyper Editor's telescopes to zoom until the event is tall and wide enough to be clearly seen.

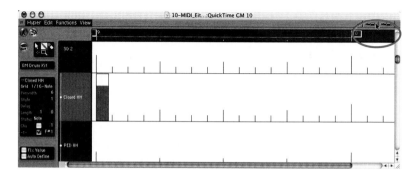

Displayed at this height, the event shows an obvious division between its white top and a gray bottom. This line between white and gray graphically indicates the note's velocity.

NOTE ▶ Velocity is a MIDI parameter that reflects how hard you strike a key on your MIDI keyboard. In general, velocity roughly equates to the volume of a note, because the harder you strike a key, the louder the note plays.

4   Using the Pencil tool, click and hold the note, then drag up and down.

The gray area grows and shrinks to follow the pointer, indicating increasing and decreasing note velocity. As you drag, the closed hi-hat plays and its volume goes up or down to follow the velocity setting. You can either set the velocity by listening to the note play or watch the Info Line that replaces the Hyper Editor's local menus as you drag to set the velocity.

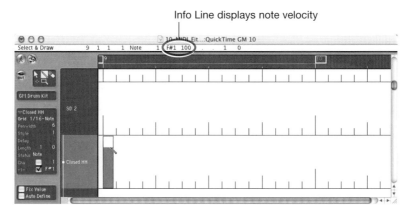

Info Line displays note velocity

Creating a Series of MIDI Events

By dragging the Pencil tool across the Hyper Editor, you can quickly create a series of MIDI events. This is a good way to program a pan that shifts between left and right speakers, a stepped volume fade, or a series of MIDI note events, as you'll do in the next few steps.

1   With the Pencil tool, set the new note's velocity to 100 (watch the Info
    Line), and then drag to the right, dipping down and back up to create
    an upside-down arc. Make sure you stop just short of bar 10, at 9 4 4 1.

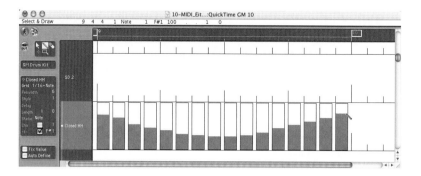

A row of notes is created in one swoop. Would you like to hear what it
sounds like? Let's loop this bar and listen to it.

2   In the top portion of the Hyper Editor's Bar Ruler, drag a cycle region
    from bar 9 to bar 10, then press the spacebar to play the song.

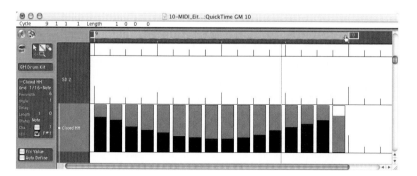

The bar loops and the closed hi-hat fades down, then up, in volume.

3 Click the Layer box, and choose MIDI Controls.

The MIDI Controls layer was empty, but it now contains a series of velocity values. These velocity values, of course, are the ones you just assigned the closed hi-hat notes using the Hyper Editor's GM Drum Kit layer. Let's next use the MIDI Controls layer to program a pan sweep.

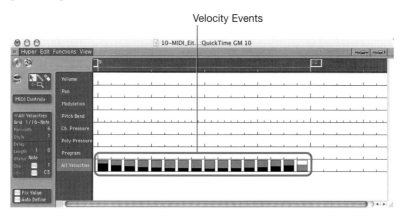

Velocity Events

4 From the toolbox grab the Crosshair tool.

Crosshair Tool

5   Click and hold the Pan row at 9 1 1 1.

The Info Line changes to display the Crosshair tool's position and value.

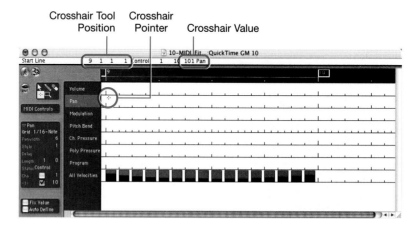

Crosshair Tool Position   Crosshair Pointer   Crosshair Value

6   Watch the Info Line and drag with the Crosshair tool to a value of approximately 100 (you don't need to be too exact), then release the mouse and move the pointer to the right.

A line trails out behind the Crosshair.

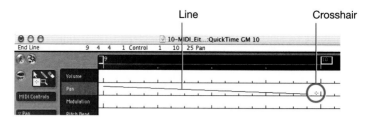

Line   Crosshair

7   At 9 4 4 1, move the Crosshair to a value of around 25, and click.

A linear series of pan events sweeps the hi-hat from left to right.

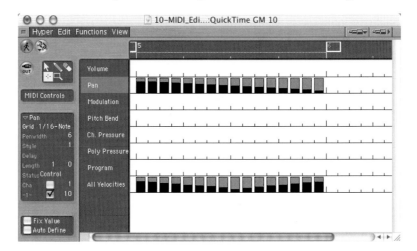

8   Press the spacebar to stop the playback, and then close the Hyper Editor.

Exploring the Matrix Editor

Keyboards provide the most common way to play notes into Logic, and the Matrix editor uses a graphic interface that parallels this type of MIDI controller. The Matrix editor's biggest advantage is its ability to show note events as horizontal beams displaying a note's velocity, length, and position in the sequence.

Opening the Matrix Editor

Let's open up the Matrix Editor and check it out.

1   Select the sequence in the QuickTime track, and choose Windows > Open Matrix Edit (Cmd-6).

The Matrix editor opens.

Matrix Editor Toolbox
Matrix Editor Keyboard   Notes   Bar Ruler

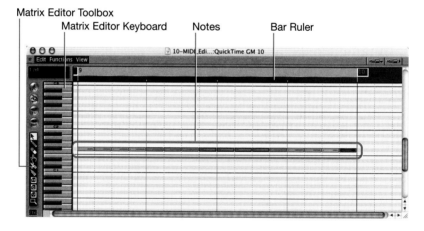

The Matrix editor currently displays a line of colored rectangles, and each of these rectangles is 1/16 of a bar—sixteenth notes! These, of course, are the sixteenth notes you entered using the Hyper Editor's GM Drum Kit interface. Along the left edge of the Matrix editor there is a keyboard, and clicking its keys with the pointer triggers playback on the current MIDI device just as if you were playing a controller keyboard.

2   Along the Matrix editor's left edge, click the keyboard's keys.

Clicking the keyboard plays the MIDI device assigned to the sequence's track (in this case, the QuickTime Synth's GM Drum Kit).

NOTE ▶ Logic's Global Preferences window has a setting labeled "Double-clicking Sequence in Arrange opens." You can set this preference so that double-clicking opens any of Logic's MIDI editors, including the Matrix editor.

Editing Notes

The Matrix editor's toolbox contains many of the same tools as the Arrange window, and indeed most of these tools function similarly in both windows. For example, the Eraser erases notes, the Scissors divides notes, and the Glue tool joins selected notes together. You've seen these tools in Lesson 9, so there's no need to cover them again. Instead, let's focus on some unique Matrix editor functions.

1 Grab any note and drag it up or down.

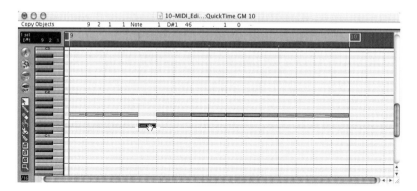

As you drag, the note moves up or down the keyboard. At each new position, the note plays to let you preview the new position's sound. You can turn this preview function off using the Matrix editor's MIDI Out button.

2 Along the left edge of the Matrix editor, click the MIDI Out button to turn the previewing off.

MIDI Out Button

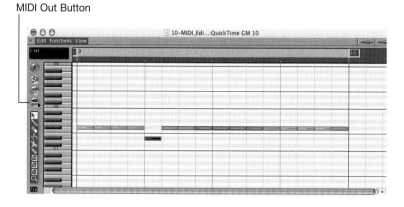

3 Once again, grab the note and drag it up or down.

Now, no sound is made and you cannot preview the edit.

4   Turn the MIDI Out button back on.

You should currently have one note out of line with the others (for now, it doesn't matter which note).

5   Grab the bottom-left corner of the note, and drag left or right.

The pointer turns into the Finger tool, and depending on the direction you drag, the note increases or decreases in duration. You can also grab the bottom-right corner of the note to stretch it in the other direction.

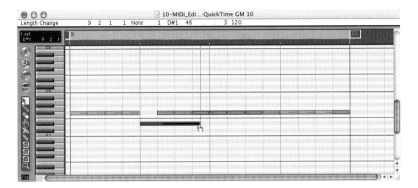

TIP From time to time you might find that Logic's Arrow tool is a bit finicky and dragging the lower corner of the note moves the note, instead of resizing it. If this happens to you, force Logic to obey your wishes by grabbing the Finger tool. This tool's only function is resizing notes, so with this tool selected, the note is sure to resize, and not move.

NOTE ▶ You probably noticed the note's edge snaps along the Matrix editor's grid as you resized it. The grid's snap settings are governed by the Matrix editor's current zoom value. To temporarily deactivate the snapping, hold down the Control key as you drag the note. To disable snapping entirely, hold down Ctrl-Shift.

6 Return the note to its original size and position in the sequence.

7 On the Matrix editor's keyboard, click the F#1 key.

F#1 Key

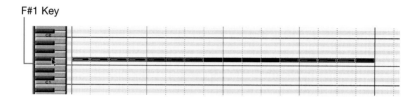

All of the F#1 notes in the sequence are automatically selected (clicking a keyboard key is similar to clicking a track in the Arrange window's Track column).

8 Grab the bottom-right corner of any note, and decrease its size a tiny bit.

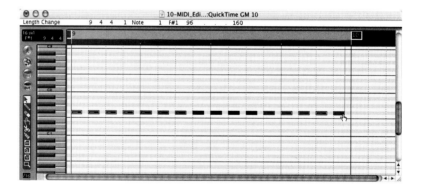

All of the selected notes decrease in size, together! Pay particular attention to this technique, because it's a great time-saver when you need to adjust the length of multiple notes at one time or to delete all the notes from a particular key.

Setting the Note Velocity

The notes in the Matrix editor are in several different colors, and these colors represent their velocity values. Each note also has a horizontal line that stretches backward from its front edge, and the length of this line in relation to the length of the note is also an indicator of its velocity. However, the notes currently in the Matrix editor are short, which makes it hard to see these horizontal velocity lines. Let's create a new, long note so this line is clearly visible, and then use this new note while experimenting with setting velocity.

Note Color vs. Velocity Value

Color	Velocity Value
Purple	01–15
Dark blue	16–31
Light blue	32–47
Light green	48–63
Green	64–79
Yellow	80–95
Orange	96–111
Red	112–127

1 From the Matrix editor's toolbox, grab the Pencil tool and click a new note anywhere in the Matrix editor.

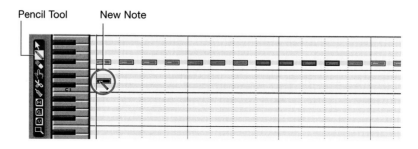

Pencil Tool   New Note

NOTE ▶ Each new note is automatically assigned the same length and velocity as the last note modified.

2 With the Pencil tool still selected, grab the bottom-right corner of the new note and stretch it across the Matrix editor.

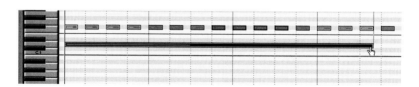

NOTE ▶ You can stretch notes with the Pencil, as well as the Arrow and Finger tools.

3 From the Matrix editor's toolbox, grab the Velocity tool.

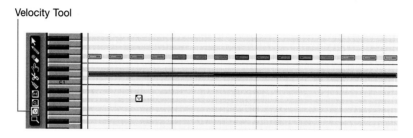

Velocity Tool

The Velocity tool has a *V* on it, and as you may have guessed, it's used to change a note's velocity.

4   With the Velocity tool, click and hold the new note, then drag up and down.

The note's color changes, and the thin line grows longer or shorter to indicate the changing velocity. As you drag, the note plays each new velocity so you can hear the results of your edit.

5   Press the Delete key to erase this new note.

You can also adjust the velocity of multiple notes at one time:

6   On the Matrix editor's keyboard, click the F#1 key.

All F#1 notes are selected.

7   With the Velocity tool, click and hold any selected note, then drag up and down.

All the selected notes change velocity together, but in a very smart way—each note keeps its velocity relative to the others. Consequently, notes with higher velocities will retain their higher velocities.

NOTE ▸ When adjusting the velocities of multiple selected notes, once any note reaches a velocity of either 0 or 127, it is no longer possible to edit any of the selected notes further.

Quantizing Notes

Quantization corrects the rhythm of notes so they conform to a specific time grid. Logic actually records two positions for each note in a sequence. The first is the note's original position, while the second is its playback, or *quantized,* position (for sequences that are not quantized, both positions are exactly the same). This fact means that quantization settings are nondestructive—only the playback (not the original note position) is changed. If you quantize a sequence but later decide you want to revert to the nonquantized version, just turn quantization off and your notes will revert to their unquantized, original positions inside the sequence.

Let's experiment a bit with quantizing the sixteenth notes in your sequence. These notes are regularly spaced, so they provide a good base for experimentation because you'll be able to easily see them snap to the new quantization settings.

1   From the Matrix editor's toolbox, grab the Quantization tool (the one with the Q on top).

Quantization Tool

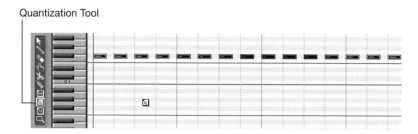

2   Click the Matrix editor keyboard's F#1 key.

All the F#1 notes are selected.

3   With the Quantization tool, click and hold any selected note.

A menu of quantization values appears.

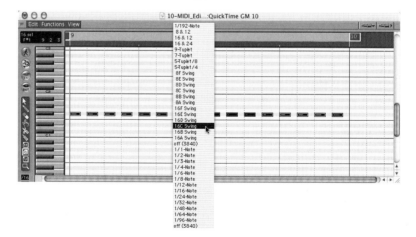

At the bottom of the Quantization menu is a section of quantization settings that snap notes directly to Logic's standard timing grid. These quantization settings work well when it comes to aligning notes with machinelike precision, but you might also find they make sequences sound *mechanical,* or inhuman. To put a bit more of an organic gloss on your MIDI sequences, the top of the Quantization menu holds several Swing settings that humanize your sequence's sound.

NOTE ▶ In the middle of the Quantization menu there's an Off setting that turns quantization off and returns the notes to their nonquantized position in the sequence.

4   From the Quantization menu, select 16C Swing.

Many of the notes shift off the standard timing grid.

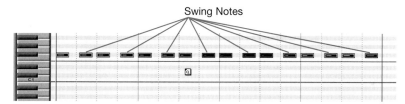

Swing Notes

5   A few exercises ago you set a cycle region to play bar 9, and this cycle region should still be active (if not, enable it now). Press the spacebar to play the cycle region, and then experiment with different quantization settings to see how they affect the selected notes.

6   Choose a quantization setting you like and then leave the Matrix editor open—you'll be using it again in the next section.

Exploring the Event List Editor

The Event List can be daunting at first glance, because it shows a long list of words and numbers that are a bit harder to read than the graphic event displays found in the other MIDI editors. Nonetheless, the Event List is a priceless tool when you need to quickly find certain types of data and make precise edits that are difficult to do using the other editors, such as finding a single program-change message in a long MIDI sequence.

Opening the Event List

Let's open the Event List now and take a look around.

▶ In the Arrange window, select the QuickTime track's sequence and choose Windows > Open Event List.

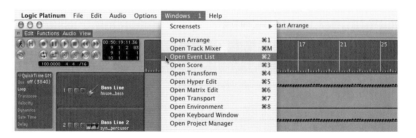

The Event List opens.

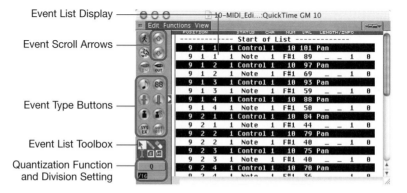

Your Event List might look a bit different from the one in the figure above, but that doesn't really matter. It still shows basically the same thing—a chart displaying MIDI events. Across the top of the Event List several headings are displayed: Position, Status, Cha, Num, Val, and Length/Info.

Position Displays the event's bar, beat, division, and tick.

Status Display's the event's type (for example, a note or control-change event).

Cha Displays the MIDI channel used to record events (this is not the channel used to play back the event!).

Num For note events, Num displays the note's keyboard position, while for control-change events it displays the controller number.

Val For note events, Val displays the note's velocity, while for control-change events Val displays the control-change value.

Length/Info With control-change events, this column shows the controller name, while for note events it shows the note's length.

Editing Event Settings

Now that you have an overall picture of what the Event List controls, let's use it to change some event settings.

1   The Matrix editor should still be open (if not, open it now). Position the Event List beside the Matrix editor so you can see both clearly.

As you experiment with the Event List, it helps to have the Matrix editor open to provide a visual display of the changes you make in the Event List (this is why you left the Matrix editor open at the end of the last exercise).

2 In the Matrix editor, select a note.

The note is highlighted in the Event List.

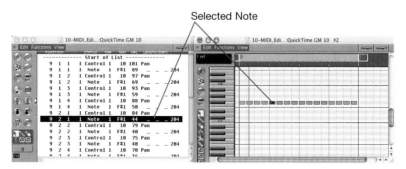

3 In the Event List, double-click the selected note's Num setting, enter *C1*, and press Return.

In the Matrix editor, the selected note jumps to C1.

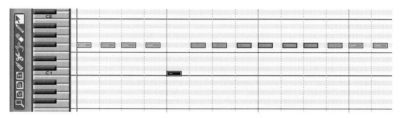

4   In the Matrix editor, grab the Arrow tool and then move the note
     back to F#1.

The Event List's Num setting reverts to F#1.

Filtering Events

The Event List is currently a mess of data, and with all these entries it's difficult to find exactly the event you're looking for. Event Type buttons to the
rescue! The Event Type buttons filter the Event List so it shows only a specific type of event, making it easier to find the event(s) you need to change.

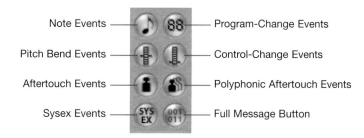

Note Events — Program-Change Events
Pitch Bend Events — Control-Change Events
Aftertouch Events — Polyphonic Aftertouch Events
Sysex Events — Full Message Button

1   Click the Note Events button.

All note events are removed from the Event List display, and it now
displays only control-change events.

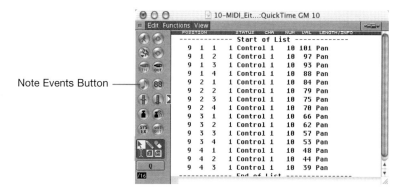

Note Events Button

2 Click the Control-Change Events button.

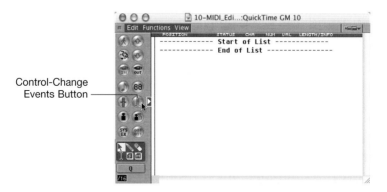

Control-Change Events Button

The QuickTime MIDI sequence contains only note and pan events. All note events are already filtered out of the Event List. Because pan events are control-change events, clicking the Control Change button filters all remaining events out of the Event List, which clears the list completely!

3 Click the Note and Control-Change Events buttons again to enable them.

Adding Events

1 Grab the Pencil tool, and click the Note Events button (the pointer remains an arrow, but don't be fooled—the Pencil tool is selected).

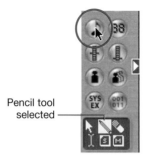

Pencil tool selected

A note is added at the current song position, as defined by the position of the SPL in the Arrange window. In the Event List display, the new note is selected and the Position area pops open a text box you can use to change the new note's position in the song.

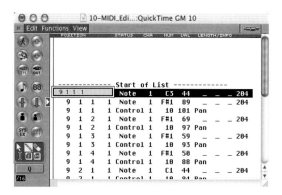

2   Set the new note's position to 9 2 1 1, and press Return.

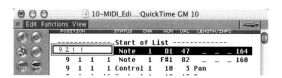

In the Matrix editor, a new D1 note appears at 9 2 1 1.

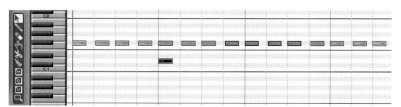

3   In the Event List display, make sure this new event is selected, and press the Delete key.

The event is erased.

4   Close the Event List and Matrix editors.

Finishing the Arrangement

Right now the QuickTime track has just a single one-bar MIDI sequence. Let's loop that sequence to the end of the song and also add a few record-scratch audio loops to act as fills. The first scratch comes right before the downbeat of bar 9 and sounds like a DJ "scratching-in" the beat. The second new audio loop "scratches-out" the beat at bar 17 (these record scratches sound like a DJ back-cuing a record, and they form a fast and catchy intro and outro to the beat sections). By the end of this lesson, your Arrange window will look like this:

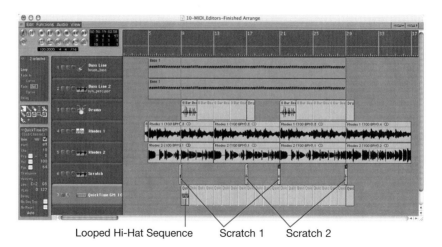

Looped Hi-Hat Sequence   Scratch 1   Scratch 2

The steps in this section are designed to give you a chance to hone the skills you've learned in the past few lessons. These steps are pretty fast-paced, but they use techniques you are already familiar with—and they're good practice—so make sure you work through them!

1   To turn off the Cycle mode so the song plays from beginning to end, click the top portion of the Bar Ruler or press C.

2   In the QuickTime track, select the one-bar sequence and turn looping on.

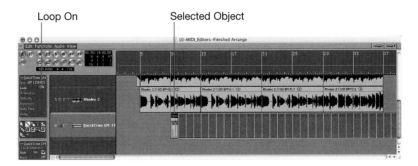

3   From the Arrange window's toolbox, grab the Pencil tool and then click at bar 29 to halt the QuickTime sequence's looping.

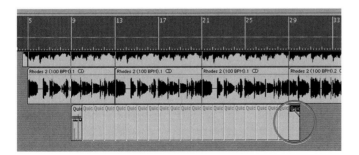

Great! Now let's add the record-scratch intros and outros. For this you will use the Scratch 1 and Scratch 2 audio files included in the Course Media folder. But first, of course, you have to add an audio track to hold these audio files.

4   Press 8 to open the Environment, then create a new Audio Object, name it Scratch, and assign its channel to Track 4.

5   Click the Scratch Object's Stereo/Mono button to make it a stereo Object.

6   Press 1 to open the Arrange window.

Remember the Create Track with Next Instrument command you learned in Lesson 6? Let's use that to quickly create a new track for the scratch samples.

7   In the Arrange window's Track column, select the Rhodes 2 track, then choose Functions > Track > Create with next Instrument (Ctrl-Shift-Return).

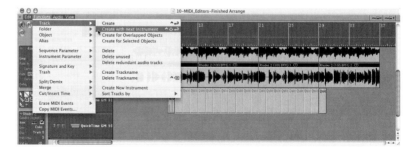

A new track is created under Rhodes 2 and automatically assigned to the Scratch Object.

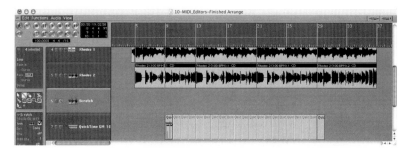

8   In the Finder, open the Course Media folder and position it beside (or below) the Arrange window.

9   Drag Scratch 1 onto the Scratch track and drop it at bar 9, then drag Scratch 2 onto the Scratch track at bar 17.

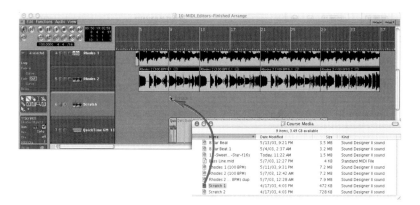

10 Double-click Scratch 1 to open the Sample editor, and then use the Sample editor to adjust the scratch region's boundaries and Anchor. It may take a few tries to get the Anchor in the correct position so it sounds like it's scratching-in the beat, but that's fine—experimentation is all part of the game!

11 Double-click Scratch 2 to open the Sample editor, and then use the Sample editor to adjust the scratch region's boundaries and Anchor point.

12 Copy Scratch 1 and Scratch 2 to bars 21 and 29, respectively.

The completed arrangement

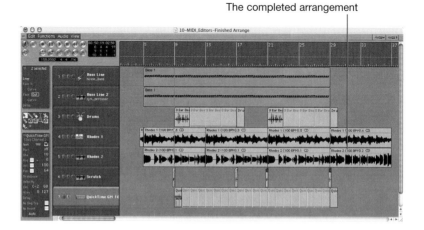

This arrangement is complete! You just did a lot in 12 steps. But that's how fast things go when you get good at using Logic!

13 Save your song.

14 Listen to the song from the beginning. If you have some free time, take a few minutes and make this song your own by arranging the sequences and regions however you like. Move things around and experiment. The song is saved and you can't wreck anything, so have fun.

TIP ▶ If your edits get a bit out of hand, choose File > Revert to return to the song's last saved version.

What You've Learned   *✗ CHAPTER 10 SUMMARY ✗*

✓ The Hyper Editor is designed to add or edit control-change data, but it also works well when it comes to creating GM drum sequences.

✓ The Matrix editor displays MIDI data graphically, showing individual notes as boxes whose size represents duration, and whose position relative to a keyboard represents pitch.

✓ In the Matrix editor, notes are colored according to velocity.

✓ When changing note velocity, you can always watch the Info Line to see an exact display of what the note's new velocity will be.

✓ Swing quantization settings can be used to humanize MIDI sequences that sound too quantized or mechanical.

✓ The Event List provides a list of MIDI events.

✓ The Event List's filter buttons are used to show or hide specific types of MIDI events.

11

Basic Mixing

Mixing is the art of adjusting the volume and pan positions of your song's tracks until each sound is sitting in its own space in the sonic spectrum. And it *is* an art, because mixing take practice. While there's no substitute for a trained ear, Logic tries hard to make mixing a painless process. For example, Audio Objects all have a channel view with a fader, level meter, and pan pot that help you visualize (as well as hear) how your song's tracks fit into the mix. There's even a dedicated window, called the Track Mixer, that's designed to mimic the layout of a hardware mixing console. With a little practice, you'll soon be using both windows to create mixes that sparkle!

Getting Started

Cycle regions are an invaluable aid when it comes to mixing, because they let you hear the section you're working on over and over again as you adjust faders, pan positions, and DSP effects. All this repetition makes you quite familiar with the song's sounds (and also keeps the song from finishing before you've finished mixing!), so let's set up a cycle region from bar 9 to bar 17. This section of the song includes a little bit of every track, ensuring that no sounds will be left out of the mix.

1   Open the song file you saved at the end of the previous lesson.

    NOTE ▶ If you didn't save your song at the end of the previous lesson, open the file named **11-Basic_Mixing-Start**.

2   In the top portion of the Bar Ruler, drag a cycle region from bar 9 to bar 17.

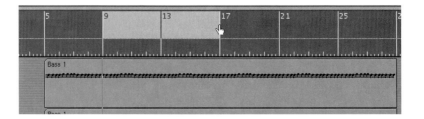

Throughout this lesson, as you play the song, these eight bars will continuously loop, giving you a good section to listen to as you mix.

Creating a Master Fader

A *master fader* is used to raise or lower the volume of your entire song. Logic provides a dedicated Object, called the Master Object, for just this purpose. Your song does not currently have a Master Object, so let's add one now.

1 In the next several steps you will need to have both the Arrange window and the Environment open on your screen, so choose Windows > Open Environment to open Logic's Environment, and then switch to the Audio layer.

2 Position the Arrange window and Environment on your screen so that you can clearly see both.

3 Create a new Audio Object and name it *Master,* and assign its channel to Master.

A Master Object is created in the Environment.

Master Object

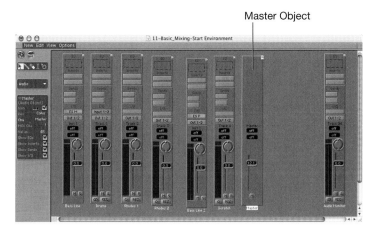

4   Press the spacebar to play the cycle region. As the song plays, raise and lower the Master Object's fader.

The song's volume raises and lowers. But notice that the level meters on the individual Audio Objects do not go up or down. This is because the Master Object boosts or attenuates (lowers) the volume of sound exiting Logic only through the outputs, and not through the individual Audio Objects themselves. This distinction will become much clearer in the next exercise.

Using an Output Object

The Master Object is limited in functionality. It does not have a level meter, and consequently it is not a good Object to use if you need to see the combined volume level of your song's tracks—an important capability when you're trying to ensure a consistent playback level that doesn't clip the output channel.

Because all your song's tracks use Outputs 1 and 2 of your audio interface, you can get the same control over volume level using an Output Object. And there are also a few advantages to using an Output Object instead of a Master Object. For starters, Output Objects *do* have level meters you can use to make sure your song's volume is at the correct level and doesn't *clip*, or spike past 0 dB. Output Objects also include a Bounce button that lets you *bounce* your song, rendering it into a stereo audio file you can burn to an audio CD or publish as an MP3 on the Internet. In fact, as the next four lessons progress, you'll really see the benefits of using Output Objects—so let's get ready by creating an Output Object now.

1   In the Environment, move the Master Object to the right side of the window (next to the Audio Monitor Object) to leave a bit of space for the Output Object you are about to create.

2 Create a new Audio Object, name it *Output 1-2*, and assign its channel to Output Stereo > Output 1-2.

3 Press the spacebar to play the cycle region. As the song plays, lower the Master Object's fader (not the fader on the Output 1-2 Object you just created).

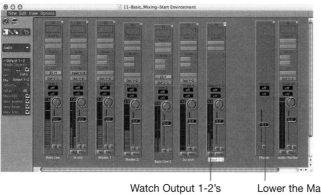

Watch Output 1-2's level meter   Lower the Master Object's fader

Notice how the new Output 1-2 Object's level meter raises and lowers as you move the Master Object's fader, while the level meters on the other Audio Objects do not change. This graphically demonstrates that the Master Object only affects the volume of your system's outputs and nothing else.

4   Return the Master Object's fader to 0.

5   Now, lower the Output 1-2 Object's fader to the bottom.

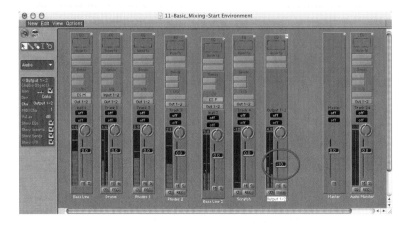

The Output 1-2 Object's level meter lowers, as does the volume of your song.

NOTE ▶ The QuickTime hi-hat track does not lower in volume. This is because the QuickTime Synth is outside Logic.

6   Hold down Option and click the Output 1-2 Object's fader.

The fader jumps back to 0.

NOTE ▶ Hold the Option key and click the Master Object's fader to quickly return the fader to its default setting of 0. Holding down Option while clicking any fader or pan pot resets the fader or pan pot to its default setting. This function also resets instrument knobs and DSP effect sliders.

7   Press the spacebar to temporarily stop playback.

Controlling Clipping

Clipping occurs when too much signal is fed through a channel. Clipping audio sounds fuzzy and distorted—you certainly don't want clipping audio in your song. Fortunately, you don't have to rely on your ears alone—all Audio Objects have a clip detector that shows you when the channel is in danger of clipping.

The clip detector is a red light that shines behind the display box at the top of an Audio Object's level meter. When too much signal is fed into the Object's channel, this detector turns red to tell you that it's time to turn down the volume. Furthermore, once a channel clips, the clip detector stays on until you turn it off by clicking anywhere on the Object's level meter. The clip detectors are very important warning devices, so let's clip the Output 1-2 channel and see what happens.

1   Press the spacebar to play the cycle region.

As the song plays, watch the Output 1-2 Object and notice how its level meter keeps peaking past the top of the scale. If you listen closely, you'll hear distortion in your audio each time the level meter spikes past its top. This is clipping.

Clip detector is on

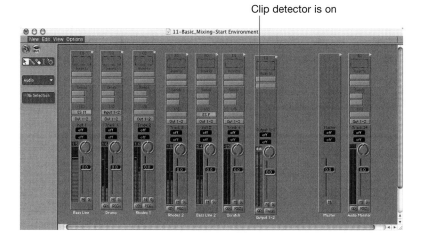

A quick glance at the other Audio Objects shows no clipping on any other channels, so why is Output 1-2 clipping? This clipping is caused by the summed effect of several distinct channels being combined together.

2   Lower the fader on the Output 1-2 Object until the level meter does not pulse past the top.

The audio coming out of your computer now sounds a lot clearer because there is no longer any digital distortion. But the red clip indicator is still on.

3   Click anywhere on the Output 1-2 Object's level meter, or directly on the clip indicator itself.

The clip detector turns off, and the red light disappears. If this red light comes back on, make sure you lower the Object's fader until the clipping stops, or your final song will have distortion in it—and that's not very professional!

NOTE ▶ If an audio channel clips, the clip indicator remains on until you manually turn it off.

4   Press the spacebar to stop playback.

Adjusting Volume Levels

All Audio Objects except the Master Object have a level meter that displays the channel's volume in decibels (dB). The bottom of this meter represents a dB value of $-\infty$ (minus infinity)—that is, silence—while the top of the meter represents 0 dB, which is the maximum allowable volume level before the signal clips the channel. As the level meter pulses up and down, the peak level is held for a few seconds, so you have time to see its value. The numerical value of the peak level is also displayed in the clip detector at the top of the level meter.

Under normal conditions, the clip detector will be off, and the numerical value it displays shows you the amount of *headroom* left above the channel's most recent volume peak. Headroom means the number of dB left before the channel clips. For example, if the clip detector is off (the background is brown), and the number it displays is 4.9, the channel can be raised a maximum of 4.9 dB before it will clip. As you saw in the last exercise, when the clip detector turns red, the channel's audio has clipped, exceeding 0 dB. In this situation, the number printed in the clip detector shows you the number of dB *over* 0 at which the channel has peaked, which in turn is exactly the number of dB by which the track needs to be attenuated, or reduced in order to avoid clipping.

Let's use the level meter to adjust the volume of the Output 1-2 Object so that it comes as close as possible to 0 dB without clipping the channel.

1   Adjust all Audio Object faders to 0, then press the spacebar to play the cycle region.

2   Adjust the Output 1-2 Object's fader so that the level meter peaks close to 0.

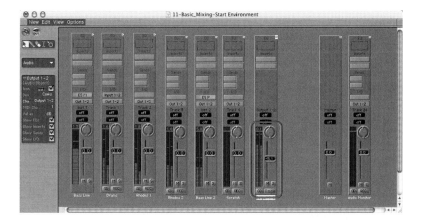

A fader setting of around –5 causes the Output 1-2 Object to peak at around 0.

NOTE ▸ The fader values given in this exercise are all approximations and may vary from the values you need to use to achieve the intended result.

3   Hold down Option and click Output 1-2's fader.

The fader jumps back to 0.

4   Watch the clip detector to determine its maximum value.

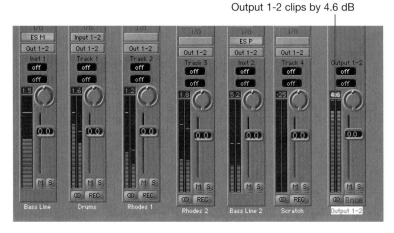

Output 1-2 clips by 4.6 dB

With all Audio Object faders set to 0, Output 1-2 clips by approximately 4.6 dB. Consequently, you know it needs to be lowered by approximately 4.6 dB to avoid clipping, so the fader needs to be set to –4.6 (0 – 4.6 = –4.6).

5   Double-click Output 1-2's fader.

A text box opens.

6   Type –4.6 into the text box, and press Return.

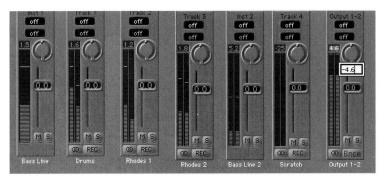

The fader jumps to –4.6, and Output 1-2 now peaks at approximately 0 dB.

NOTE ▶ By default, level meters show a channel's volume as adjusted by the fader. If you'd like to see the volume of a channel's source track, choose Audio > Pre-Fader Metering.

7   Press the spacebar to stop playback.

Cleaning Up the Audio Layer

Your Environment's Audio layer has many Objects on it, and unless you've hand-positioned them, they're probably spread haphazardly across the window like the Objects in the figures above. Logic has an automatic clean-up function used to align Objects nicely one beside the other. Let's use this function to make the Environment a bit more organized and easy to use.

1   Rubber-band select all of the Audio layer's Objects except the Audio Monitor.

The Audio Monitor is not really part of your song, so it can remain off to the layer's right side.

2   From the Environment's local menus, choose Options > Clean up > Align Objects.

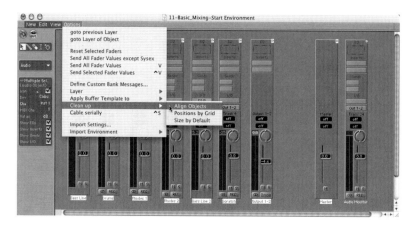

The selected Objects snap together!

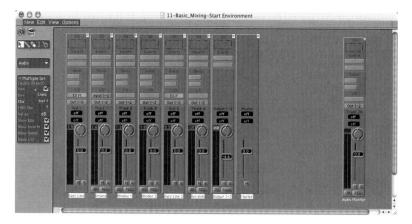

3   Close the Environment window.

Exploring the Track Mixer

In the last few exercises you used the Environment's Audio layer to make some simple changes to the level of your entire song. However, when it comes to mixing, Logic's Track Mixer window is really the place to be. One major advantage of the Track Mixer is that it displays MIDI tracks right alongside audio tracks so that you can mix all your song's tracks in one convenient window.

Opening the Track Mixer

Let's open up the Track Mixer and position it under the Arrange window so that both are clearly visible.

1 Choose Windows > Open Track Mixer (Cmd-2).

The Track Mixer opens. Logic automatically creates a mixer based on the tracks currently available in the Arrange window. The order of these tracks, from left to right, mirrors the order of the Arrange window's tracks from top to bottom. Pay particular attention to the QuickTime track on the right. It has been supplied with a MIDI channel strip that transmits control-change data so that you can mix this MIDI track alongside your audio tracks.

NOTE ▶ As tracks are added to or deleted from the Arrange window, they automatically show up or disappear from the Track Mixer.

2   Position the Track Mixer under the Arrange window in such a way that you can clearly see both windows at the same time.

TIP ▶ Don't forget about the Windows > Tile Windows horizontally command! This is a great command for laying the Track Mixer under the Arrange window, or vice versa.

3   In the Track Mixer, select a track.

The track is outlined in red. Back in the Arrange window, the track is also selected.

4   In the Arrange window, select a track.

The track is automatically selected in the Track Mixer and outlined in red. As you can see, the Track Mixer is clearly connected to the tracks in the Arrange window.

Filtering Tracks

The *filter buttons* along the Track Mixer's left edge are used to display only the tracks you're interested in. If you have dozens of tracks in your project, these buttons make it easier to find the exact track you're after.

Let's experiment with filtering the Track Mixer display so that it shows only certain tracks.

> **NOTE ▶** These filter buttons are actually just shortcuts to some of the settings available in the Track Mixer's Tracks menu.

1   On the left edge of the Track Mixer, click the MIDI button.

    All tracks disappear except for the QuickTime MIDI track.

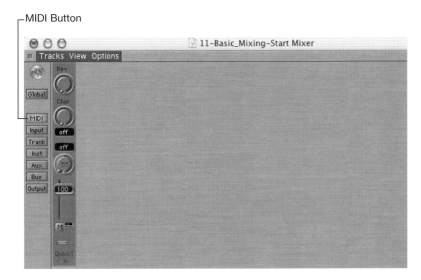

2   On the left edge of the Track Mixer, click the Track button.

    The Track Mixer now displays only Audio tracks.

3   Click the Track button once again to revert the Track Mixer back to its normal display mode.

4 On the left edge of the Track Mixer, click the Global button.

Global Button

The Global button displays all Audio and MIDI Instrument Objects that exist in the Environment. With the Global button turned off, you don't have access to your Master or Output 1-2 Objects, which makes it difficult to adjust the volume level of your entire song at once. Clicking the Global button takes care of this problem.

NOTE ▶ Clicking the Global button causes the track order to change. First, the MIDI instruments are displayed, followed by Input, Track, Instrument, Auxiliary, Bus, Output, and finally Master Objects that exist in the Environment.

5 Click the Global button once again to revert the Track Mixer back to its normal display mode.

Exploring the Fader Area

The bottom half of each channel displays the fader area. You've already explored some of this area's functions, such as the fader and level meter, but let's take a moment to look at a few of the others, including panning, muting, soloing, and setting up mix groups (automation modes and record enabling will be explored in later lessons).

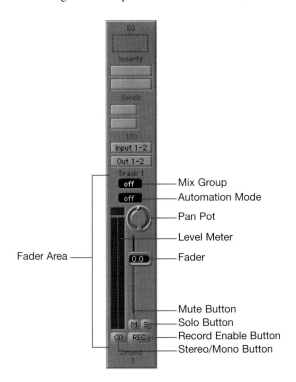

Panning Tracks

Your song is like a panorama of sound. Visualize your song as a properly composed photograph. The subject of the photograph is usually right in the center, while all other supporting parts of the image are spread out toward the edges. Your song should use the same formula. For example, vocals and important rhythmic elements such as kick drums and the bass line are often centered in the mix, while hi-hats, snares, rhythm guitar, keyboard, and other supporting sounds are panned to the sides.

Imagine that this picture is a song, and each person in the picture is a sound. In the photo, you wouldn't want everyone standing right on top of the person in the center. Similarly, in the song you don't want all your sounds in the middle of the sonic panorama.

The fader area's pan pot controls the channel's panorama setting, or more specifically, how much of the channel's sound is sent to the left versus the right speakers. The pan pot's function differs for stereo and mono channels. For a mono channel, the pan pot determines the position of the channel's sound in the stereo image by moving the sound left or right. For stereo channels, the pan pot acts as a balance control that determines relative volume level of the left versus the right side of the channel. This is an important distinction to understand, because you might guess that you could pass the sound in stereo channels from one channel to the other by twisting the pan pot—but this is not the case. For example, if there's a hi-hat panned hard left in a stereo drum track, twisting the pan pot to the right will not move the hi-hat into the right channel. Instead, the sound of the hi-hat just disappears.

In your song, the Rhodes 1 and Rhodes 2 tracks are currently fighting for space in the middle of the mix. Let's give them some room to breathe by panning the Rhodes 1 track left and the Rhodes 2 track right.

1   Check the Stereo/Mono buttons of all audio tracks to ensure that they are set to stereo playback.

2   Press the spacebar to play the cycle region.

Watch the QuickTime track's pan pot. Notice how the pan pot automatically moves from left to right? This reflects the pan curves you drew in the last lesson, using the Hyper Editor.

3   Click and hold the Rhodes 1 track's pan pot, and drag *down* until the value in the center of the pot reads −24.

NOTE ▶   To adjust pan pots, do not drag in an arc around the pot. Instead, drag up in a straight line to move the pot right, and down to move the pot left.

The Rhodes 1 track plays out of the left speaker more than the right one.

NOTE ▶ Pan is measured on a scale that has 127 numbers. The middle is 0, and the left has a maximum range of −64, while the right has a maximum range of +63.

4   Double-click the Rhodes 2 track's pan pot.

A text box opens.

5   Type *24* into the text box, and press Return.

The Rhodes 2 track pans to the right. Your mix should now sound a bit brighter and more alive.

The song is starting to sound great (and you haven't even applied any DSP effects yet!). Before going any further, take a moment to refine the mix.

6   Experiment with the pan settings and fader levels of the each track until the tracks are all playing at a volume level and pan setting that sounds good.

You've just created a basic mix! But there's a bit more to learn about mixing, so read on.

Muting and Soloing in the Track Mixer

At the bottom of the fader area there's a button with an *M*, and beside that there's a second button with an *S*. These are the Mute and Solo buttons. The Mute button, when clicked, turns off a track's sound, while the Solo button turns off the sound of all tracks except the one being soloed.

1   Press the spacebar to start playback.

2   On the Rhodes 1 track, click the Mute button.

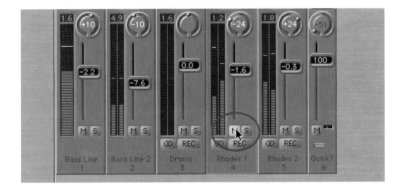

The Rhodes 1 track stops making sound.

3   Click the QuickTime track's Mute button.

The QuickTime track also stops making sound.

4   Click the Rhodes 1 track's Mute button again to turn the sound back on (but leave the QuickTime track muted for now).

5   Next, click the Rhodes 1 track's Solo button.

Now all other tracks stop making sound except the Rhodes 1 track.

6   With the Rhodes 1 track soloing, click the Rhodes 2 track's Solo button.

The Rhodes 2 track starts playing along with the Rhodes 1 track.

7   Click both the Rhodes 1 and Rhodes 2 tracks' Solo buttons to disable Solo mode.

8   Unmute the QuickTime track.

All of the tracks are now playing.

9   Press the spacebar to stop playback.

Using Groups to Link Channels Together

Logic 6 introduces a new feature called *groups*. Groups let you link multiple channels together so that you can control them all at once. For example, if multiple channels are assigned to a group, you can increase the volume of one channel and all the other channels in the same group will also increase in volume.

This is a great technique to use when you need to preserve relationships between tracks. For example, you've probably assigned the Rhodes 1 and Rhodes 2 tracks different volume levels. If you later decide that the combined sound of the Rhodes tracks is too loud or too quiet, you currently have to change each track's volume individually. This makes it very easy to lose the relative relationships between these tracks' volume levels. By assigning the tracks to a group, you can change the volume of one, and the others automatically follow.

1   On the Rhodes 1 track, click and hold the Group box.

The Group pop-up menu appears.

2   From the Group pop-up menu, select Group 1.

This initializes the group, and the Group Settings dialog opens.

The settings in this dialog dictate which edit operations affect grouped tracks. By default, Volume and Mute are enabled.

NOTE ▶ The Group Settings dialog automatically opens when you first initialize a group (if you assign a track to a group but the Group Settings dialog doesn't open, it means that the group has already been initialized). After that, you can open the Group Settings dialog at any time by selecting Open Group Settings from the Group pop-up menu.

3   Select the Pan check box.

4   On the Rhodes 2 track, click and hold the Group box, and choose Group 1 from the pop-up menu.

    The Rhodes 1 and Rhodes 2 tracks are now both assigned to Group 1.

5   Adjust the Rhodes 1 track's fader and pan pot.

    The Rhodes 2 track's fader and pan pot also adjust relative to the Rhodes 1 track.

6   In the Group Settings menu, deselect the Enable check box.

7   Once again, adjust the Rhodes 1 track's fader and pan pot.

The Rhodes 2 track does not follow the Rhodes 1 track, since you have temporarily disabled the group.

8   On the Group Settings menu, reselect the Enable check box and then close the Group Settings menu.

> **NOTE ▶** To temporarily disable a group, you can use the Toggle Group Clutch key command. When you press the Toggle Group Clutch key once, Logic temporarily disables all of your song's groups, allowing you to adjust individual faders and pan pots. Pressing the Toggle Group Clutch key a second time reenables all groups. Logic 6 uses the G key as the default Toggle Group Clutch key, though you may have to visit the Key Commands window and assign the G key to Toggle Group Clutch before this command will work (make sure you do this, because it's a very handy key command).

9   Close the Track Mixer.

Quantizing MIDI Sequences

In Lesson 10 you used the Matrix editor's Quantization tool to fix the timing of notes inside a MIDI sequence. This is a great way to quantize individual notes, or even several notes at the same time, but if you want to quantize all of the notes in a MIDI sequence, the Sequence Parameter box is just the ticket.

At the top of the Sequence Parameter box there's a Quantization setting that affects the MIDI sequence currently selected in the Arrange area. This Quantization setting works exactly the same as the Quantization tool in the Matrix editor, so if you've read Lesson 10, it will present you with no surprises. Let's take it for a test drive.

> **NOTE ▶** In Logic, quantization affects only notes and not control-change data in MIDI sequences.

Sequence Parameter box's Quantization setting

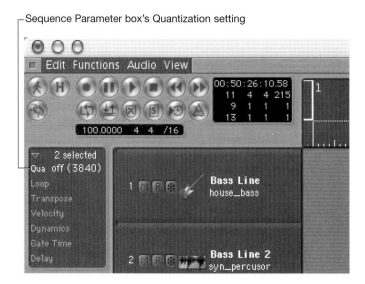

1   Press the spacebar to play the cycle region, and listen to the bass line.

The bass line in this song uses sixteenth notes that are very evenly placed along Logic's timing grid. Only the most skilled musicians can play with such machinelike perfection. As a result, the bass line sounds very mechanical—as if a computer is playing it, and not a real person. Let's use the Sequence Parameter box's Quantization settings to add some swing to the bass line.

2   In the Arrange window, rubber-band select the Objects in both the Bass Line and Bass Line 2 tracks.

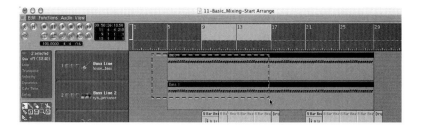

Because both sequences make up the bass line, you will most likely
want to adjust both sequences' quantization settings together
(although you don't have to—using different quantization settings
for each sequence can lead to some interesting effects, so feel free
to experiment).

3   In the Sequence Parameter box, click and hold the Quantization setting, above off(3840).

The Quantization menu appears.

4   Choose 16C Swing.

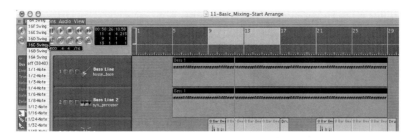

Does the bass line sound more natural?

5   Experiment with other Quantization settings until you find one
you like.

NOTE ▶ Remember, in Lesson 10 you learned that Logic actually
records two positions for each note in a sequence. The first is the
note's original position, while the second is its playback, or quantized,
position. Because of this, quantization is a nondestructive edit and
you can't hurt anything, as the note's original position is still stored
by Logic. To revert back to the nonquantized setting, just choose
off(3840) from the Quantization pop-up menu.

6   Press the spacebar to stop playback.

Transposing MIDI Sequences

Transposing a MIDI sequence shifts its notes by a certain number of semitones. Similar to quantization, transposing is a nondestructive function, so if you later decide the transposed notes don't sound right, you can easily revert to your pre-transposed sequence by turning the transpose function off.

In your song, the Bass Line 2 track's MIDI sequence contains notes that sound a bit high for a bass line. Using the transpose function, you can quickly move all the MIDI sequence's notes down into the bass range.

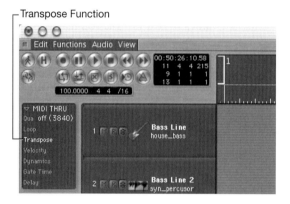

1   Press the spacebar to play the cycle region.

2   Select the MIDI sequence in the Bass Line 2 track.

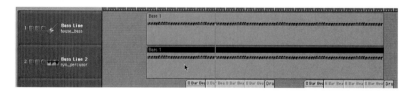

3   In the Sequence Parameter box, double-click beside the empty space to the right of the word Transpose.

A text box appears.

4   Type in *–12* and press Return.

All of the notes in the MIDI sequence are adjusted down by 12 semi-tones. Twelve semitones is a full octave, so Bass Line 2's sequence now plays an octave lower than before.

You can also adjust transpose values in real time as you listen.

5   In the Sequence Parameter box, click and hold to the left of the word Transpose, then drag up and down.

Bass Line 2's sequence transposes up and down in real time.

6   Return the transpose value to –12.

7   Press the spacebar to stop playback.

Creating Fades

The Arrange window has a dedicated tool for making fades, and as you may have guessed, it's called the Fade tool. Fades created with the Fade tool are nondestructive, which means your audio files are not permanently altered in any way. Instead, when the song begins playing, a fade audio file is created on your hard disk, with one region for each fade, and Logic refers to this fade file as it plays the fades.

Let's experiment a bit with creating a fade-in, a cross fade, and some other fades.

1 From the Arrange window's toolbox, grab the Magnifying Glass tool and zoom in on the first region in the Rhodes 1 track.

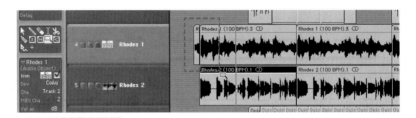

Fades are hard to see unless you zoom in very close. With the first audio region filling the Arrange area, it's easy to see the fades you'll make in the following steps.

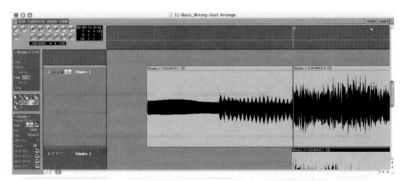

2 From the toolbox, grab the Fade tool (the one with the sideways *V* on it).

Fade Tool

3   Drag the Fade tool over the beginning of the first region in the
Rhodes 1 track.

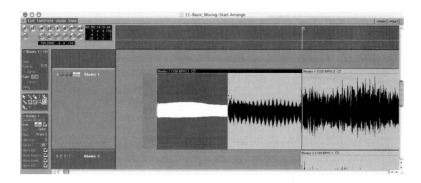

A fade-in is created. The length of this fade-in is displayed in the
Region Parameter box.

Fade-In

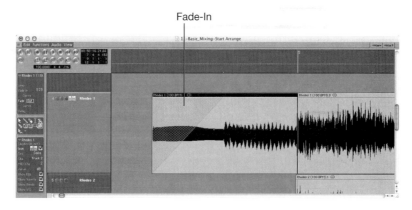

Fades are measured in milliseconds. A fade length of 1000 is 1 second,
2000 is 2 seconds, and so on. You can make adjustments to the fade
length by changing the number in the Region Parameter box.

4   In the Region Parameter box, double-click the number beside the words Fade In and enter *400*.

The fade adjusts to be exactly 400 milliseconds long.

NOTE ▶ You can also adjust the Region Parameter box's fade values by dragging the values up or down.

Under the Fade In parameter, you may have noticed a parameter called Curve. This parameter changes the fade from a straight line to a curve. Both positive and negative values between 0 and 99 can be entered here.

5   In the Region Parameter box, double-click the blank area beside the word Curve, enter *–50,* and press Return.

The fade changes into a curve.

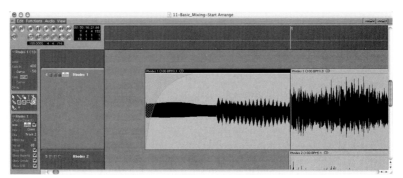

The Region Parameter box's Curve setting gives you close control over the value of the fade curve, but if you're a more freehand type of person, you can draw quick fade curves right in the Arrange area using the following technique:

6   With the Fade tool still selected, hold down Control and click and drag up or down on the fade.

Hold down Control while
dragging up or down on the fade

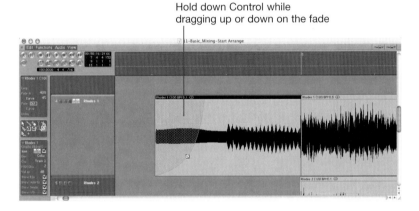

The fade curve follows the pointer.

A cross fade is created in exactly the same way as a fade-in, except instead of dragging the Fade tool over the beginning of a region, you drag across the boundary between two adjacent regions.

7   Drag the Fade tool over the boundary between the first and second regions in the Rhodes 1 track.

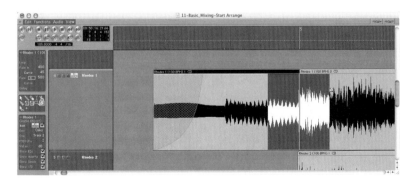

Logic creates a cross fade.

Cross Fade

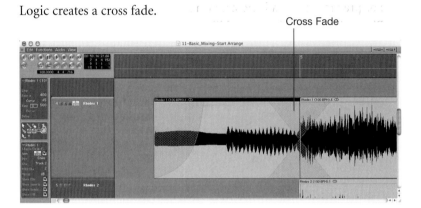

Unless you were very careful, the fade does not cross exactly where the two regions meet. This is easy to fix.

8 Hold down Control and drag the cross fade up or down.

The fades' cross point moves right or left.

9 Hold down Option and click the cross fade.

The cross fade-in is deleted.

And that's all there is to it! So, what about fade-outs? Fade-outs are created in exactly the same way as fade-ins and cross fades, but instead of dragging over the beginning of an audio region (fade-in) or the intersection of two audio regions (cross fade), you drag over the end of an audio region. Other than that, all the same principles apply to each of the three different types of fades.

10 For practice, go ahead and create a few fades. When you're done, click Play to hear what they sound like.

Before Logic plays your song, it calculates a fade file that contains the added fades.

Creating Fade(s)

"Rhodes 1 (100 BPM).3"

NOTE ▶ If your computer is quick, or if the fades are small, the dialog pictured above might not appear.

This fade file is stored in the same folder as the faded region's audio file, and is named after the song, with the extension *-f16m* for 16 bit recordings, or *-f24m* for 24 bit recordings.

Fade File

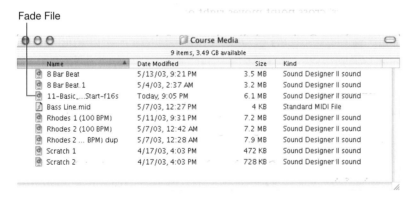

Name	Date Modified	Size	Kind
8 Bar Beat	5/13/03, 9:21 PM	3.5 MB	Sound Designer II sound
8 Bar Beat.1	5/4/03, 2:37 AM	3.2 MB	Sound Designer II sound
11-Basic_...Start-f16s	Today, 9:05 PM	6.1 MB	Sound Designer II sound
Bass Line.mid	5/7/03, 12:27 PM	4 KB	Standard MIDI File
Rhodes 1 (100 BPM)	5/11/03, 9:31 PM	7.2 MB	Sound Designer II sound
Rhodes 2 (100 BPM)	5/7/03, 12:42 AM	7.2 MB	Sound Designer II sound
Rhodes 2 ... BPM) dup	5/7/03, 12:28 AM	7.9 MB	Sound Designer II sound
Scratch 1	4/17/03, 4:03 PM	472 KB	Sound Designer II sound
Scratch 2	4/17/03, 4:03 PM	728 KB	Sound Designer II sound

9 items, 3.49 GB available — Course Media

NOTE ▶ If this fade file is moved out of the folder or goes missing, it's not a big deal. Logic will simply create a new fade file the next time you play the song.

What You've Learned *✱ CHAPTER 11 SUMMARY ✱*

✓ A Master Object controls the volume level of all audio interface outputs simultaneously.

✓ Output Objects control the volume of specific audio interface outputs, and also contain a level meter and inserts used to apply DSP effects to an entire mix.

✓ The clip detector at the top of each level meter lights red if a channel's volume is too high.

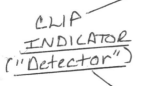
CLIP INDICATOR ("Detector")

✓ If the clip detector is black, the number in it shows how many dB below 0 the channel peaks at. If the clip detector is red, it shows how many dB *over* 0 the channel peaks at—which, in turn, tells you the number of dB by which you need to attenuate the channel to bring its volume level back under 0 dB.

✓ Level meters hold the channels' peak levels for a few seconds, making it easy for you to see volume peaks.

✓ The Track Mixer displays the same channels as the Arrange window, in the same order.

✓ The Track Mixer's filter buttons are used to hide or display specific track types.

✓ Fades created in the Arrange window are nondestructive and do not change the original audio files.

✓ To create a curved fade, hold down Control and drag up or down on a fade.

12

Lesson 12
Sweetening the Mix

In the last lesson you learned how to set volume levels and pan positions to create a basic mix. This is a good first step in finding the sound you're after, but the final polish is added with such DSP effects as dynamic range compression, delay, reverb, and chorus effects. And Logic has plenty of these to offer. For example, Logic Platinum provides 53 different DSP plug-ins, while Gold users get 42, and Logic Audio, 28. This lesson shows you how to add these effects to your song, and also covers some important mix techniques, such as creating an Aux channel, using system busses, and freezing tracks to free up system resources for other important things (like adding more plug-ins!).

Monitoring System Performance

Digital audio editing is a system-intensive process. With multiple audio files zipping around your computer and DSP effects chewing up your CPU power, your computer is working hard! As you apply more and more DSP plug-ins to your song's tracks, you'll notice your system beginning to slow down. At the end of this lesson you'll learn how to use Logic 6's brand-new Freeze function to combat this problem, but in the meantime, your single biggest asset in monitoring your computer's performance is Logic's CPU window.

The CPU window shows you how much of your system's resources are being devoured by your song. Let's open the CPU window and watch it work.

1   Set up a cycle region from bar 9 to bar 17, and then play your song.

2   Choose Audio > System Performance (Option-Y).

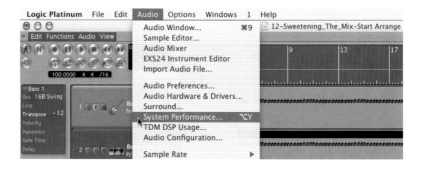

The CPU window opens.

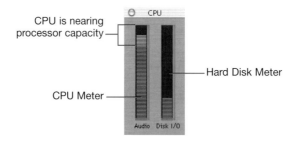

CPU is nearing processor capacity

CPU Meter

Hard Disk Meter

The Audio meter on the left of this window monitors your CPU's performance. As you apply more and more DSP effects, this meter will pulse higher. At the very top there's a bright yellow band, which is the warning band. When the Audio meter level nears this band, it's time to take action to free up system resources, because your system will start to bog down and become slow. (If this occurs, you'll need to freeze some tracks! But more on that later.)

The Disc I/O meter on the right keeps track of the strain on your hard disks as audio is pulled off of them. This meter follows a very simple rule: The more audio tracks used in your song, the more strain is put on your hard disks. A slow hard disk, such as the 4200 rpm disks that come with PowerBooks, will not let you use as many tracks as a faster disk like the 7200 rpm discs in Power Mac G4s.

MORE INFO ▶ *In digital audio, fast hard disks are king. While 5400 rpm hard disks are attractive due to their low cost, you should avoid them like the plague. They'll work for a while, but digital audio can put considerable strain on these low-rpm disks, which will dramatically decrease their lifespan. To avoid the horror of seeing your hard disk crash, stick to hard disks of 7200 rpm or higher. If you're a PowerBook user, you should take particular note of this fact and consider upgrading your system with an external FireWire hard drive.*

3 Place the System Performance (CPU) window in the bottom-right corner of your screen, and refer to it often as you progress through this lesson.

Using Plug-Ins

Plug-ins are power! These essential tools can turn an OK mix into a chart topper by taking good sounds and making them truly sparkle! Logic comes with a full suite of extremely useful plug-ins. If Logic's stock plug-ins don't provide exactly the sound you're after, not to worry—there are dozens of third-party plug-in manufacturers that make every type of sound-processing plug-in imaginable. However, keep this in mind: Logic 6 for OS X *only* supports Audio Unit plug-ins. VST, AS, or any other plug-in formats no longer work (if you're running Logic 6 in OS 9, you can still use VST plug-ins).

> **TIP** ▸ In digital audio there's a saying: Garbage in, garbage out! While plug-ins can take a good sound and make it better, they are only marginally successful at making bad sounds good. For this reason, always start your songs with the best possible source files.

Inserting Plug-Ins

You insert plug-ins into the Insert slots at the top of each channel strip, whether you're in the Environment, the Track Mixer, or Logic 6's new Arrange-window channel strip. By default, each of these objects provides two Insert slots. But you're not limited to two—as you insert plug-ins, new Insert slots appear. Depending on your version of Logic and the speed of your computer, you can insert up to 15 plug-ins on each channel! Let's insert one to start things off.

> **NOTE** ▸ Logic Platinum provides 15 inserts per channel, while Logic Gold provides 8, and Logic Audio, 4.

1   Press Cmd-2 to open the Track Mixer.

2   At the top of the Drums track, click and hold the first Insert slot.

A menu appears, showing all of Logic's available DSP plug-ins.

3   From the Inserts menu, choose Stereo > Logic > Dynamic > Silver
Compressor.

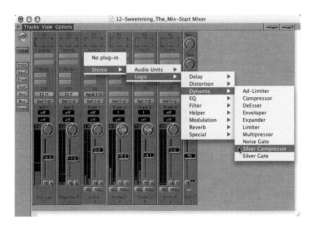

The Silver Compressor is assigned to Insert 1 of the Drums track, and
the track instantly becomes louder. This is the result of the Silver
Compressor's dynamic range compression.

4   If the Silver Compressor *did not* automatically open after the last step,
double-click the insert to open the Silver Compressor.

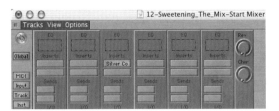

The Silver Compressor opens in a plug-in window. Leave this plug-in
open for a bit, because you are going to work with it through the next
several exercises.

5   In the Track Mixer, adjust the Drums channel's fader until its volume
mixes properly with the rest of the song's tracks.

Automatically Opening Plug-Ins

If assigning a plug-in to an insert does not automatically open the plug-in
window, you must double-click the plug-in's Insert slot to manually open
the plug-in window on your screen. This is an extra step that sucks up
time, and you can get around it by setting the following preference:

1   Choose Audio > Audio Preferences.

The Audio Preferences window opens.

2   Near the middle of the Audio preferences window, click the check box
next to "Open plug-in window on insertion."

Now, each time you assign a plug-in to an insert, it will automatically
open!

Bypassing Plug-Ins

Bypassing a plug-in turns it off so that you no longer hear its effect.
Bypassed plug-ins do not drain system resources, and visiting the Bypass
button lets you perform a simple A-B test to compare the affected audio
against the channel's nonaffected sound, which in turn lets you make sure
the plug-in is actually having a good effect on the signal.

1   In the Silver Compressor window, click the Bypass button.

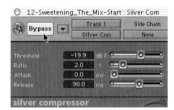

The Silver Compressor stops affecting the Drums track. In the Track
Mixer, the Silver Compressor Insert slot is no longer colored blue,
which indicates that it's currently turned off.

2   In the Track Mixer, hold down Option and click the Silver
Compressor's Insert slot.

The Silver Compressor turns on. Back in the Silver Compressor window, the Bypass button is no longer enabled. Holding down Option while clicking an Insert slot toggles the insert's Bypass status. This is a great shortcut to keep in mind, because it allows you to quickly bypass a plug-in without opening the plug-in window.

Using Plug-in Presets

Almost all plug-ins come with a few presets stored in the Settings menu, which is accessed by clicking the downward triangle to the right of the Bypass button. Presets are named for their intended use. For example, the Silver Compressor has a preset called Drums. You've inserted the Silver Compressor on the Drums channel, and as you might expect, this Drums preset is the one you are going to choose. From there you can change the plug-in to suit your sound, and then save the preset for future use.

1   In the Silver Compressor window, click and hold the downward triangle to open the Settings menu.

The Settings menu appears. At the bottom of the Settings menu, there is a Factory option that opens a submenu displaying the plug-in's presets.

2 This is a drums track, so choose the #Factory > Drums preset.

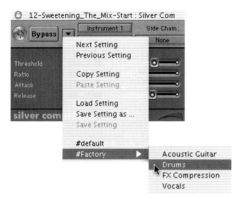

Listen to how the Drums preset affects the Drums track.

3 Adjust the Silver Compressor's sliders until the Drums track sounds the way you want it to.

4 Choose Settings Menu > Save Setting as.

The "Save Setting as" dialog opens, and Logic has automatically selected a destination folder to save your custom preset into. Do not navigate to a new folder—Logic has picked the proper folder for this preset. You need only type in a name for your custom preset.

5 Type a name for your preset setting (make sure you keep the *.pst* extension, which stands for *Plug-In Setting*), and click Save.

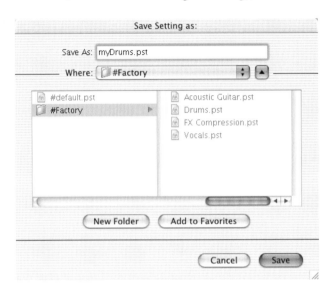

By saving your custom preset in the folder that Logic suggests, you ensure that it will always be available from the Settings menu.

6 Click and hold the Silver Compressor's Settings menu.

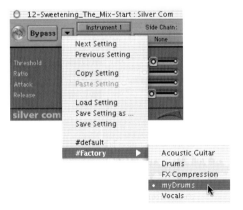

Your custom plug-in setting is now listed as a preset!

The plug-in settings themselves are stored in the Plug-In Settings folder located in the same folder as the Logic Audio Application icon. Logic needs all Plug-In Settings files (or aliases to those files) to be located in this folder, or it will not see them.

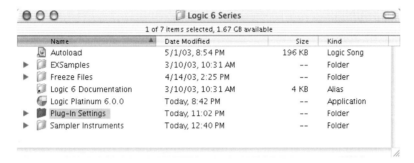

TIP Don't forget about the Next and Previous Plug-In Setting key commands you assigned to Option-N and Option-B. These key commands work great when it comes to skipping through plug-in presets! If you didn't set up these key commands, revisit Lesson 5 to learn how.

Opening Multiple Plug-in Windows

Right now, each time you open a plug-in, it replaces the last plug-in onscreen. This helps conserve screen real estate, but it's not too handy if you want to compare the settings of two plug-ins or adjust several plug-ins at the same time. To have multiple plug-in windows open onscreen, you need to use this trick:

1   On the Scratch channel, click and hold the first insert, and then
    choose Stereo > Logic > Delay > Tape Delay.

Scratch Channel

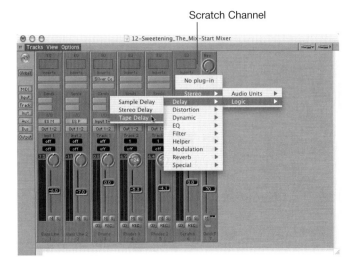

The Tape Delay opens, replacing the Silver Compressor.

2   In the Tape Delay plug-in window, click the Link button to turn it off
    (the Link button is the one with a chain on it).

In Lesson 3 you learned that the Link button ties an editing window to
things selected in other Logic editing windows, and the Link button on
the plug-in window is no different. With the Link button enabled (violet), each time you open a new plug-in, it replaces the old plug-in in the
currently open plug-in window. Disabling the Link button changes this
behavior, and each new plug-in opens in its very own plug-in window.

3   In the Track Mixer's Drums channel, double-click the Silver
Compressor insert.

The Silver Compressor opens in its own plug-in window.

Silver Compressor   Tape Delay

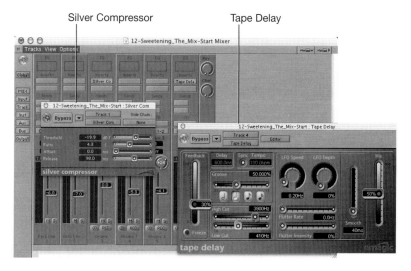

4   Listen to the effects, and adjust them as necessary.

Using Sends

When you insert a DSP plug-in into a channel's Insert slot, 100 percent of the channel's sound passes through the plug-in, so all of the channel's signal is processed by the effect. For equalizers or dynamic range compression, this is perfect because you want to equalize or compress the entire signal. But for other effects such as reverbs and delays, you will normally want only a portion of the signal to be processed so you can control how *wet* the signal is (the amount of reverb compared with the amount of the source signal). While a Mix slider is used with these types of effects to adjust the amount of reverb compared with the amount of source signal, in many situations *Sends* provide a far better method for working with these types of effects.

Sends split a portion of a channel's sound out and *send* it through a system bus to another Audio Object. The signal that travels out through a Send is exactly the same as the signal passing through the channel itself.

Setting Up an Aux Channel

Sends provide a great way to conserve CPU power, because they allow you to process multiple channels using just one occurrence of an effect. For example, your song's two Rhodes tracks would sound nice with a reverb applied to give them some warmth and make them sit a bit farther back in the mix. You could apply a reverb to each Rhodes channel, but this would result in two different occurrences of the reverb—a senseless waste of CPU resources. Instead, let's set up the reverb on an Aux channel and send a portion of each Rhodes track to it.

Before using a Send, you must have a destination ready to receive the Send's signal. Sends transfer signal to a system bus, and Aux (Auxiliary) channels can use a system bus as an input, so Aux channels provide an appropriate destination for a Send's signal. To see how this works, let's set up an Aux channel now.

1   Press 8 to open the Environment, and switch to the Audio layer.

2   Create a new Audio Object, name it Aux 1, and assign its channel to
Aux > Aux 1.

3   Click the Aux Object's Stereo/Mono button to make sure it's a stereo
channel.

4   Click and hold Aux 1's first Insert slot, and then choose
Stereo > Logic > Reverb > SilverVerb.

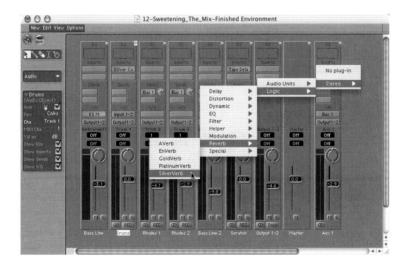

The SilverVerb plug-in window appears onscreen.

5   At the top of the SilverVerb window, click and hold the Settings menu and choose the Ambience preset (you can change the preset to something different at a later point in time, if you so desire).

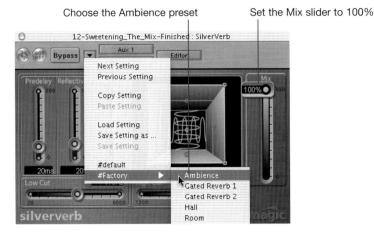

6   Set the SilverVerb's Mix slider to 100%.

Why 100%? The Mix slider adjusts the ratio of processed signal to source signal. In this case, the Aux channel is there to provide only processed sound, and you don't want any of the original signal sneaking through—the Rhodes tracks themselves provide enough of that! So, setting the Mix slider to 100% means that the Aux channel's output contains only reverb.

7   Close the SilverVerb plug-in window, and press 1 to open Screenset 1.

Screenset 1 opens to display the Arrange window and Track Mixer. The Track Mixer does not currently display the Aux 1 channel. Let's fix that.

8   On the Track Mixer's left edge, click the Global button.

Click the Global button   Aux 1 channel appears

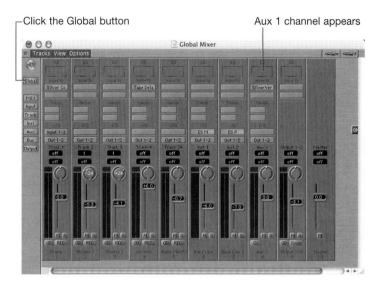

The Aux channel is now visible on the Track Mixer's right side. This
Aux channel is now ready to accept signal, so let's initialize a Send and
transfer some sound to it.

Initializing Sends

With the Aux 1 channel set up with a reverb, it's time to initialize the
Sends on the Rhodes 1 and Rhodes 2 tracks, and send some signal into the
Aux channel.

1   Press the spacebar to start playback.

2   In the Track Mixer, locate the Rhodes 1 channel, then click and hold
the first Sends slot and choose Bus > Bus 1.

The Send is assigned to Bus 1, and a Send Level control appears to the
right of the Send slot. The Send Level control is currently set to the off
position –∞.

Send Slot   Send Level Control

3   Drag the Send Level control up to set it to 0.

As you drag, the Send slot temporarily changes to show you the value
of the Send Level control.

TIP ▶ Setting the Send level to 0 is called *normalizing the Send level*.
You can quickly normalize the Send level by holding down Option
and clicking the Send Level control.

4   Repeat steps 2 and 3 for the Rhodes 2 track.

Signal has now been split from the Rhodes 1 and Rhodes 2 channels
and sent to Bus 1. All that remains is to transport Bus 1's signal into
the Aux 1 channel.

5   Click and hold Aux 1's input slot, and choose Bus > Bus 1.

Aux 1's level meter jumps to life, and you can hear reverb being
applied to the Rhodes tracks. This is the SilverVerb you are hearing!

6 On the Aux 1 channel, click the Mute button.

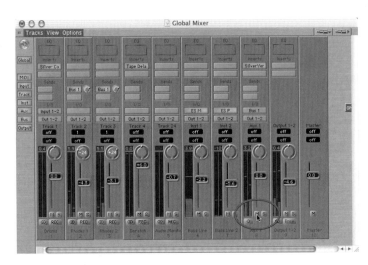

Clicking the Mute button temporarily stops Aux 1 from making sound, which lets you hear the Rhodes tracks without reverb.

7 Click Aux 1's Mute button again to turn muting off, and then adjust Aux 1's volume fader until the reverb sounds loud enough. If you'd like, you can also open the SilverVerb itself and experiment with its presets and other settings.

Exploring Pre and Post Sends

Channel Sends can be set to pre or post fader. *Pre fader* ensures that the Send signal remains constant regardless of the channel's main Volume fader setting, while *post fader* means that the level passing through the Send changes as the channel's main fader is raised or lowered. Sends default to post fader, and in most situations this is exactly what you want. For example, with the Sends set to post fader, lowering the Rhodes tracks transmits less signal to the Aux 1 channel, which means that lowering the volume of the Rhodes tracks also causes the volume of the reverb to lower. If you were to set the Sends to pre fader, raising or lowering the Rhodes tracks' Volume faders would have no effect on the volume of the reverb.

Explaining how pre and post fader Send settings work is much harder than demonstrating by example, so let's experiment with the Rhodes tracks now.

1   If the song is not playing, press the spacebar to begin playback.

2   Click and hold Rhodes 1's first Send slot, and choose Pre from the pop-up menu.

3   Repeat step 1 for the Rhodes 2 channel.

Did you notice that the sound of the SilverVerb became louder?

4   Lower the Rhodes 1 track's fader to the bottom.

At the end of the last lesson you grouped Rhodes 2 with Rhodes 1, so Rhodes 2's fader follows Rhodes 1's to the bottom. Both tracks no longer transmit signal, but you can still hear the reverb coming out of Aux 1. This is because the signal traveling from the Sends to Aux 1 is pre fader, and thus the Sends pay no attention to the Rhodes tracks' Volume fader.

5   Click and hold Rhodes 1's first Send slot, and choose Post from the pop-up menu. Do the same for Rhodes 2.

The Sends are reset to post fader, and Aux 1 stops producing sound! Why? Because the signal traveling from the Sends to Aux 1 is now post fader. But the fader is at $-\infty$, so no sound is traveling to Aux 1.

6   Raise Rhodes 1's Volume fader.

The SilverVerb raises along with the Rhodes tracks.

7 Press the spacebar to stop playback.

8 Close the Track Mixer.

Using the Freeze Function

Freezing tracks is a new Logic 6 feature that greatly increases Logic's power to process audio. If your system resources monitor (the CPU window) begins peaking too close to the top of its meter, you can click the Freeze button and then keep working.

Freeze performs an offline bounce for each frozen track. In other words, it renders the track and its plug-ins into a *freeze file*, and then automatically plays back this freeze file instead of the original one. The track along with all of its plug-ins are temporarily deactivated and place virtually no strain on your system until you unfreeze the track.

The Freeze button appears on every audio and audio instrument track in the Arrange window, and it looks like a little ice crystal. In a few moments you'll click this button to freeze the Drums track. But before doing so, there's something you need to know …

Setting the Song Start and End Markers

Freeze files are always rendered between the song start and song end markers. This has significant implications for short songs like the one you're working on because if you click the Freeze button now, you'll have to sit and wait as Logic freezes a lot of empty space at the end of the song. Fortunately, this is a waste of only time, and not disk space—Logic automatically trims all silence from the end of a freeze file. Still, time is money, so let's take a moment to snug the song start and end markers up to the active part of the song.

> **MORE INFO** ▶ *The song start and end markers also form the default bounce region, as you'll learn in Lesson 14.*

1   Grab the song start marker and drag it to bar 4 (the song start marker
looks like a white outlined rectangle at the beginning of the Bar Ruler).

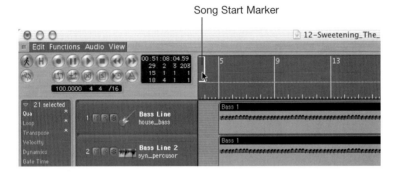

NOTE ▶ Clicking the song start marker has a side effect: All Objects
in the Arrange area are automatically selected. Logic does this for a
reason—if you so desire, you can grab all the selected Objects and
then drag them forward toward the song start marker at bar 1,
instead of dragging the song start marker toward the Objects.
However, to keep pace with these steps you should move the song
start marker back to bar 4.

The song end marker is currently way down the Bar Ruler. You can
scroll down until you find it, and then drag it forward to the end of
your song, but a far easier method involves using the Transport window's song end setting.

2   Choose Windows > Open Transport (Cmd-7).

The Transport window opens. In the bottom-right corner of the Transport window is a box that displays the number of the bar where the song currently ends.

Song End Setting

NOTE ▶ The song end setting is available only in the Transport window—the Arrange window's Transport panel does not give you access to this setting.

3   Double-click the song end setting, type *38* into the text box that appears, and press Return.

Why 38? A quick glance at the Arrange area shows that all Objects finish by bar 37. Here's the reason: Providing an extra measure at the end of the song gives a bit of room to catch reverb or delay tails. Because the Rhodes tracks now play through the SilverVerb, there's a bit of a reverb tail you need to catch, so bar 38 is a good place to end this song.

After you press Return, the song end marker jumps to bar 38.

Song End Marker

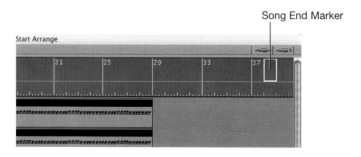

4   Close the Transport window to get it out of the way.

Freezing Tracks

The Freeze process uses 100 percent of the available CPU resources. If the track you are freezing (along with all its plug-ins) takes up 25 percent of the CPU power to play, its freeze file will be created at four times the real-time playback speed, which means a track that's 1 minute long will take 15 seconds to freeze. If the track uses 50 percent of CPU power, a track that's 1 minute long takes 30 seconds to freeze.

Let's freeze the Drums track and see how the process works.

1   In the Track column, click the Drums track's Freeze button.

Nothing happens right away. Logic waits until the next Play command to freeze the track, which provides you the opportunity to freeze more than one track at the same time.

2   Press the spacebar to initiate a Play command and, by association, the Freeze process.

The SPL races through your song, following the process of the Freeze function, and the Freeze progress dialog appears.

Logic renders out the track, along with all associated plug-ins assigned to its Insert slots. Until you unfreeze the Drums track by clicking the Freeze button again, Logic will play the Drums freeze file instead of the original audio track.

The freeze file itself is stored in a new Freeze Files folder that Logic automatically creates in the same folder as the song's project file. This freeze file remains only as long as the track is frozen. The instant you unfreeze this track, Logic deletes the new freeze file.

3   Press the spacebar to play the song.

The Drums track sounds just like it did before, and you can still hear the effect of the Silver Compressor, but the strain on your CPU is lower.

What You've Learned *✱ CHAPTER 12 SUMMARY ✱*

✓ The CPU window is used to monitor your computer's performance.

✓ To insert DSP-effect plug-ins, you apply them to the Insert slots found at the tops of channels in the Environment and Track Mixer.

✓ Each time you open a plug-in window, it replaces the previously opened plug-in. To open multiple plug-in windows at the same time, click the plug-in window's Link button to disable it before opening new plug-ins.

✓ The Bypass button in the top-left corner of every plug-in window lets you temporarily turn off a plug-in, so that you can quickly compare the channel's sound with and without the plug-in. Bypassed plug-ins do (not) drain system resources.

✓ Plug-in presets are stored in the Settings menu, which is opened by clicking the button with the downward triangle next to the plug-in window's Bypass button.

✱ PLUG-INS

✓ A Send (located below a channel's Insert slots) splits a portion of a channel's sound out and *sends* it through a system bus to another Audio Object.

✓ The Freeze button, which looks like a little ice crystal, appears on every audio and audio instrument track in the Arrange window.

✓ When you freeze a track, Logic renders the track and all its plug-ins into a high-quality audio file that it plays instead of the original track. All plug-ins are temporarily deactivated and place no further strain on your system until you unfreeze the track.

✱ FREEZE (function) BUTTON

13

Automating the Mix

Some high-end hardware mixing consoles can actually record fader movements, and if you've ever seen one of these mixing consoles in action, it looks like ghostly hands are moving its faders up and down to create automated volume adjustments. This is called *automation*, and as you may have guessed from this lesson's title, Logic can automate fader movement, too. But even better, Logic does not stop at automating faders. In fact, it can automate all MIDI controller data, and even the sliders and knobs on every DSP plug-in, including software instruments and effects such as delays and EQs. Automation really is the icing on the sonic cake, because it takes an otherwise straight-ahead mix and breathes life into it by changing its sound over time to create a constantly evolving ambience. If you want to make your mixes truly shine, automation is the answer.

There are two different forms of automation in Logic: HyperDraw and Track Automation. HyperDraw automates MIDI control-change data inside MIDI sequences themselves, while Track Automation is recorded or modified in Arrange window tracks, independent of the Objects in the track. HyperDraw data is tied to Objects and always moves with the Object it belongs to, but Track Automation belongs to the track itself and does not behave the same way. The choice of which automation method to use—and when to use it—depends upon what you want to achieve with your edit, so let's begin exploring automation by looking at HyperDraw.

Using HyperDraw

First, don't confuse HyperDraw with the Hyper Editor—they are completely different things. While the Hyper Editor also is, in fact, used to modify MIDI control-change data such as volume or pan messages, it works in a totally different way than HyperDraw. For starters, the Hyper Editor does not give you access to the same range of MIDI controller data as HyperDraw does (unless you create custom Hyper sets). In the default Hyper Editor, you can only edit basic control-change messages such as volume, pan, or velocity, but in HyperDraw, Logic Gold and Platinum users have access to all 127 MIDI controllers. Additionally, HyperDraw uses nodes to indicate controller points and then interpolates a line between those points, giving you smooth transitions between control-change messages.

Exploring HyperDraw in the Matrix Editor

HyperDraw is located in the Matrix editor, Score editor, and Arrange window. It works exactly the same way in each editor, so for the purpose of experimenting, let's open it up in the Matrix editor and enable

HyperDraw. But before doing so, a quick word of advice: As you experiment with editing nodes, remember Cmd-Z (undo)! It's easy to make mistakes when editing nodes, so Cmd-Z can be a real lifesaver.

1   Open the song file you saved at the end of the previous lesson.

> **NOTE** ▸ If you didn't save your song at the end of the previous lesson, open the file named **13-Automation-Start**.

2   Select the first Object in the QuickTime GM track, and choose Windows > Open Matrix Edit (Cmd-6).

The Matrix editor opens.

3   From the Matrix editor's local menus, choose View > Hyper Draw, and take a look at the choices presented in the HyperDraw menu.

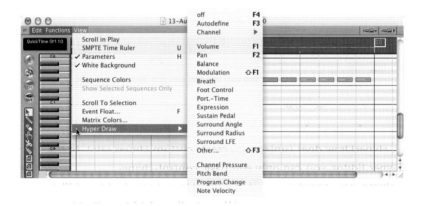

The HyperDraw menu lists all of the standard control-change, or MIDI controller, types you will commonly use while editing your sequences, including Volume, Pan, Modulation, and so on.

> **NOTE** ▸ If you need a MIDI controller not displayed in the HyperDraw menu's main list, choose the Other option, and a dialog will open to let you enter any controller you need.

4 From the HyperDraw menu, choose Pan.

The HyperDraw area appears at the bottom of the Matrix editor and displays the sequence's pan data.

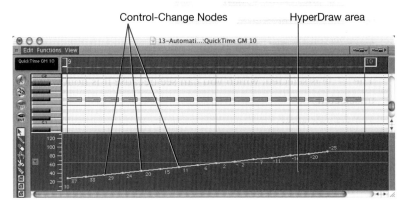

The HyperDraw area currently displays a few dots, called *nodes,* with lines between them. The nodes represent the pan positions you set using the Hyper Editor (way back in Lesson 10), and as you can see, they show a straight right-to-left pan sweep. Beside each node there's a number that reflects the node's value.

NOTE ▶ HyperDraw will always display node values, unless there is not enough room between nodes for the values to be displayed.

Selecting and Moving Nodes

Logic is very intelligent in the way it deals with nodes, and in most cases you'll find node editing to be an intuitive process. For example, to move a node, just grab it and drag it around the HyperDraw area. However, there're still a few tricks to keep in mind, so let's practice moving a few nodes.

1 From the Matrix editor's toolbox, grab the Arrow tool.

2   Click and hold the last node in the HyperDraw area.

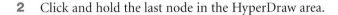

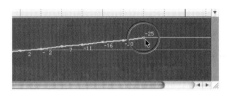

The node is selected, which you can see because it is hollow, while the unselected nodes are solid. Let's move the selected node around the HyperDraw area.

NOTE ▶ If you quickly click a node, it is deleted! To select a node without deleting it, either click and hold the node, or else *slowly* click the node with a long press of the mouse button.

3   Drag the node up or down.

TIP ▶ To restrict node movement either horizontally or vertically, hold down Shift as you drag the node. The node's movement will be restricted to whichever axis you first begin dragging along.

The node follows the pointer movements. You can also move multiple nodes together.

4   Hold down Shift and click every second node in the line.

This is a good exercise, because by selecting alternating nodes, you can see how intuitively HyperDraw works.

5   Grab any of the selected nodes and drag up.

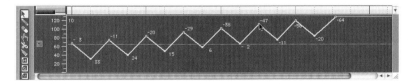

As you might expect, the selected nodes rise, while the other ones remain right where they were.

6 Click the HyperDraw area's background to deselect all nodes.

7 Grab any line between two nodes, and drag it up or down (make sure you grab directly on the line).

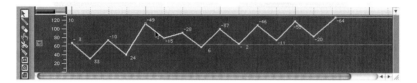

The line turns white, and the nodes at either end move in unison.

Deleting Nodes

Logic provides three different ways to delete nodes, so let's try out each one and learn how it works. The first method is one you may have learned earlier—the hard way—if you clicked a node too quickly during a previous exercise.

1 Quickly click a few nodes.

They are instantly deleted.

2 Select the node at the far right side of the HyperDraw area, and drag it to the left (don't release the pointer).

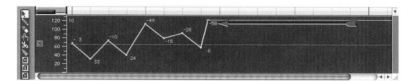

As you drag the node, each time you pass another node, the passed node disappears. However, these nodes are not gone for good, and as long as you continue to hold down the mouse button, you can backtrack this edit.

3   Drag the selected node back toward the right.

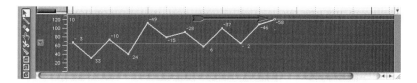

The erased nodes reappear! This is a great feature that really shines in those moments when you accidentally drag a node too far.

4   Hold down Shift and rubber-band select all nodes in the HyperDraw area.

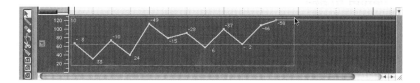

NOTE ▶ To rubber-band select nodes, you *must* hold down the Shift key. If you don't, trying to rubber-band select nodes instead creates new nodes, as you'll learn in the following exercise.

5   Press the Delete key.

All nodes are erased from the HyperDraw area.

Creating and Copying Nodes

With the Arrow tool, all you need to do is click in the HyperDraw area to create a new node. Logic automatically interpolates a line between the new node and the nodes immediately to its left and right.

1   With the Arrow tool, click in the HyperDraw area to create three nodes
at 9 1 1 1, 9 2 1 1, and 9 3 1 1, as pictured in the following figure:

NOTE ▶ If an extra node is created right at the beginning of the
HyperDraw area, just give it a quick click to delete it.

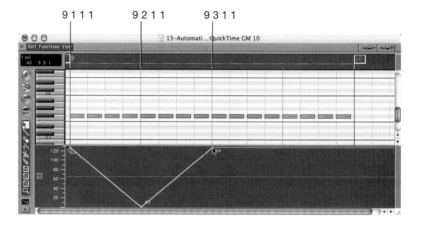

With a little practice, creating nodes becomes a quick and intuitive
process. Copying nodes is easy as well. The following steps show you
how to copy several nodes at the same time, though you can use these
techniques to copy single nodes as well.

2   Hold down Shift and rubber-band select all three nodes.

3   Hold down Option, click and hold any selected node (or any line
between the selected nodes), and then drag to the right until your
HyperDraw area looks like that shown in the following figure (be sure
to hold down the Option key until *after* you release the mouse button):

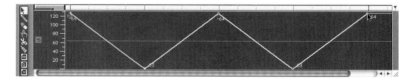

Holding down Option is a great way to copy nodes, and indeed it's a method you'll often use because it's convenient. However, you can also copy and paste nodes in the HyperDraw area.

4   Press Cmd-Z to undo the last edit.

The copied nodes disappear, and the first three nodes are reselected (if they are not, press Shift and rubber-band select them now).

5   Press Cmd-C to copy the selected nodes.

The selected nodes are copied to the Clipboard. You'll paste these nodes back into the HyperDraw area in a second, but first you have to move the SPL to the place where you want the first node to be pasted, because Logic always pastes copied nodes beginning at the SPL's position in the song.

6   In the Bar Ruler at the top of the Matrix editor, click at approximately 9 3 1 1 to move the SPL halfway through bar 9.

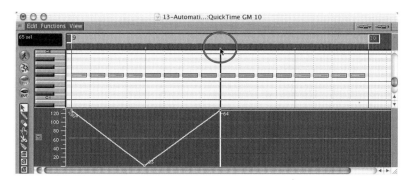

7   Press Cmd-V to paste the copied nodes back into the HyperDraw area.

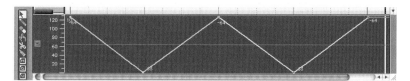

Creating Curves

If you're using Logic Platinum, automation curves are arguably the coolest feature of Logic's HyperDraw area, because they let you quickly create complex automation sweeps, such as customized volume fades, or, for the purpose of this example, smooth pan sweeps from one side of the stereo spectrum to the other.

> **NOTE ▶** Automation curves are available only to Logic Platinum users.

1   Hold Ctrl-Option and drag down the line between the first two nodes.

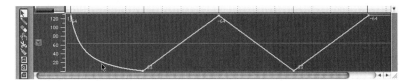

A sweeping automation curve is created.

There are four different types of automation curves, each of which you create by holding down Ctrl-Option and dragging a line in one of the following four directions: down (to create a concave curve), up (convex curve), right (horizontal S-curve), or left (vertical S-curve). Let's try creating one of each.

2   Hold down Ctrl-Option, and then drag the first of the remaining three lines up, the second right, and the last one left.

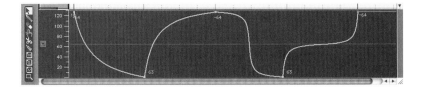

If you decide that a curve isn't exactly what you want, you can revert to the straight line by using the following trick:

3   Hold down Ctrl-Option and quickly click one of the curves.

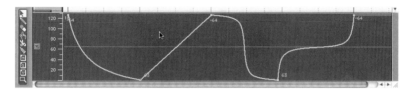

The curve reverts to a straight line.

Using the HyperDraw Arrow menu

On the left edge of the HyperDraw area sits a small downward-pointing arrow button that serves as a shortcut to the HyperDraw menu.

HyperDraw Menu Button

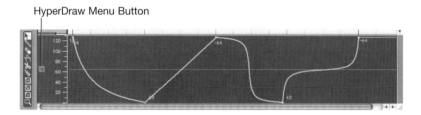

1   Click and hold the HyperDraw menu and take a look at the options.

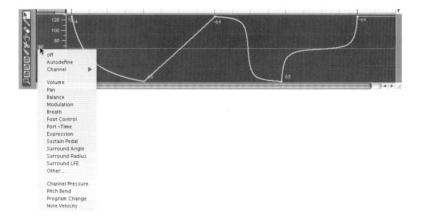

This menu lists all the same options as the HyperDraw menu that's accessible from the Matrix editor's View menu.

2   At the top of the menu, choose "off."

The HyperDraw area is hidden.

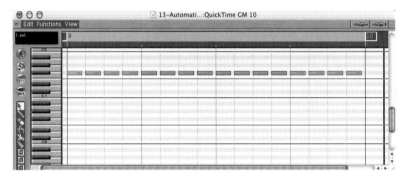

3   Close the Matrix editor.

Using HyperDraw in the Arrange Window

HyperDraw is also available in the Arrange window, and HyperDraw works exactly the same way here as it does in the Matrix editor—with an extra benefit: Enabling HyperDraw in the Arrange window saves you from opening the Matrix editor, which in turn conserves screen real estate. As an added bonus, you can enable HyperDraw for several different sequences and then compare their settings.

Let's see how to access HyperDraw in the Arrange window.

1   Select the first Object in the QuickTime GM track.

2   Choose View > Hyper Draw > Pan.

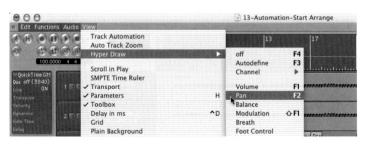

The selected QuickTime GM Object turns blue, and the pan data entered in the Matrix editor's HyperDraw area is displayed. The following figure shows a close-up of the QuickTime GM track's first Object:

3   To edit this HyperDraw data, use the techniques you learned in the above sections of this lesson. That's all there is to it!

Using Track Automation

Track Automation is quite similar to HyperDraw, but as its name suggests, Track Automation is tied to specific tracks in the Arrange window, and not to individual Objects as is the case with HyperDraw. Right now, Track Automation is not enabled, and all Objects in the Arrange area look normal. With Track Automation enabled, a gray automation track appears, as we'll see in the next exercise.

Exploring Track Automation

Let's enable Track Automation and automate some changes in volume.

1   Choose View > Track Automation (or press F4).

If this is the first time you've enabled Track Automation for your song, the following dialog appears (if this dialog does not appear, skip the next step).

2   Choose All Tracks.

The dialog closes, and Track Automation is turned on.

In the Arrange area, each track now has a gray area with a data line through it. This is the Automation track itself. The Track column also expands to display a few new areas, including an Automation Type panel and an Automation fader, which displays the current setting of the parameter displayed in the Automation Type panel.

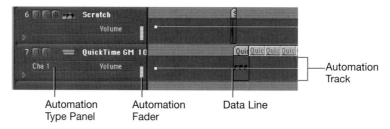

3   In the QuickTime GM track, grab the Automation fader and drag it up or down.

As you drag, the pointer turns into a crosshair, and the Automation track's data line moves up or down to follow the Automation fader's movements. This Automation fader comes in very handy when you need to make "set-and-forget" changes to a track's volume, pan position, or other controller data, because it provides a convenient fader right in the Arrange window. However, set-and-forget changes only work when the track contains no automation data, as the next steps demonstrate.

4 From the Arrange window's toolbox, grab the Magnifying Glass tool and zoom in on the first Object in the QuickTime GM track.

Make this Object big!

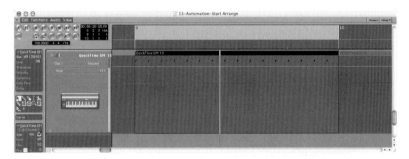

If you look closely at this Object, you can see a line of black dots curving through it. This is the pan controller data you drew into the HyperDraw area in the first part of this lesson. We'll come back to this pan data in a minute. But first, let's add some new automation data.

5 Grab the Arrow tool, and then click in the Automation track to add nodes in the approximate positions shown in the next figure:

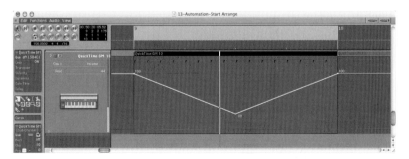

The Automation Type panel says Volume, and indeed, volume automation has been added to the track. As you can see, adding automation nodes works exactly the same way as adding nodes to the HyperDraw area. This includes creating, copying, deleting, and moving nodes. Of course, automation curves are also available to Logic Platinum users, and they work exactly like curves in HyperDraw.

Let's play this volume automation to see what it does.

6   Create a 1-bar cycle region from bar 9 to bar 10, and then press the spacebar to play this cycle region.

As the cycle region plays, the hi-hat line in the QuickTime GM track decreases and then increases in volume. In the Track column, the yellow Automation fader goes down and up. You've just automated the QuickTime GM track's volume!

7   Use the horizontal telescope to zoom out until bars 4 through 10 are visible in the Arrange area.

8   Hold down Shift, and rubber-band select all of the volume-automation nodes, including the one at the very beginning of the automation track.

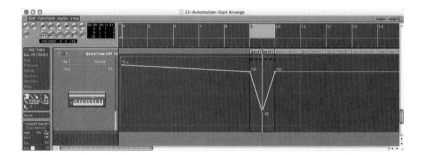

9   Press the Delete key.

All volume-automation nodes are deleted. Make sure you delete every volume-automation node! If any are left over, the following steps will not act as they should. You can tell that all automation nodes are deleted because the Automation track's data line will turn from solid to a dash.

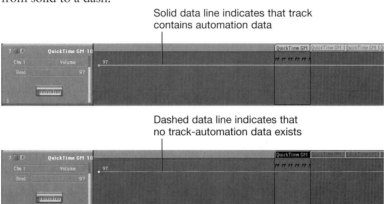

Solid data line indicates that track contains automation data

Dashed data line indicates that no track-automation data exists

Switching Automation Types

The Automation Type panel displays the parameter you are currently editing. In the case of MIDI tracks, such as the QuickTime GM track, this panel shows all 127 MIDI controllers, just as HyperDraw does. For audio tracks and audio instruments, these MIDI controllers are replaced by the automatable parameters available to the track's plug-ins. You'll look at automating plug-ins later in this lesson. For now, let's concentrate on the QuickTime MIDI track as we look at how to switch from one automation type to another.

1   Click and hold the QuickTime GM track's Automation Type panel.

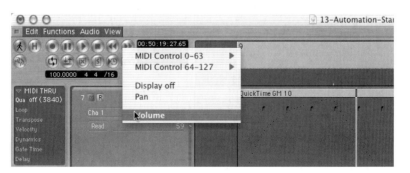

A hierarchical menu appears, which you can use to select any of the 127 MIDI controllers available to MIDI tracks. For quick changes, the most common MIDI controllers, volume and pan, are displayed at the bottom of the menu, but others, such as modulation wheel, pitch change, and portamento, can be selected from the hierarchical menus.

2   Select Pan.

The Automation Type panel changes to say Pan instead of Volume, and the automation track's data line now shows the QuickTime GM track's pan automation (or lack of pan automation, because the QuickTime GM track currently has none—all automation is currently in HyperDraw).

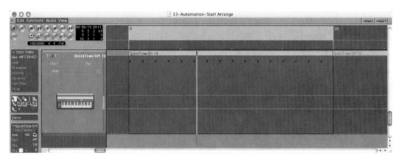

3   Press the spacebar to play your song. As it plays, watch the data line.

Even though there's no pan track automation, the data line sweeps up and down, reflecting the pan settings you drew using HyperDraw in the first part of this lesson. But you can't see the pan curves you drew into the HyperDraw area. This fact solidifies an important point: HyperDraw and Track Automation are completely separate things! Let's explore the differences between the two.

4   Press the spacebar to stop playback.

Comparing HyperDraw and Track Automation

As you've just seen, Track Automation is very similar to HyperDraw. For example, both use nodes to manipulate controller information, and nodes are created, deleted, copied, and moved in exactly the same way. However, there are some important differences in how HyperDraw and Track Automation data are attached to sequences and regions. Exploring these differences will help you to understand when to use which option.

Exploring the Differences Between HyperDraw and Track Automation

The key difference between HyperDraw and Track Automation is this: HyperDraw data is stored in the individual Objects, while Track Automation is stored in the Arrange window track. If you move a sequence or region, all HyperDraw data moves with it, while the Track Automation data may or may not move (the choice is yours).

Let's try moving Objects with both kinds of data and see what happens.

1   Select the QuickTime GM track's first Object, and drag it to bar 5.

> **NOTE ▸** To select the QuickTime GM Object with Track Automation enabled, you must grab the thin bar at its top. Trying to select in the Automation track creates new nodes. Whoops! If you accidentally create new nodes, either click them quickly to delete them or press Cmd-Z to undo the edit.

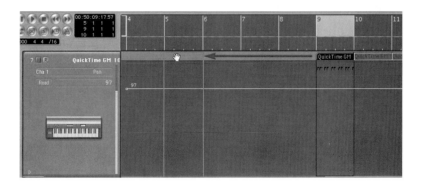

The Object drags to bar 5 as expected. Now, watch this next step carefully:

2   Choose Options > Track Automation > Move Current Object Data To Track Automation.

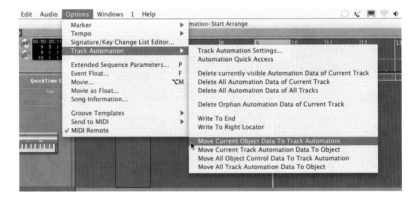

The pan controller data is removed from the Object and jumps into the Automation track.

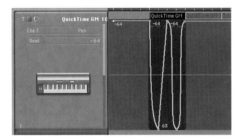

3   Grab the QuickTime GM Object and try dragging it back to bar 9.

A dialog appears, asking if you'd like to move the Automation data. You didn't get this dialog when the pan data was part of the Object, did you?

4 Choose Don't Move.

The QuickTime GM Object jumps back to bar 9, but the automation data stays at bar 5. This is because the automation data is now part of the track, and not part of the QuickTime GM Object!

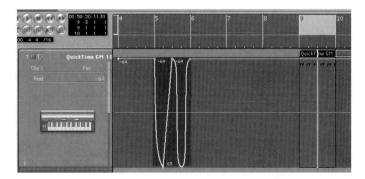

5 It doesn't make much sense to have the pan data sitting out there all by itself, so press Cmd-Z to undo the Object move.

In step 3, you were faced with a dialog that asked if you wanted to move the automation data with the Object. You can avoid facing this dialog by setting an option in the Track Automation Settings window, as follows.

6 Choose Options > Track Automation > Track Automation Settings.

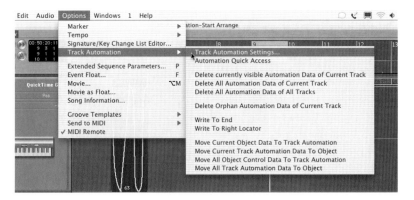

The Track Automation settings window opens.

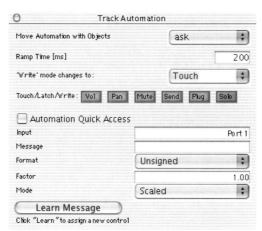

At the top of this window there's a setting called Move Automation with Objects, and it's currently set to "ask."

7   Set Move Automation with Objects to "always."

8   Now, move the QuickTime GM Object back to bar 9.

The pan Track Automation moves with it, and no extra dialog appears. As you can see, the Track Automation settings window holds some important settings, and it's a good idea to have this window open whenever you are working with Track Automation. You'll use this window again soon, so for now, leave it open.

When to Use HyperDraw vs. Track Automation

As you've seen above, Track Automation data belongs to the track, while HyperDraw data belongs to an Object in a track. Your decision to use Track Automation or HyperDraw will depend on your situation and what you are trying to accomplish. In general, though, you'll want to use HyperDraw whenever you are programming control changes that should always affect the Object, such as the panning of the hi-hat in the QuickTime GM Object. Use Track Automation, however, for programming control changes that are not necessarily tied to the Object, such as a volume fade or cutoff sweep. Why? It all comes down to moving, copying, or looping the Object itself, as demonstrated in the following steps.

1   Create a 2 Bar cycle region spanning bars 9 and 10.

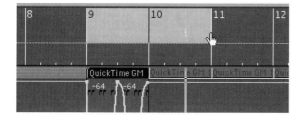

2   Press the spacebar to play the cycle region.

As the cycle region plays, watch the Automation fader. In bar 9 it moves to reflect the pan automation, but at bar 10 it sticks in place and doesn't change.

NOTE ▶ If the Automation fader doesn't move, click an extra node or two into the middle of the automation track in bar 10 to "wake automation up." Then delete this new node(s) with a quick click.

As you can see, the looped QuickTime GM Object only pans in bar 9, and this is a problem, because you want the looped Object to behave exactly the same in every loop as it does in the original Object. Let's change this incorrect behavior by moving the Track Automation back into the Object.

3   Choose Options > Track Automation > Move Current Track
Automation Data To Object.

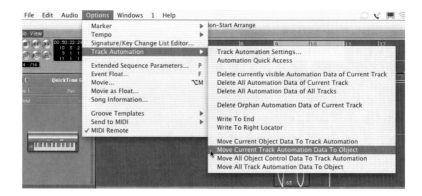

The pan Track Automation is repacked inside the MIDI sequence, and
the MIDI sequence turns blue. What's happened here is that Logic has
automatically enabled HyperDraw for the Object, so you can see that
the pan automation has indeed moved into the Object. That's great,
but you are not done with Track Automation, so let's turn it back on.

4   Click and hold the Automation Type panel, which now says "Display
off," and choose Pan.

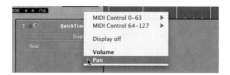

Pan Track Automation is reenabled, and there's no longer any data in
this automation track—it's all been moved to the sequence.

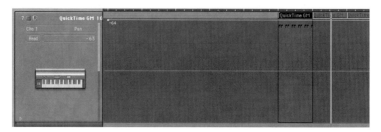

5   Press the spacebar to play the cycle region.

Notice that now the Automation fader moves not only in bar 9, but also in bar 10. For the purpose of setting the QuickTime GM Object's pan position, you can now see that HyperDraw is better than Track Automation, because you want the panning to affect not only the original Object, but all its loops as well.

Using Live Automation

In the steps above, you've experimented with *offline automation*, a process in which you enter nodes by hand. Live automation records automation data as you move faders and plug-in knobs inside Logic, letting you effectively perform Track Automation in real time.

1   Use the Arrange window's telescopes to zoom out until all the song's Objects are visible in the Arrange area.

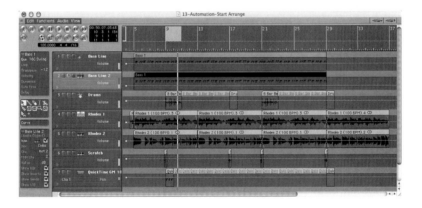

2   The Bass Line 2 track is the one you will use to experiment with live automation, so select it now.

3   On the left edge of the Arrange window, collapse the Sequence/Region Parameter box and the Object Parameter box by clicking the triangle in the top-left corner of each.

Triangle

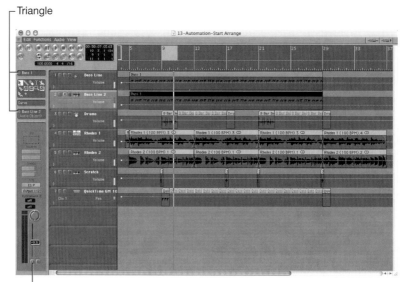

Arrange Window Channel Strip

With the Sequence/Region Parameter box and Object Parameter box collapsed, the Arrange window Channel Strip comes into view (you may have to pull the bottom of the Arrange window down a bit to fully see this channel strip). The Arrange window Channel Strip is new with Logic 6, and it updates to show you the channel view of any track selected in the Arrange window. With the addition of this channel strip, you can now mix most songs right in the Arrange window, so there's less need to switch to the Track Mixer when it comes time to mix your song.

4   On the Arrange Channel Strip, make a mental note of the Bass Line 2 track's volume level (you'll want to return it to this level later), then grab the Volume fader and move it up and down.

Watch the Bass Line 2 track as you do this. Notice how the Bass Line 2 track's Automation fader moves up and down, as does the Automation track's data line.

The Automation fader follows the   ... and so does the
Channel Strip's Volume fader ...   Track Automation data line

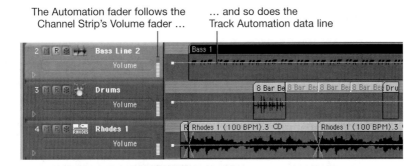

These are real-time edits!

5   On the Arrange Channel Strip, double-click the Bass Line 2 track's input (the ES P button).

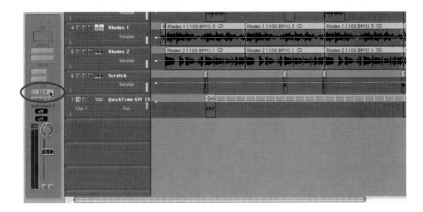

The es-p synth opens. This synth has many automatable settings, including the Frequency, Resonance, and in fact, every other slider on its surface! Let's check out the cutoff automation.

NOTE ▶ Cutoff is a frequency control that filters out all harmonics above a certain threshold, and it's set using the es-p's Frequency knob.

6   In the Track column, click and hold the Bass Line 2 track's Automation Type panel, and then choose 1 ES P > Cutoff from the pop-up menu.

The Automation Type panel changes to say 1 ES P Cutoff.

This step demonstrates a powerful feature of automation in Logic: If a plug-in with automatable settings is assigned to a track, that plug-in will automatically be listed in the Automation Type panel. Logic sets this up for you, and there's no extra work to do. Just select the parameter you want to automate, and you're off to the automation races!

7 On the es-p synth, grab the Frequency knob and drag it up and down (not in a circular motion around the knob, just up and down).

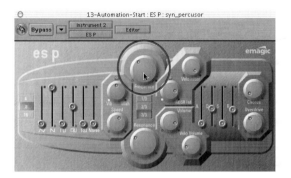

While you're adjusting the Frequency knob, watch the Bass Line 2 track in the Arrange window. Just as adjusting the channel strip's Volume fader moved the data line for volume automation, moving the Frequency knob adjusts the data line for cutoff automation! Once again, this happens in real time. This is pretty cool stuff, so let's move on to the next exercise and learn how to record these real-time changes to automate the Bass Line 2 track's cutoff.

Recording Live Automation

Track Automation has its own recording system, which functions independently of Logic's other recording features, and the Transport's Record button has nothing to do with it! That's right—Logic can record automation during regular playback. To accomplish this feat, Logic uses Track Automation modes. There are six different Automation modes available, each with a slightly different purpose.

Off Automation is turned off and Track Automation will neither be sent nor received. In other words, Logic ignores all Track Automation for each track with the Automation Mode panel set to "off."

Read All existing automation data will be read, but moving any fader (or DSP plug-in slider) inside Logic will not result in any new automation data being written to the track.

Touch Logic writes new automation data whenever a fader is *touched*. When you stop touching, or moving, the fader, Logic stops writing automation data and the fader returns to the pretouched level.

Latch Similar to Touch mode, but Logic continues recording automation data as long as playback continues, even if you stop touching the fader.

Write Overwrites all existing data for all the data types selected in the Track Automation Settings window (the Track Automation settings window is discussed in the next exercise). In general it is better to use Touch or Latch mode, because these modes only overwrite the data for moved faders, while Write mode generally overwrites all automation data. Period.

MIDI Disconnects Track Automation from faders and knobs inside Logic, though faders will still send MIDI data.

Well, that's the theory—now let's put it into action by automating a filter sweep for the Bass Line 2 track!

1   In the Arrange window, turn off Cycle mode, and position the SPL at bar 4.

2   Use the Arrange window's vertical telescope to increase the size of the tracks until the Automation Mode panels are visible.

Automation Mode Panels

The Automation Mode panels are hidden until you vertically zoom
the track so that there's enough space to show them—keep this fact
in mind!

3 Click and hold the Bass Line 2 track's Automation Mode panel, and
choose Latch from the pop-up menu.

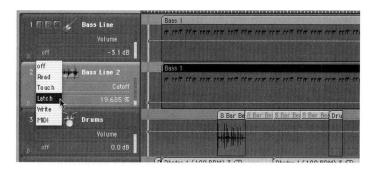

This track is now ready to be automated. All you need to do is play
the song while adjusting the es-p synth's Frequency knob.

4 Press the spacebar to start playing the song.

5 Adjust the es-p synth's Frequency knob.

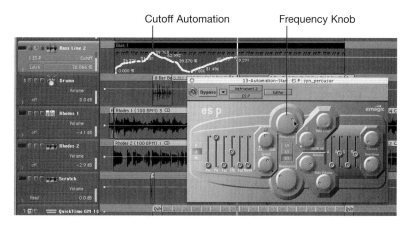

Cutoff automation data is recorded into the Bass Line 2 track! Note that you did not have to click the Transport's Record button. Setting the Automation Mode panel to Latch and twiddling the es-p synth's Frequency knob as Logic plays is all you need to do to automate this plug-in's cutoff. Congratulations—you've just automated a filter sweep!

6   Press the spacebar to stop playback.

7   Press Cmd-Z to undo the cutoff automation you just created.

We're not yet finished exploring Track Automation, so get this first pass of cutoff automation out of the way by undoing it.

Controlling Automation types

In the Track Automation settings window there's a line of buttons labeled Touch/Latch/Write. These buttons tell Logic which types of automation to record. By default, all these buttons except Solo are enabled, which means that Logic will record automation data for Volume, Pan, Mute, Send-level, and plug-in settings. To avoid accidentally automating something you shouldn't have, it's a good idea to turn off all the settings you don't want to automate.

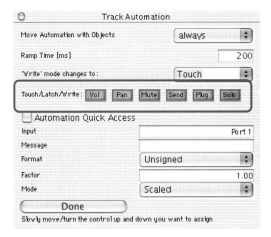

1   If the Track Automation settings window is not open, choose
Options > Track Automation > Track Automation Settings.

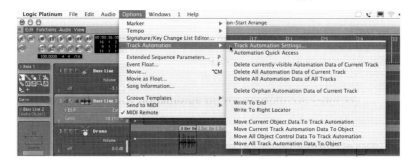

2   For the purpose of demonstration, click all the buttons in the
Touch/Latch/Write section of the Track Automation settings window
to disable them.

3   Move the SPL to bar 4, and press the spacebar to play your song.

4   Adjust the es-p synth's Frequency knob.

No automation is recorded, because the Track Automation settings
window's Plug button is currently disabled.

5   Click the Plug button (plug-ins) to reenable it, and then adjust the
es-p synth's Frequency knob.

Cutoff automation is once again recorded.

Keep the Track Automation settings window open onscreen as you
automate your tracks! To avoid accidentally automating something
you shouldn't have, enable only the type of automation you want to
record. For example, right now only the Plug button is enabled, which
means that only plug-in parameters can be automated. If you need to
automate volume or pan, you'll have to enable those buttons first!

6   Press the spacebar to stop playback.

7   Once again, press Cmd-Z to undo the cutoff automation you've created.

In the next step you are going to learn a far better way to automate the es-p synth's cutoff, using Automation Quick Access.

Using Automation Quick Access

In the previous exercise you adjusted the es-p synth's Frequency knob to automate its cutoff. Wouldn't it be great to make these automation adjustments using a knob or slider on a hardware MIDI controller, instead of adjusting the relatively nonintuitive knob in the plug-in window? Well, in Logic 6 you can, using a feature called Automation Quick Access!

Quick Access assigns a slider or knob on your hardware MIDI controller keyboard that can be used to modify Track Automation data. The bottom of the Track Automation settings window has a section dedicated to Quick Access, and here you turn Quick Access on or off. Let's set up Quick Access now and then take it for a test drive.

1   In the Track Automation settings window, click the Automation Quick Access check box to select it.

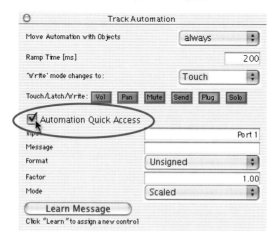

Quick Access is now turned on.

At the very bottom of the window there's a button labeled Learn Message. This button is key to Quick Access, because it tells Logic to listen for an incoming MIDI controller signal and then apply that controller to Quick Access. What this means is that you can click the Learn Message button and then turn any knob or slider on your MIDI controller—for example, the pitch wheel or the modulation wheel—to assign it to Quick Access. Or even better, if you are using a controller keyboard, such as the Midiman Oxygen 8, that has several controller knobs on it, you can turn one of those knobs to assign it to Quick Access, leaving the pitch and modulation wheels free to do their real jobs.

For the purpose of this demonstration, let's assign Quick Access to the modulation wheel (you can always change it later).

2   Click the Learn Message button.

The Learn Message button changes to say Done, and under it appears a tip, which says, "Slowly move/turn the control up and down you want to assign." Let's follow the instructions.

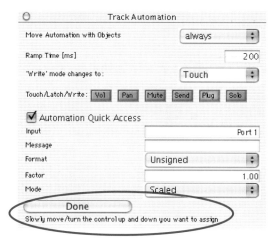

3   On your MIDI controller keyboard move the modulation wheel.

The Message box updates to show the MIDI controller you've moved.

4   Click Done to lock this controller into Quick Access.

5   Move your MIDI controller keyboard's modulation wheel, and watch both the Automation track for Bass Line 2 and the Frequency knob on the es-p synth.

They both move as you adjust the modulation wheel! Great—let's record these movements.

6   In the Arrange window, make sure that the Bass Line 2 track is selected and the Automation Mode panel says Latch.

7   Position the SPL at the beginning of bar 4.

8   Press the spacebar to play the song.

9   On your MIDI controller, move the modulation wheel as the song plays.

Presto! Automation data is now entered using your MIDI controller's modulation wheel. This provides a much smoother and more intuitive way to enter this data than turning the software knob of the es-p synth, doesn't it?

10 Have fun.

Add a DSP plug-in such as a reverb or delay to the Bass Line 2 track, and try automating some of its parameters (Feedback and Mix are always good to start with). Go ahead and automate a few other track settings. The bottom line here is: Have fun and create some exciting, constantly evolving music. After all, that's what automation is all about.

11 When you're finished automating, choose Options > Track Automation > Automation Quick Access.

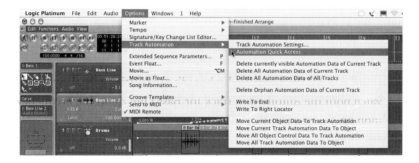

This is a shortcut you can use to toggle Quick Access on or off without having the Track Automation settings window open.

12 Close all windows except the Arrange window, and save your song.

What You've Learned *CHAPTER 13 SUMMARY*

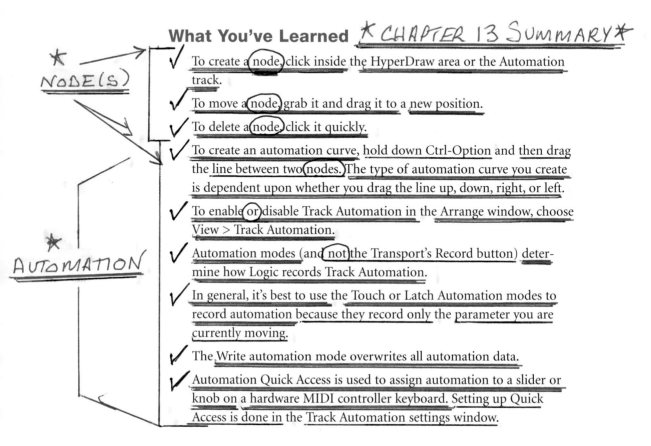

✓ To create a node, click inside the HyperDraw area or the Automation track.

✓ To move a node, grab it and drag it to a new position.

✓ To delete a node, click it quickly.

✓ To create an automation curve, hold down Ctrl-Option and then drag the line between two nodes. The type of automation curve you create is dependent upon whether you drag the line up, down, right, or left.

✓ To enable or disable Track Automation in the Arrange window, choose View > Track Automation.

✓ Automation modes (and not the Transport's Record button) determine how Logic records Track Automation.

✓ In general, it's best to use the Touch or Latch Automation modes to record automation because they record only the parameter you are currently moving.

✓ The Write automation mode overwrites all automation data.

✓ Automation Quick Access is used to assign automation to a slider or knob on a hardware MIDI controller keyboard. Setting up Quick Access is done in the Track Automation settings window.

NODE(S)

AUTOMATION

14

Start	14-Finishing-Start
Complete	Final Mix.wav
	Final Mix.mp3
	Final Mix MIDI.mid
Time	Approximately 30 minutes
Goals	Create a final mix of your song
	Make an MP3 of your song
	Consolidate your project
	Export information from your song to another system

Finishing Your Song

Now that you have a completed mix, it's time to consider a few final questions: How do I allow others to hear my song? How do I archive my song so that I can make changes later if I wish? How can I continue to work with my song at a studio that doesn't have Logic?

Creating a Final Mix

Some people like to make music just for themselves, but most want to share their music with the rest of the world. Unfortunately, not everyone in the world has Logic. In order for you to share your creation with everyone else, you need to create a final mix of your music and prepare it for delivery in a format that Joe or Jane Public can play.

Bouncing Your Song

Bouncing (as it applies to audio) typically refers to combining several tracks of audio into one file. This is exactly what you need to do, as most people do not have the type of equipment necessary to play back multi-track recordings. Another advantage is that this bounced file will be much smaller than your entire Logic song and supporting audio files. Since listeners don't care about editing your tracks or tweaking your mix, they need only the audio that represents your final mix, not the individual tracks.

In Logic, bouncing is a function of output Audio Objects. When you listen to your song file, what you hear is the product of an Output Object that is being sent to your computer's speakers. When you use the Bounce function in Logic, you're taking the same product of that Output Object and saving it to a new audio file on your hard drive. That new file contains a perfect copy of the signal that passed through the Output Object.

If you like what you hear, then it is simple to bounce an audio file of it. This bounced file will be much more practical for those who don't have Logic.

But before you begin the process of bouncing your song, let's discuss some of the bounce options you'll need to set—and which settings are most appropriate for files you want to use with audio CD–burning software:

File Format The File Format setting determines the audio-file format of the resulting bounce file. Wave (WAV) is the most popular uncompressed file format for sharing across multiple platforms.

Resolution The Resolution setting determines the bit resolution of the bounced file. With higher resolutions, the digital data reproduces the audio waveform more accurately, the dynamic range of the audio is expanded, and the signal-to-noise ratio is increased. However, recording at higher resolutions increases file size dramatically—and not all audio hardware can handle 24 bit files. A setting of 16 Bit is appropriate for files you want to burn to an audio CD.

Stereo File Type Since you are bouncing a stereo Output Object, the resulting bounce can end up either as two mono files (one for left and one for right) or in a single interleaved format, which is a single file that contains both channels of audio. Most CD-burning programs require interleaved files for stereo playback.

Surround Bounce Surround Bounce should always be off, unless you're working in surround sound. You can learn how to create and bounce a surround sound mix in Lesson 16.

Dithering This is a process of reducing an audio signal from a higher bit resolution to a lower one. All audio processed within Logic is done at a 32 bit resolution. A CD can only play files saved in16-bit resolution. Different types of dithering, and noise shaping, can produce subtle differences in how the audio sounds once the bit resolution is reduced. These differences are mostly a matter of personal preference. You may want to experiment with using different dither settings, but keep in mind that the sonic differences are very minute.

Bounce Mode The Bounce Mode setting affects whether the bounce is done in real time or offline. Real-time bouncing will cause Logic to play the song just as you've been playing it. You will hear the song play, and Logic will record the audio you are hearing to the bounce file on the hard drive. Offline bouncing allows the computer to process the file as fast as it can. You will not hear the song play, but you will see the SPL move across the Arrange window as the file is being bounced. The faster your computer, the faster the bounce will happen. After the bounce process is finished, the bounce window will automatically close.

Now that you understand the options you're going to encounter, it's time to bounce!

1   From the lessons folder, open the file **14-Finishing-Start**.

2   Open the Environment window, and choose the Audio layer. (Screenset 8)

3   Play back the song, and make sure the clip meter on the Output 1-2 Object does not turn red.

It's very important that you do not clip the final output. Even though your individual tracks may not be clipping, cramming all of those tracks through a single Audio Output Object could cause it to overload. Play your entire song from beginning to end, and pay close attention to the main output meter. No clips!

4   Raise the Output 1-2 channel fader so that the clip meter (not the fader value) at its highest point reads about 1 dB below 0. It's best to play the song from beginning to end and simply look at the value in the clip meter to see how you are doing.

You also want to make sure that you have a strong level on your final output. Ideally you want the meter to read as high as possible, but without clipping. It's always better to be a little low with your level than to clip the track. If you end up a little low in your peak level, don't worry. The next exercise will show you how to automatically compensate for any subtle changes that will be needed to maximize your output level.

5   In the lower-right corner of the Output 1-2 Object, click the Bnce (for Bounce) button.

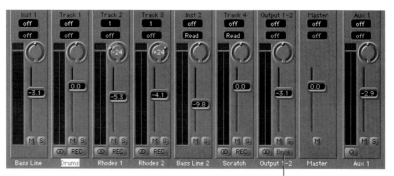

Bnce Button

The Bounce settings dialog opens.

6   Set the range for your bounce from 4 1 1 1 to 38 1 1 1. As with setting locate positions, you can do this by clicking and holding the mouse on the bar number and dragging up or down to change the value. You can also double-click the Start or End Position values to type in the numbers.

Typically you want to be sure to leave a little extra room after the last note of your song. This ensures that any decays for synths, reverbs, delays, and so on, will be heard. This song starts just before bar 5, with a few pickup notes, so it's necessary to start a little before that at bar 4.

7   Set the options to match those shown here:

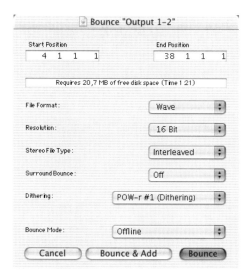

These settings are appropriate for bouncing a file that can be used with most audio CD–burning software.

TIP ▶ It's recommended that you bounce a file as a 24 bit file as well, so that you have a master mix-down file with the highest resolution.

8   Click Bounce & Add.

A Save dialog opens.

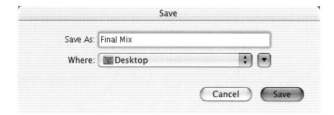

After selecting Save, you'll see a lot of action. Sit back and watch. You're going to do one additional process to the file after the bounce, which is why you chose the Bounce & Add option. This will cause the bounced audio file to be automatically imported into the Audio window. You'll take a look at it in a few steps.

TIP ▶ If you want to further polish your final mix, you may also want to experiment with adding plug-ins to the Output 1-2 Object. A little equalization or compression across the entire mix may be what you need to make it sizzle.

NOTE ▶ You may notice that this version of the song doesn't have the QuickTime track that was playing some of the percussion lines. That's because the QuickTime music synth does not output audio through Logic's Output Objects. As with any MIDI sequence, bouncing won't pick it up unless it's recorded as an audio file. To avoid confusion about this QuickTime track, we removed it from the Start file for this exercise.

Normalizing Your File

Now that you've bounced your final mix, you should make sure that it is every bit as good as it can be. Actually, in this case, *bit* is the key word. The bit resolution of a recording is used to represent the dynamic (volume) accuracy of a recording. Although you took the time to make sure that your levels were strong but not too strong, there may still be a little room to raise the level of your overall mix.

Normalization works by scanning a selected area of digital audio for the highest recorded level. If that highest peak value was recorded at –3 dB, then 3 dB of digital gain will be added to the entire file. This means that the peak level will now be at 0 dB. The relative values for the song will remain the same, because 3 dB were added to everything in the file, not just the peak position. As far as overall volume goes, normalizing helps your song compete with other recorded audio out there. There are other factors that can cause one song to sound louder than another (EQ, compression), but normalizing helps to level the playing field—so let's go ahead and normalize your bounced file now.

1   Go to the Audio window (Cmd-9) and scroll down until you find the bounced file **Final Mix.wav**.

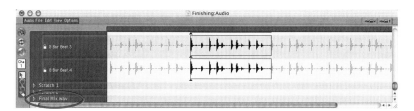

2   Click the triangle next to the filename to reveal the waveform view of the region you just bounced.

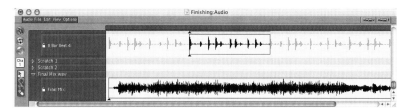

3 Double-click the waveform to open the Sample editor.

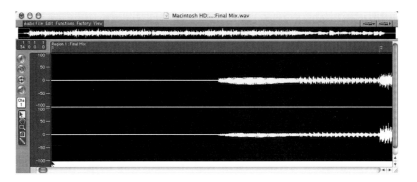

The entire waveform is selected. Keep it that way.

4 In the Sample editor local menu select Functions > Normalize, or use the Ctrl-N key command.

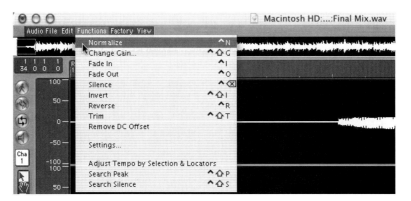

5 Confirm the procedure by clicking Process in the dialog that opens.

6   When asked if you would like to create a backup, click No.

You'll see the samples being processed.

NOTE ▶ If a dialog that says the file is already normalized appears, then simply confirm it. This simply means you did such a good job of setting your final output level that there is no need to normalize the file.

7   After the file is processed, close the Sample editor window. You'll be asked if you want to make the last edit permanent. Click Yes.

Now you're ready to burn! The file you've created can be imported into any CD-burning software such as Apple's iTunes or Roxio's Toast. Nothing can be more satisfying than taking the music you've worked so hard on, popping it into that CD player, and hearing it play—or, better yet, hearing it blast from your car speakers as you're cruising down the highway.

Creating an MP3 File

If you haven't heard of MP3s by now, then you may want to crawl out from that rock you're under. CDs have been a great consumer standard, as they do not compromise the quality of your audio. MP3s can compromise the sound quality; however, the files sound nearly as good as CDs and have a much smaller file size. This small file size makes them great for things like Internet audio distribution and portable MP3 players.

MP3 files use lossy data compression to achieve small file sizes, and this compression involves a sacrifice in sound quality. The art of creating MP3s comes down to finding the right balance between file size and sound quality.

Logic for Mac OS X can encode MP3 files directly. It is actually possible to choose MP3 as the audio file format when bouncing, but typically you want to retain a high-resolution file as your master copy. It's easy to convert your highest quality original to an MP3, but you can't do it the other way around.

Let's go ahead and create an MP3 version of your file.

> **NOTE** ▶ MP3 encoding is a feature available only in the OS X version of Logic. If you are using OS 9, please skip to the next exercise.

1   In the main menu bar, select Logic Platinum > Preferences > MP3 Export. The MP3 Preferences window opens.

2   Notice the various options of the encoder.

Match your settings to those in the figure, which are a typical good balance of file size and sound quality. Most MP3 encoders have these options. To learn more about MP3 encoding options, visit one of the dozens of MP3-related Internet sites that explain these options fully, such as www.mp3-converter.com.

3   Close the MP3 Preferences window.

4   In the Audio window select the Final Mix.wav file (not the region).

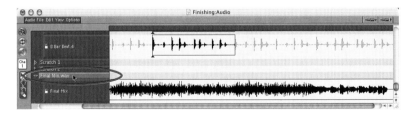

5   In the Audio local menu, select Audio File > Convert to MP3.

A Save dialog opens.

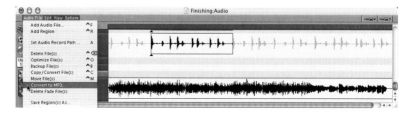

6   Select the location where you want to store your MP3 file, and click
Save.

The file that was saved will not appear in your Audio window but
rather in the folder on your hard drive that you saved it to. That file is
one that can easily be sent via email. Give it a try!

Using the Save as Project Command

Now that you've bounced your final mixes, you may want to back up and
archive your song in its existing project state so that you can return to it
later and make changes to the arrangement or mix. Perhaps you'll want to
take your song to a studio for additional recording. You won't be able to
do this if your only copy of the song is a bounced file. Remember, your
song doesn't include only the Logic song file; it consists of multiple audio
files that may be coming from various places on your computer's hard
drive. For many projects, trying to consolidate all these different files can
get pretty confusing and time-consuming. In addition, if you move your

source audio files, your current Logic song file will no longer be able to find them—which means you have to relink Logic to the new locations of the audio files.

Save as Project is the simple solution to the problem of consolidating a Logic song into one folder and automatically repointing the Logic song file to the new location of the audio files. Once this is done, you can easily move the folder to another location, such as a different hard drive or computer, or even a backup disk—without having to manually collect all the necessary files and associate their new positions with the song.

Let's see how Save as Project works.

1   From the File menu, select Save as Project.

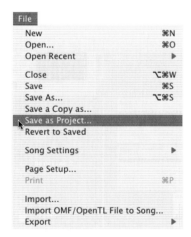

2   Confirm that Logic will need to save your song first.

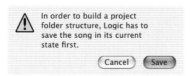

3   Select the folder where you want the song and all of its files to be stored. Click Choose.

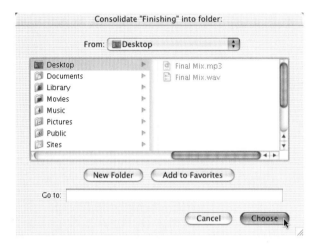

The Consolidate Song: Options window appears.

4   For the folder name, enter *Logic Course Complete*, and then click OK.

All necessary files are put into a new folder, which has the name you gave it.

Now, everything you need to play the song is wrapped up in one tidy package. This folder could also be burned as a data CD or DVD as a backup to the project.

Exporting Your Song

In some cases you may want to transfer elements of your song to another audio or MIDI program. A problem you may encounter is that most musically based audio and MIDI software programs store their songs in their own unique formats. They will not be able to understand a Logic song file format. Fortunately, you can get around this problem, for the most part, in a couple of ways: by exporting in Standard MIDI format (in the case of MIDI tracks) and by freezing (in the case of audio tracks).

Exporting a Standard MIDI File

Standard MIDI is a common file type that almost any MIDI sequencer can read. In Logic, you can export selected MIDI sequence Objects as a Standard MIDI File. Remember that MIDI is not audio, so this will not work for your audio tracks. Also consider that MIDI represents only the performance information (which note was played, when, how hard, and so on), so the sounds of Logic's virtual synthesizers will not accompany the MIDI file to another program. Once the MIDI tracks arrive at their destination, they will have to be reassigned to new sound sources.

Let's step through the process of exporting a Standard MIDI file.

1   Choose Screenset 1 to automatically close the Audio window and open the Arrange window.

2   Make sure that no tracks are frozen. Also make sure that any muted MIDI sequences are removed from the song. This step is necessary because muted Objects will behave as if they had not been muted when they are delivered within a Standard MIDI file.

> **TIP** ▶ The Select Muted Objects function is an easy way to get rid of unwanted muted sequences. In the Arrange local menu go to Edit > Select Muted Objects. Then simply press Delete.

3   From the Arrange window local menu, select Edit > Select All (Cmd-A).

Only selected MIDI sequence Objects get exported to the Standard MIDI file. Selected audio sequences will not get included, so the Select All command is an easy way to ensure that you don't miss anything.

4   From the main menu bar, choose File > Export > Export Selection as MIDI File.

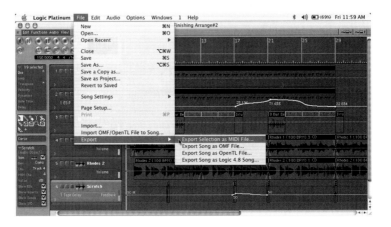

5   Choose your directory, name the file, and click Save.

This file saved on your hard drive is ready to be delivered to just about any MIDI sequencer around.

NOTE ▸ Logic's real-time sequence parameters (quantize, transpose, gate time, and others) are not exported, which may cause the MIDI file not to play exactly as it did in Logic. To prevent this problem, use the Normalize Sequence Parameters and Fix Quantize functions (described in detail in the Logic Reference manual).

Freezing an Audio Track for Export

The audio files that Logic creates can typically be read by other audio editing software. This seems like great news, except for one very important problem: The other audio program won't know which file to play at what time. The song you've created has several tracks of audio that have multiple audio regions within them. Importing these raw files into another program without the proper positioning of the audio edits you've made is of little use to you. Re-editing the parts is typically impractical.

The solution is to render each of the audio tracks as one large continuous audio file. This way, when you import the tracks into your destination program, you need only make sure the beginnings of all the audio files are aligned with each other. The Freeze function is a great way to do this. You've seen Freeze before as a way to relieve the DSP load on your computer, but the audio files that Freeze creates work perfectly for exporting audio tracks.

Let's go ahead and see how easy it is to freeze your audio tracks.

1   In the main menu bar, select Preferences > Audio Preferences.

2 In the Preferences window, for the Freeze File Format option select 24 Bit, and click OK to confirm your settings and close the window.

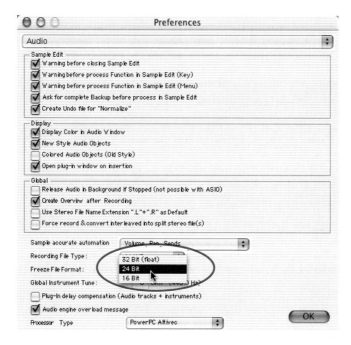

Other audio systems may not support 32 bit files directly, so switching to 24 bit will ensure greater compatibility.

NOTE ▶ When you Freeze at 24 Bit resolution, there is far less head room than with 32 Bit (float). A track that does not sound distorted in Logic's native 32 Bit mode may reveal distortion when set to 24 Bit. To avoid distortion, make sure the levels on the track's meters stay below 0 dB.

3 Click the Freeze button on all tracks (where possible), and click Play.

TIP ▶ You may not want Logic's plug-ins to be part of the exported files. In that case, simply bypass all the plug-ins inserted directly on the files you wish to freeze.

4 Freeze files are always kept in a special folder. On your hard drive, locate the folder that contains the current song. Open the Freeze Files folder, which will be located in the same folder as the current Logic song file.

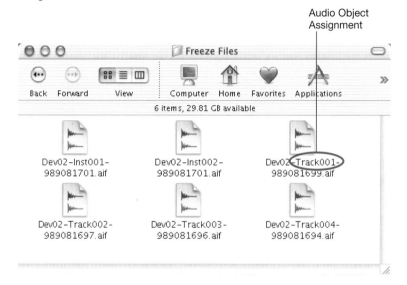

Logic automatically generates the names of the resulting audio files. Most of the characters in the filename won't be meaningful to you, but notice that part of each filename is named after the Instrument or track assignment.

NOTE ▶ Freeze files are always in the AIFF audio file format. This is a fairly common audio format on Macintosh computers. If you need to change the file format, you can import these files into the Logic song and convert them using options in the Audio window.

5 Go back to the audio Preferences window and reset the Freeze File Format back to 32 bit.

If you don't reset this format, all frozen files from this point on in any new songs will be in 24 bit format, which is fine for exporting audio to take to other programs, but you want to keep the 32 bit setting for freezing files during the course of creating your song in Logic.

TIP ▶ Although you can import the frozen files into most other audio editing applications, there will be no tempo map, so the bar lines won't match. To prevent this from happening, you can try also exporting a Standard MIDI file (even if you don't have any MIDI data in the song), and then, if possible, importing the Standard MIDI file into the other program; the resultant file will have a tempo map. When you import your frozen files into the other audio editing program, as long as the audio files are aligned at the beginning of bar 1, the bar lines should line up with the audio files throughout the song.

NOTE ▶ Users of Logic Platinum can also export Logic songs in either OMF or Open TL format. These formats can remember what audio file plays on what track at what time, allowing the file to retain all the edits within a track. This greatly simplifies moving the audio of a Logic project to systems that support these formats.

Congratulations! You've just completed the last steps in producing a song in Logic from start to finish. You've should be feeling great about that! Now the real fun begins. You've learned a lot about Logic by way of the demo files used with this book, but now it's time to stretch your wings and let your own original ideas become reality. Have fun in the next chapter learning how to get those ideas out of your head and recorded into Logic!

What You've Learned *CHAPTER 14 SUMMARY*

- Bouncing an output Audio Object is how you create a final mix file of your song.
- It's important to set final output levels carefully before you bounce your song.
- Normalization can help to maximize the final level of your recording after you bounce your file.
- Logic can process audio files directly into MP3s (OS X only).
- The Save as Project command lets you group all files necessary to play back a Logic song and consolidate them into one folder.
- Logic can export Standard MIDI files so that other MIDI-based applications can read and play MIDI sequences you create.
- Freezing tracks is a great way to move the audio from a track within Logic to another audio editing system.

15

Start	15-Recording-Start
Time	Approximately 30 minutes
Goals	Set up a song for recording audio and MIDI
	Configure the metronome
	Use Realtime, Autodrop, and Punch on the Fly modes
	Learn differences between how MIDI and audio can be recorded
	Use step-time recording

Recording

This is most likely the moment you've been waiting for. Up to this point in the book you've seen a myriad of different ways in which a musical creation can be twisted and turned to suit your every whim. You've learned this by using the provided examples, which is a great way to get familiar with the inner workings of Logic. However, it's likely that you've been thinking of how you will use these newfound tools to realize the unique songs playing in your head. Once you know how to record your own material, you'll be off and running!

This lesson has been structured to show you how the recording process works for both audio and MIDI. As you've learned by now, each has its own purpose and unique advantages. You don't have to be a virtuoso musician or an accomplished vocalist to get through these exercises. The point is to know how the recording process works in Logic, not how to be a great performer. You will, however, need to be able to count out loud from one to eight and be able to press a few keys on your MIDI controller. Can you handle that?

NOTE ▶ As you should know by now, all information that comes in or out of Logic passes through Objects in the Environment. To keep the focus on recording, this lesson has already been configured with two tracks and their corresponding Environment Objects. You may want to take this time to review Lessons 4 and 5 if you are unsure of how these Objects and tracks were created.

Setting Up the Metronome

Logic was designed from the ground up as a system with which to create music. For that reason, the primary way Logic references time over the course of a song is via bars and beats, as opposed to minutes and seconds (although it can do that, too). It's rare that you would hear one musician say to another, "Let's take it from 1 minute and 32 seconds." They're much more likely to say, "Let's start at bar 42." In order to ensure that you and Logic are in sync with where the beats are, you must play along with Logic's metronome. In the next steps you will set up the metronome to click out your song's tempo as you record.

1   Open the file **15-Recoding-Start**.

2   In the Transport panel, click and hold the Metronome button (the one with a picture of an old-fashioned metronome). In the pop-up menu select Metronome Settings.

The Song Settings window opens to display Metronome Settings.

3   Make sure that "Click while recording" is enabled and that "Count-in" is set to 1 Bar.

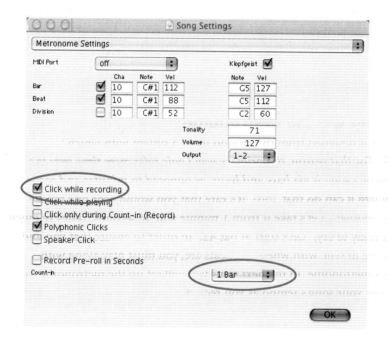

"Click while recording" allows the click track to automatically be heard each time you enter the Record mode.

Where the window says 1 Bar, it is indicating an automatic count-in. A count-in gives you a bit of a head start before recording occurs by starting the SPL one bar early. This gives you time to get ready to play after entering Record mode.

NOTE ▶ If one bar is not enough time to get ready, the Count-in menu will let you set up to six bars as a count-in.

4   Click OK to confirm your settings, and close the Song Settings window.

5   Select the Instrument 1 track.

You don't actually want to record anything just yet. At this point, you're just going to test the metronome. MIDI-based tracks do not record anything unless you generate MIDI data, so for now you'll use the MIDI track to check your metronome.

6   Position the SPL at bar 5, and click the Record button (press * on the numeric keypad).

The Bar Ruler turns red (for record); the SPL jumps back to bar 4 and then starts playing. This one-bar jump-back represents the 1 Bar count-in you selected in step 3. During this one-bar count-in, nothing will be recorded, but the metronome still clicks along to get you into the tempo and prepare you to record.

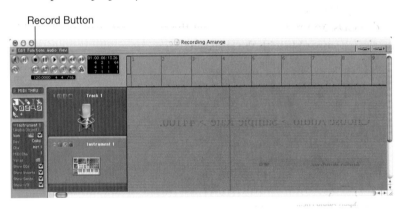

7   Press the spacebar to stop recording.

Setting Audio Options

Before you record audio into Logic, we need to address some basic functions and features. Think of Logic as being like a high-end professional camera. It offers a lot more features and flexibility than that cheap throwaway. With that flexibility you have many options that give you much more control over the final image that is created. Before you snap that picture, however, you need to make sure that all the settings are just right so that they'll create the best possible image. Some of these options are set just once, before you start to record, while others may need changing during the process of creating your song. For some options, you'll choose settings based purely on personal preference. Nevertheless, its best to think through all your setting choices before you begin your work.

Choosing a Sampling Rate

We first addressed sampling rate when you changed the Rhodes 2 (100 BPM) file from 48 kHz to 44.1 kHz, back in Lesson 8. It is extremely important that you are aware of your song's sampling rate setting, because it greatly affects your computer's performance. Logic can support sampling rates up to 192,000 samples per second, but a rate that high takes well over four times the disk space and four times the digital signal processing power as the standard 44,100-samples-per-second rate used on audio CDs. You must make sure that the sample rate you've selected in Logic is compatible with the audio interface you are using. Most audio interfaces support 44,100 samples per second (44.1 kHz), so you'll use the 44,100 setting when recording audio in this lesson.

1   Choose Audio > Sample Rate > 44100.

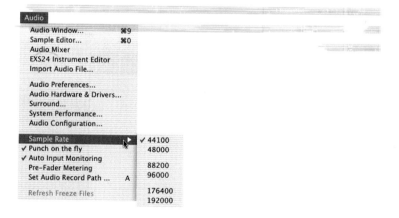

2   If the sample rate is set to 44100, then leave it in its current value; if not, change it to 44100.

Choosing Hardware Driver Settings

The Audio Hardware & Driver Preferences window is starting to become an old friend. In Lesson 5 you visited this preference window both to increase the track count available to Logic and to explore the driver options available. Let's take a moment to check out a few of its other settings.

Setting the I/O Buffer Size The buffer setting in Logic controls how big of a bite the computer tries to chew at one time when working with audio. This setting, which is measured in samples, can dramatically change the way in which your system performs, especially when recording. Typically, the bigger the buffer size, the more recorded channels of audio can be played at the same time, and this reduces the processing power required by your computer's CPU. However, bigger buffers make the system react more slowly when recording. For example, with a large buffer setting you may notice an audible delay between playing a note on your MIDI controller and hearing one of Logic's soft-synths react to that note. Latency can also occur when recording audio. For example, you may hear an audible delay between when you sing into a microphone and then hear it through the speakers. This is called *latency*.

To avoid latency, you may want to use a smaller buffer. The downside to a smaller buffer is that your computer's CPU must work harder, which means that fewer total audio tracks, plug-ins, and soft-synths can play simultaneously.

With these considerations in mind, start with a buffer setting of 64. If you later find you need more tracks, plug-ins, or soft-synths, you can increase the buffer size.

1 From the main menu, choose Audio > Audio Hardware & Drivers.

The Preferences window opens to display the Audio Driver pane.

2 In the I/O Buffer Size pop-up menu select 64.

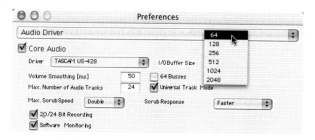

3 When changing a buffer setting, you'll be asked to reboot Logic. Click the button that says Try (Re)Launch.

Logic will initialize your driver settings, and you won't have to shut down and reboot the program. You're going to change a few more items in this window, so for now, leave it open.

Setting the Bit Resolution Logic can record using 16 or 24 bit resolution. The higher the bit resolution, the more accurately Logic can represent the audio waveform. The reason the Audio Driver pane says 20/24 is because some audio interfaces only support 20 bit resolution. When you choose 20/24 Bit Recording, Logic records the 20 bit audio it receives in a 24 bit format. Using 20/24 instead of 16 bit resolution will require more processing power from your computer's CPU and take slightly more disk space when you start to record audio. However, with the current generation of technology, 24 bit recording has become quite standard.

▶   If 20/24 Bit Recording is not already selected, select it.

Enabling Software Monitoring

When you're recording an audio track, software monitoring allows you to hear the signal in your speakers after it has already passed through all the Audio Input, Track, and Output Objects you have created in Logic's environment. This allows you to hear how settings such as level, panning, and plug-ins affect the audio as you are recording it. The potential drawback is that since you are recording the audio live, the computer can't look ahead at what's coming. If you have a slower computer or are using high buffer settings, you may notice a delay between when the audio is created and when you hear it. Hardware monitoring is a solution for this, but it is a feature of your audio interface and not of Logic. The disadvantage of hardware monitoring is that you are not able to hear how Logic is processing signal until you finish recording the sound and play it back.

Since you're not going to want to hear a delay as you record, let's turn software monitoring on.

1   If Software Monitoring is not already selected, select it.

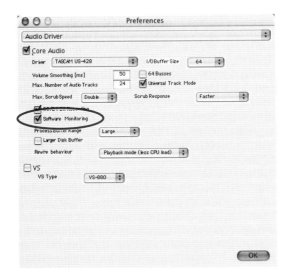

2   Click OK to confirm your settings, and close the window.

Selecting a File Type

When Logic records audio, the audio is stored in separate audio files on your computer's hard drive. Logic can create your choice of WAVE, AIFF, or SDII audio files. These file formats do not use data compression as MP3 files do, which means that they maintain the best possible audio quality. WAVE files are the most common type of uncompressed audio files, so let's choose WAVE as the file type for your audio files.

1 Click-hold the pop-up menu at the top of the Preferences window, and select Audio.

2 Set the Audio Recording File Type parameter to WAVE.

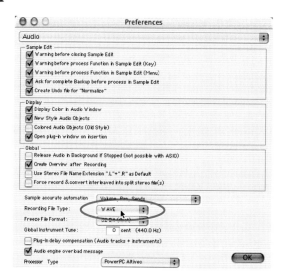

3 Click OK to confirm your settings and close the window.

Specifying a Record Path and Name

Unlike MIDI data, which is stored directly within the Logic song file, audio files are stored separately on your computer's hard drive. Audio files can be kept anywhere on your hard drive. It is very important to know where your audio files will be recorded, so you should set a record path before you record audio for the first time.

Each audio file you record also needs a unique filename. Instead of manually naming each one, you can have Logic automatically use the name
of the track as the filename. Logic will automatically add numbered extensions to the filename to prevent duplicates when you record on the same
track multiple times.

Let's specify an appropriate record path and naming basis for your
audio files.

1   From the main menu bar, choose Audio > Set Audio Record Path (A).

2   Make sure that the pop-up menu above the Core Audio area is set to
    Song Recording Path.

    You can specify a global location to store all your audio, or you can
    specify this on a per-song basis.

3   Make sure that Use Audio Object Name for File Name is selected.

    Having Logic use the Audio Object name as a basis for filenames
    is especially useful when you're recording multiple tracks at the
    same time.

4   Click the Set button in the Core Audio area, and navigate to a location
    where you want to store your audio.

    NOTE ▶ If you do not choose a record path ahead of time, you will
    be prompted to choose a record path the first time you record-enable
    an audio track.

5   Click OK to confirm your settings, and close the window.

Selecting Auto Input Monitoring

An audio track either can output the audio regions it finds as the SPL moves across them, or it can output the signal it receives from its input. Typically you want to hear the audio regions during playback and hear the input in the following two situations: when the track is record-enabled but the transport is still (so you can set levels), and when the transport is moving and in Record mode (which is the actual act of recording). Enabling Auto Input Monitoring automatically switches between the signals that are to be monitored, depending on the conditions just described.

Since this automatic switching is very helpful, let's go ahead and select Auto Input Monitoring.

1   Select Audio in the main menu bar to open the pull-down menu.

2   If there isn't a check mark next to Auto Input Monitoring, select it. If there already is a check next to Auto Input Monitoring, simply release the mouse to close the menu.

Enabling Replace Mode

In most cases when you are recording, you'll want to use something called Replace mode. This simply means that when Logic is recording onto a track, any information that was on that part of the track is overwritten with a new Object. In other words, Logic behaves just like a regular audio-cassette recorder. However, Logic does not actually rewrite or delete the previously recorded audio on the hard drive. This gives a huge advantage over the cassette recorder: You can always undo your recording and go back to where you were before!

> **NOTE** ▶ Recording without Replace mode can get very confusing. Without Replace engaged, Logic will present multiple recorded Objects on the same track. In the case of an audio track, only one of these Objects can be heard at a time, but in the case of a MIDI track, multiple Objects can be heard from the same track. Sometimes the Objects overlap to the point where you can't see other Objects underneath. This can be very problematic, as you may be hearing things you can't see in the Arrange window.

▶ Click the Replace button in the Transport panel.

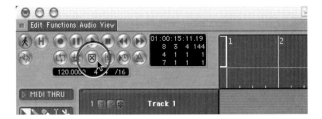

Recording Audio

For the next set of exercises, you'll need a microphone plugged into one of your audio interface inputs. In order for this to work correctly, a microphone needs a preamplifier. Many audio interfaces have mic preamps built into them. If yours doesn't, then you will need an external preamp, which you will connect to one of your interface's line inputs.

NOTE ▶ It is possible to do this exercise without a microphone. If you have any device that sends out a line-level signal, you can use it instead of speaking the parts. Instead of counting (as indicated in the exercise), just play a note for each word instead.

Adjusting Track Settings

In the last section you had to deal with a lot of general settings. Fortunately, those are primarily set-and-forget kinds of options that you will not need to change during the course of your song. The following settings may need to be changed each time you record a track, depending on what you are recording.

Choosing Mono or Stereo As you know by now, Logic can work with either mono or stereo audio tracks. Before recording, select whichever option is appropriate for what you are trying to record. In this case, you are going to be recording in mono.

1   Go to the Track Mixer (Cmd-2)

2   Make sure the Mono/Stereo button on the Track 1 channel is set for mono (single circle).

Setting an Input Now you will need to assign the audio track's input. This should correspond to the physical input that you have your microphone hooked up to. Many audio interfaces (including the stock audio inputs of your computer) only have stereo inputs labeled L (left) and R (right). In this case Input 1 in Logic represents the left input of your audio interface, and Input 2 represents the right input.

▶   Select the input that is appropriate for your studio.

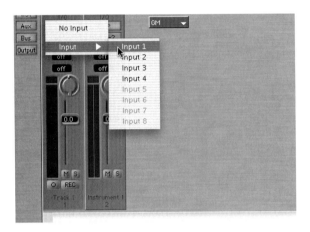

In this case, physical Input 1 is being selected.

Preparing a Track for Recording   Now you need to designate that you want to record onto a specific track by record-enabling it. Once a track is record-enabled, you can see and hear the signal going through the track without actually recording. Before you record, you want to make sure that the input levels are strong but not clipping.

> **NOTE** ▶ For this exercise you will be recording only one track at a time, but if you have multiple tracks created, it is possible to record to more than one track at a time by simply clicking the Record Enable buttons on the tracks. For example, you might do this to record a drum kit for which you need to record kick, snare, overhead, and tom tracks simultaneously.

TIP Avoid feedback by making sure your speakers aren't turned up loud and your microphone isn't pointed directly at them—or by using headphones instead of speakers.

1   From the Track Mixer click the Record Enable button on the Track 1 channel.

2   Speak into the microphone, and adjust the level on your preamp until you get a strong level without clipping

Record Enable Button

TIP Many people feel more comfortable having some kind of effect on their voice, like a reverb or delay. You can plug in an effect directly on the record track and hear the effect live. The effect will not actually be recorded onto the audio file that's created.

Making a Recording

Now you have your canvas ready, and all that's left to do is to apply your brush. The next set of exercises will help you understand the various techniques you can use to create the picture in your mind.

Recording Your First Take Here it is—the big moment! You are about to make your first live recording. Read through this recording exercise to get the big picture of what is about to happen. Once you feel comfortable, proceed with the following steps.

1   Return to the Arrange window, and make sure the SPL is at bar 1.

2   Click the Record button or press the asterisk (*) key. You will hear a one-bar count-off (four clicks). Simply count the bar numbers out loud as the SPL reaches them, 1 through 8. Click Stop or press 0 on the numeric keypad after bar 8.

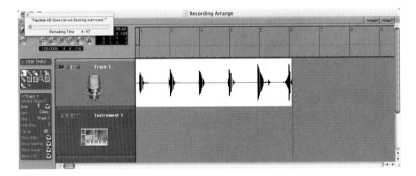

While recording, notice the remaining-time indicator that appears. After you click Stop, Logic will quickly create a waveform overview. The new sequence will have the track Object name, with a version number added.

NOTE ▶ If you've clipped your recording, Logic will notify you just as a precaution. Simply click Continue.

3   Listen to what you have recorded. Make sure the SPL is at bar 1, and click Play.

That's you! Don't worry if you don't like the way it sounds; most people tend to not like the way their voice sounds on a recording. If you messed up, don't sweat it—the next exercise addresses what to do.

Deleting and Redoing Your First Take   It's likely that your first performance won't be what you had hoped. Fortunately, you can easily get rid of your last take.

1   Press the Delete key.

The Object you just recorded will already be selected, so hitting the Delete key is all you need to do.

2   When asked if you want to delete the selected audio file, click Delete.

Deleting removes the file from the drive. Selecting Keep removes the file from the Arrange window but keeps the file on your drive and in your Audio window. Keeping old files that you know are not going to be used will begin to fill and clutter your hard drive.

3   Record yourself speaking the numbers again in the exact same way to prepare for the next exercise.

Recording Over Existing Audio You may find that you want to record over only a certain section of your previous recording. Here's what you can do.

1   Move the SPL to bar 6.

2   Click Record. You will still get the 1-bar count in. Recount bars 6 and 7, but stop before you get to bar 7.

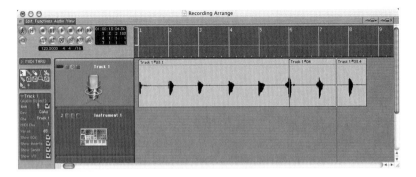

Notice that even though Logic was recording during the counting, the region starts exactly at bar 6. Sometimes this can cut off part of the audio that you want to hear.

3   If necessary, drag the start point of the new region from bar 6 to just before bar 6 so that you can hear the entire number.

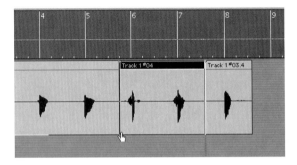

Punching

Punching in and out on a recording is a concept that goes back to traditional analog multitrack recorders. This is not something that your typical consumer tape deck can do. The basic idea is that you may want to play the track you've just recorded up to a certain point, then start recording, and then revert back to playback in one continuous process. This is handy for replacing certain parts of track that don't sound right. Trying to record right at the offending part (as in the past exercise) makes it difficult to hear and feel the context of the part you are trying to replace.

> **NOTE ▶** Only the tracks that are record-enabled will be affected by punching.

There are two ways to punch: by predefining punch-in and punch-out points with Logic's Autodrop feature, or by using key taps to punch in and out as you record (that is, punching *on the fly*).

Using Autodrop Autodrop is Logic's way to predefine the area you want to punch. You use a process similar to creating a cycle region to set punch-in and punch-out points. Once you define this area, the recording happens only between these two points, in your *autodrop zone*—even if you start record or playback from before the area you want to punch. In this exercise you're going to rerecord yourself speaking the number four, using the Autodrop feature.

1   Click the Autodrop button in the Transport panel.

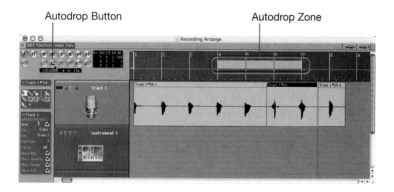

Something that looks similar to a cycle region appears in the Bar Ruler.

2   Move the Autodrop zone to start at 3 3 1 1 and end at 4 3 1 1.

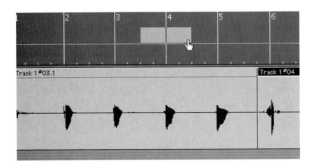

Use the locators in the Transport panel to confirm your position.

3   Place the SPL at bar 1 and click Record. Say the number four when it gets to bar 4.

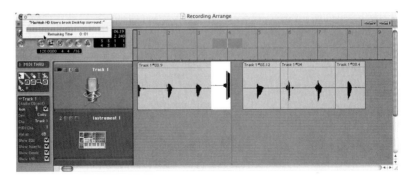

Notice that Logic automatically punched you in and out where you told it to. You should now have a new Object in the area that you dropped in on. If you make a mistake, simply undo it (Cmd-Z) and try it again.

NOTE ► Undoing a record operation does not erase the file from the drive. The file will still remain in the Audio window. You'll learn how to clean up unused files in just a few exercises.

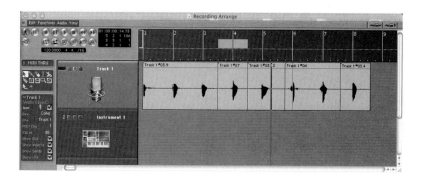

4   Turn Autodrop mode off.

Punching on the Fly   Instead of predefining the area you want to record, you can tap keys to punch in and punch out whenever and wherever you want. For this to work, Logic needs to be in Punch on the Fly mode. This lets it know to be ready for a recording at any time.

When you're punching on the fly, it's important to initiate each punch-in and punch-out by using a command called Record Toggle. Although it's possible to punch in by simply hitting the Record button while in playback, this is not recommended, as Logic tends to behave sluggishly under these circumstances. Record Toggle is only accessible through a key command that is not assigned in the default Logic key command set. If you need to, review the "Using Key Commands" section in Lesson 3 to see how to set the Record Toggle function to Shift-* (on the numeric keypad). This key command simply toggles you between playback and Record mode. During playback you simply tap Shift-* to punch in, and Shift-* again to punch out. You can actually do this multiple times throughout the same track.

1   From the main menu bar, click Audio to open the pull-down menu. If "Punch on the fly" is not already checked, select it.

2   Position the SPL at bar 1.

3   Click the Play button. Just before bar 3, press Shift-* and say "three" at bar 3. Just after you say it, press Shift-* again to punch out. You should end up with a new Object around bar 3 for the area that you recorded.

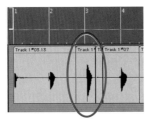

This may take some practice. Remember, if you mess up, just undo it and try again.

TIP ▶ You may want to assign the Record Toggle function to a single-stroke key command that doesn't require a modifier key like Shift.

Merging

Once you've punched in and out a few times, you'll notice that the track has been divided into several different Objects. This is not a problem until you want to move the entire passage. Having to select multiple Objects can get confusing, and mistakes can easily be made. In this case, once you're sure that everything sounds correct, you can simply glue all the Objects back together again. This will not change the sound of the track at all!

1 Select all Objects on Track 1.

2 Click any of the Objects with the Glue tool.

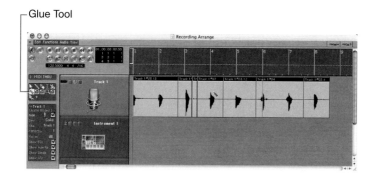

3 Select Create when asked if you want to create a new audio file.

Notice that you now have a brand-new continuous region. This should sound identical to what you had before you merged the Objects.

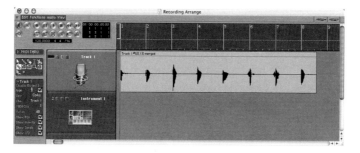

Cleaning Up

After a session of tracking audio, you will most likely have a lot of audio that was recorded but is no longer used. Remember when you punched in over your track? The audio you recorded over is still on your hard drive, eating up precious space. This is very different from what happens on a conventional tape deck. When you record over something, it's gone! The advantage of Logic's method is that if you need to, you can always undo your actions and get back to where you were, because the original audio isn't erased. However, you must go back and get rid of any unused audio, once you're satisfied with the complete work. The steps in this exercise show you how to do this cleanup easily, without accidentally throwing out something you need.

1   Go to the Audio window (Cmd-9).

You are likely to have many audio files and regions in your list.

2   From the local Edit menu, choose Select Unused.

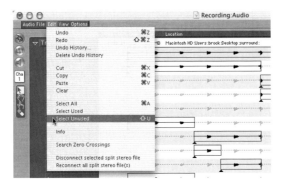

3   From the local Audio File menu, select Delete File(s).

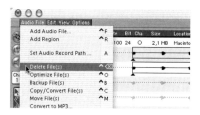

4   Confirm the deletions.

Now things should be nice and tidy, with only the audio files that are used in the song appearing in the Audio window.

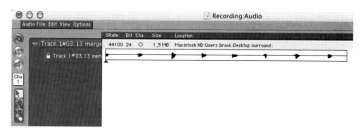

5   Close the Audio window.

Recording MIDI

Now that you have the process of recording audio down, recording MIDI will be a snap. For the most part, recording MIDI data onto tracks works in the same way as what you've learned with audio. The actual processes of recording and punching in and out work the same, but there are a few differences you need to be aware of, plus some cool things that aren't possible with audio.

In the following exercises, you'll choose whether or not to hear the recording of yourself counting aloud. If you don't want to hear it, simply mute the track. On the other hand, leaving it unmuted is a good way to hear how you can build MIDI tracks over audio that you have already recorded.

As far as a sound source for the MIDI track, this song has been set up with an es-p virtual synthesizer ready to go. To review how virtual synthesizers work, go to Lesson 5, "Setting Up the Audio Environment."

Enabling MIDI Recording

You may have noticed in other exercises that the Record Enable button automatically engages when you select a MIDI track. Selecting a different track automatically causes the newly selected MIDI track to become record-enabled, instead of the previous MIDI track. This probably occurs because 99 percent of the time you will need to record only one MIDI track at a time.

1   Disable the Record button for Track 1.

2   Select the Instrument 1 track.

It is automatically record-enabled.

3   Play your controller. You should hear the default preset for the es-p synth, which has already been set up for you.

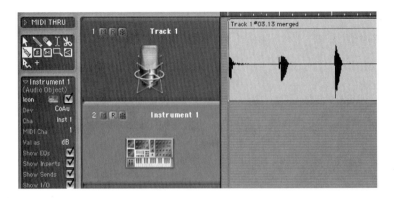

Filtering Input

MIDI controllers can generate a variety of different MIDI commands. In addition to note-on and note-off information, they also send information like continuous control numbers and *aftertouch* (pressure) commands. In some cases, you may not want to record every type of information that your controller is generating. For example, you may not want to record aftertouch information if you have a sound that reacts strangely to after-touch and you sometimes inadvertently press too hard on the keys. You can use input filtering to prevent this information from getting to the track.

1   From the main menu bar, select File > Song Settings > MIDI Options.

2   Deselect the Note button, and play the keyboard.

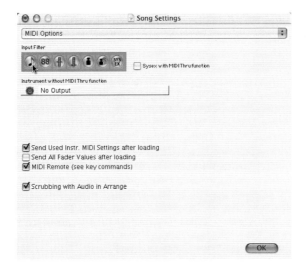

Notice how you won't hear anything because you've filtered all incoming notes on messages so that they never make it into Logic's sequencer.

3   Click the Note button to reselect it, and play the keyboard. Click OK to confirm the settings.

Recording in Real Time

Real-time recording simply means that you are playing the part live.
Operations like punch-in and options like Autodrop work the same way
for MIDI as they do for audio. However, MIDI data is not recorded as a
separate file. All MIDI information is stored within your Logic song file.
This type of information takes up virtually no space, so you'll never have
to worry about running out of disk space.

Let's record some MIDI information and see how easy it is.

1   Place the SPL at bar 1, and click Record.

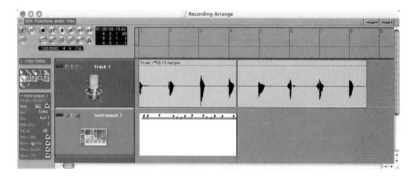

2   Play your controller for a few measures and then hit Stop.

Notice that there is no waveform view, but there is a rough musical
notation of your note positions.

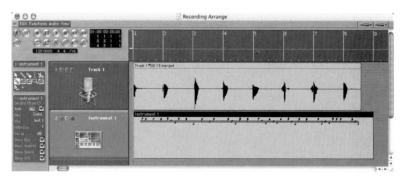

Once you stop, you should have a nice new MIDI Object!

Just have fun with this. You really can't mess it up. Go back through some of the exercises for recording audio, and see how things work the same for MIDI tracks.

Retrospective Recording

Ever had a great performance and then said to yourself, "I wish I had recorded that!"? For MIDI, Logic is actually able to record your last performance even if you weren't recording! It can be done with a feature called "Capture last take as recording." This feature is available only through a key command that is not defined in Logic's default key command set. If you need to, review the "Using Key Commands" section of Lesson 3 to see how to set the "Capture last take as recording" function to Ctrl-*.

Let's see how this option works.

1   Select all Objects on the Instrument 1 track, and delete them.

> **NOTE** ▸ When you delete MIDI Objects, they are gone. There is no MIDI window as with the Audio window. Move MIDI Objects that you might want later to No Output tracks for safekeeping.

2   Play the song from bar 1, and play your controller while in Playback mode.

3   After stopping, press Ctrl-*.

Step Recording

Step recording is similar to the process of what composers do when they write music. One at a time, notes are carefully placed on the paper with all of the appropriate position, duration, and dynamic markings. These carefully written markings are eventually played in real time by a musician to create the music the composer was seeking. You can do step recording in Logic even if you have no formal music training.

1   Delete all recorded Objects on the Instrument 1 track.

2   Select the Pencil tool from the toolbox and click in the open space in the Instrument 1 track at bar 1.

This creates a blank Sequence Object, which will serve as the paper for you to write your music upon.

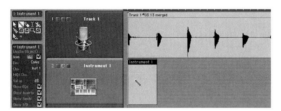

3   Drag the end position of the Object to the beginning of bar 9.

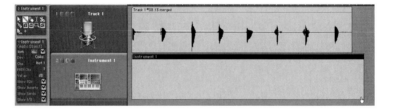

Now you have a little more room to work with.

4   With the new Object selected, open the Matrix editor.

5   Click the MIDI In button.

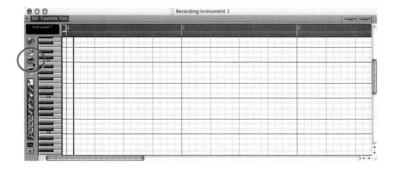

The button turns red. Make sure not to double-click it, or a small dot will appear in it; the dot selects another mode.

6   Play several notes one after the other on your controller.

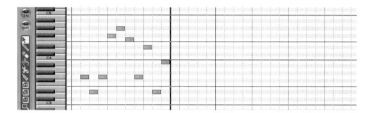

Notice how a new bar appears each time you press a key. Also note that each new note is automatically advanced to the next step in time.

7   Change the Time Division value in the lower left of the Matrix window to /4, and play some more notes.

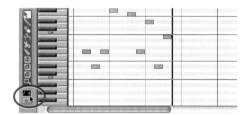

Notice that the steps and note lengths are longer in duration.

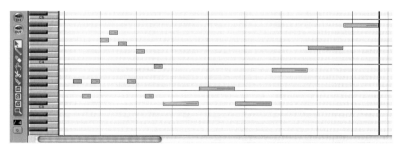

8 From the main menu bar, select Windows > Open Keyboard Window.

This is handy if you are working without a controller, as you might do with a laptop.

9 Click the virtual keys.

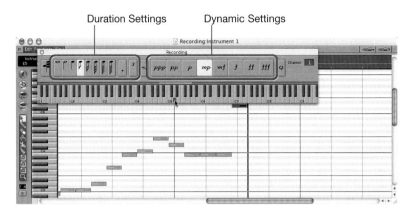

10 Click a different note duration setting, and click some more keys.

NOTE ▶ The dynamic buttons (such as pp and ff) change the velocity value recorded.

That's it! You should now be able to capture your musical and sonic ideas with Logic. Assuming that you've mastered the rest of this book, you can now transform your raw recordings into the finished vision you have in your mind—or perhaps create some sounds you never dreamed of!

By the way, you don't need to save this lesson unless you really love the sound of yourself counting to eight while doodling on the keyboard.

What You've Learned *CHAPTER 15 SUMMARY* *

✓ You can configure the metronome as an audible-click track guide.

✓ Buffer settings allow you to control track count and audio latency.

✓ You can use input monitoring to hear what you're recording in real time.

✓ Audio files are recorded independently of the Logic song file to an area directory you define on the hard drive.

✓ You can use the Audio window to view, manage, and delete audio files within your song.

✓ Autodrop and Punch on the Fly help you re-record areas of a track.

✓ The Glue tool lets you merge Objects after punching to create one seamless Object.

✓ MIDI recordings are kept within the song file.

✓ MIDI performances can be recorded even if Record mode wasn't engaged, by using the "Capture last take as recording" command.

✓ You can apply input filters to prevent certain types of information from being recorded into a track.

✓ The MIDI In button allows you to step-record notes one at a time. The Keyboard window can be used in place of your controller keyboard.

*
STEP
RECORDING

16

Working with Surround Sound

Have you ever noticed that if you watch a movie on a really big screen, you almost start to feel like you are in the movie? This works because the screen is so large that it fills your entire field of vision. The screen doesn't need to extend behind you, because your eyes can only see what's in front of you. Is that true for sound? Can you only hear what's in front of you? Of course not. So why do people typically listen to music played only through speakers that are sitting in front of them? Why not put speakers around them, allowing them to hear a prerecorded sound from all directions, as they normally hear sound in nature? This is something that the movie industry has understood for quite some time. Now people are bringing this idea home with the huge popularity of surround sound home theater systems.

Since it's now not so unusual for the general consumer to have a surround sound playback system at home, and it typically consists of five or six speakers, why play music through only two of them? In recent years there has been a movement for surround sound music production. New audio-specific formats such as DVD-Audio and Super Audio CD are making their way into the market as ways to deliver surround sound music to the masses.

Logic gives you the tools you need to produce surround sound audio, whether it be to support a movie or for music only. If you've never experienced surround sound music, then you owe it to yourself to check it out. Here's how you can do it for yourself using Logic!

> **NOTE** ▶ To hear the results of this lesson, you will need an audio interface with six outputs wired to the inputs' six-channel surround sound playback system. If you do not have this type of system, you can follow through the lesson steps, but you will hear your results only in stereo.

Configuring the Playback System

Of the various surround sound formats introduced over the years, the one that's emerged as most common is called 5.1. With this format, you typically play your audio through five full-frequency speakers, which are fed by five independent channels (left, right, center, left surround, and right surround), plus one dedicated low-frequency subwoofer, which is fed by a channel referred to as an LFE (Low Frequency Effect). Many manufacturers make package systems that include the speakers and amplifiers to play back 5.1 audio. If you're looking to purchase a system, make sure it has six analog inputs, so that it can receive signals from the outputs of your audio interface.

As far as placing your speakers, there are a lot of different ways you can go about it. The following diagram shows an overview of a common layout designed specifically for monitoring 5.1 music playback. The basic idea is that the speakers are all placed at an equal distance from where you (the black dot in the center) typically listen. The numbers indicate degrees of separation. Looking directly ahead, the center speaker is considered to be 0° off center. The right front speaker is 30° to the right of the center speaker, and the right rear speaker is 110° to the right of the center. The left front and left rear speakers are mirrored on the left side. The LFE is not indicated in the diagram because subwoofers tend to sound dramatically different depending on where you put them in the room. Exact placement of the subwoofer will be unique for every room, but typically it is placed on the floor in alignment with one of the front three speakers.

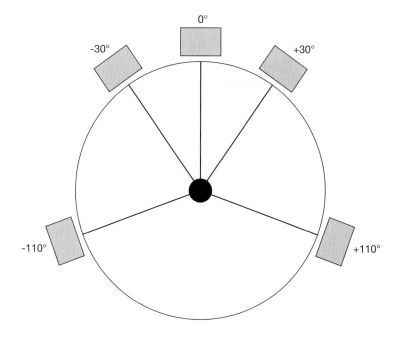

Configuring Logic

You'll need to do a little preliminary work in Logic to get it prepared for surround mixing.

Assigning the Outputs

In order for this to work, you will need not only the speakers, but also an audio interface with at least six independently addressable audio outputs. Emagic's own EMI 2-6 interface is a good example of one that will work well. Logic will then need to know which outputs are connected to what speakers. Otherwise, when you tell Logic you want a track to be played out of the center speaker, it may come out of the left rear one.

1   Open the file **16-Surround-Start**.

2   From the main menu bar, select Logic Platinum > Preferences > Surround.

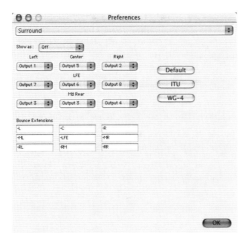

The Surround Preferences window lets you configure various options related to your speaker output. Most important, it shows you which audio interface outputs are designated for which speaker positions.

You can assign a hardware output to each surround sound channel by choosing an output from the pop-up menu under each channel. The buttons on the right can be used to automatically select different output order standards.

As in Lesson 14, "Finishing Your Song," the goal is to create a final mix file by bouncing—but in this case, that mix is in surround sound. For a surround mix, extensions are added at the ends of the filenames of the bounced files to indicate the speaker position that each file represents. You can change these extensions as needed.

3   Choose 5.1 from the "Show as" pop-up menu.

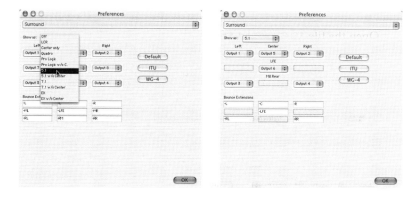

Logic can work with various surround sound formats. Selecting 5.1 for this option simply helps to avoid confusion, by causing this dialog to show you only the speakers that will be used in your surround playback system.

4   Click OK.

Adding Output Objects

When you created your final mix in Lesson 14, you paid very close attention to the level on your main stereo output meter. Now, as you create a new 5.1 mix, you'll need to pay careful attention to the meters of six channels. To do this, you need to add more Output Objects into the Audio layer of your environment.

1   Select the Environment's Audio layer (Screenset 8).

2   Select and delete the Output 1-2 Output Object. Move the Aux 1 and Master Objects over to make better use of your space.

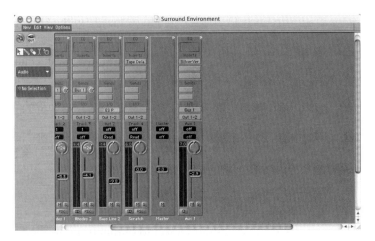

3   Create six new Audio Objects by choosing New > Audio Object from the Environment's local menu.

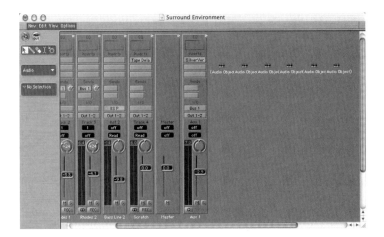

Logic doesn't have a single surround sound Object, so creating six Output Objects works just the same.

4 Now assign the new Objects to output channels, and name them to match their speaker positions, as follows (if you need to refresh your memory of how to do this, see the "Using Audio Objects" section of Lesson 5):

▶ Assign the first new Output Object to output 1 (in the Object Parameter box), and change the name to Left.

▶ Assign the second new Output Object to output 2 (in the Object Parameter box), and change the name to Right.

▶ Assign the third new Output Object to output 3 (in the Object Parameter box), and change the name to Rear Left.

▶ Assign the fourth new Output Object to output 4 (in the Object Parameter box), and change the name to Rear Right.

▶ Assign the fifth new Output Object to output 5 (in the Object Parameter box), and change the name to Center.

▶ Assign the sixth new Output Object to output 6 (in the Object Parameter box), and change the name to LFE.

5 Select all the new Output Objects, and then deselect the Show EQ, Show Inserts, Show Sends, and Show I/O check boxes.

This will make the screen less cluttered when the Objects are expanded into a channel view.

6 Double-click each Output Object to display its channel view.

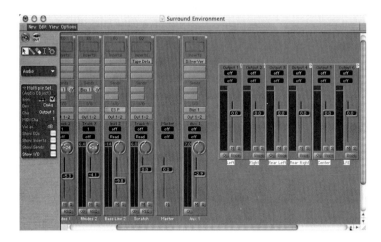

7 Rearrange the Output Objects so that the meter positions better reflect the actual speaker positions. Compare them with the figure.

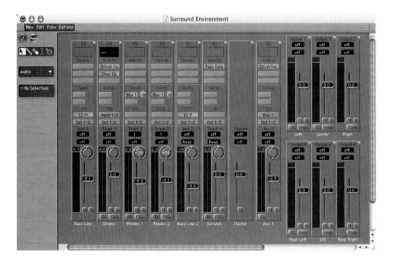

This layout makes it easier to understand at a glance what each meter represents.

NOTE ▶ Most audio interfaces lack a single volume control for working with surround sound. In this lesson, you already have a Master Object, and its fader will serve as a volume control for your entire surround mix.

Using the Surround Control

Now is where the real fun begins! By default, tracks in Logic assign themselves to stereo outputs. You will need to redirect them to your surround output. Once you have them assigned, you will want to control which of the speakers you want each track to be heard from. This is done by way of a surround control. The concept of the surround control is similar to that of the pan control; it's just a little more complex. The surround control has to distribute sound not only between the left and right positions, but also between the front and back positions. Don't worry—it's pretty simple to understand once you get into it.

Displaying a Surround Control

You've used the stereo pan control in all the other lessons, but this control is not sufficient for mixing in surround sound. Now you'll convert the stereo pan control in the channel view of each track to a surround control.

1   On the Drums channel, click and hold the output assignment, and select Surround from the pop-up menu.

Surround Channel Panner

Notice how the channel panner changes from a stereo type to a surround type with a dot in the middle of a circle.

NOTE ▶ The default position is for the dot to be in the center of the circle. This position indicates that the sound for the track will be distributed to all of the speakers shown in the surround control. Since this is a stereo track, the left channel of the drums will be played partially from the center speaker and partially from the two left side speakers, while the right channel will be played partially from the center and partially from the two right speakers.

2   Do the same for the remaining channels.

TIP ▶ You can do this quickly by selecting all the channels for which you want to change the output settings, and then holding down Option as you make the output selection.

NOTE ▶ In Logic, it is possible for you to assign some channels to the surround outputs, while others remain on the standard stereo output. Those assigned to the standard outputs (1-2) will simply have their audio mixed into the left and right outputs in the surround mix.

3   Play the song. While the song is playing, adjust the master fader. Return it to 0.0.

Notice that the volume of the entire surround mix changes.

4   While the song is playing, grab the dot in the Base Line surround control and move it around.

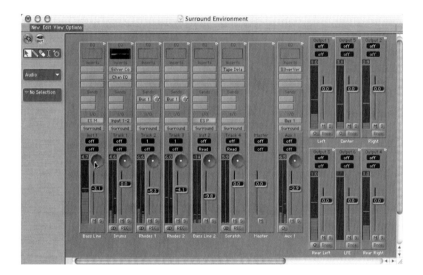

Listen to the movement of the Bass Line as you move the dot. Also notice the output meters and how they reflect your movements. If you want to get a more isolated listen to what's happening, solo the Bass Line.

5   Option-click the Synth surround control.

This is a quick way to return a dot to the center position of a surround control.

Using the Pan Window

The Pan window is an enlarged view of the surround control. It allows you to control the pan position with greater accuracy—and gives you access to some very cool features to enhance your panning control.

1   Double-click the surround panner on the Bass Line channel.

2   Move the dot around.

Notice how this moves the channel panner on the Bass Line as well.

3   Click the edges of the surround panner.

This will cause the dot to jump to the position you clicked.

Now that you know the Pan Window basics, it's time to learn some tricks with the Command and Control keys.

4   Hold down the Command key.

A line appears across the Pan window.

5   While the Command key is held down, drag the dot in the Pan
window.

The dot moves only on the path indicated by the line.

6   Release the Command key. Drag the dot, and hold the Command
key again.

Notice that the angle of the line is determined by where the dot is
in the panner.

7   Release the Command key. Move the dot somewhere other than
dead center.

8   Hold down the Control key.

A circle appears in the Pan window.

9   While holding down the Control key, drag the dot around in a circle.

The position of the dot when the Control key is held down changes the size of the circular path. Using the Control key is the way you can create perfect circular pan moves.

10 Option-click the dot to reset it to the exact center of the control.

Changing the Output Assignment In some cases you may want to intentionally assign the output of a track to something other than the 5.1 setting you have now. An example is when you want to make the track play from the traditional stereo position (playing equally out of the left and right speakers), and not the center speaker. This is often referred to as the *phantom center position.* The problem is that if you position the dot in the front center position, the sound will come from the center speaker. Here's how to get around that.

1 Set the Bass Line to Solo mode. Then, working in the Pan window, place the Bass Line's dot on the center speaker. Play the song, and notice how the meters show that the signal is coming only from the center speaker.

2 Click and hold the surround output assignment in the upper-left part of the surround panner, and change the output assignment to 5.1 w/o Center.

3 Play the song back. Notice that the Bass Line is now played from the left and right output channels.

Working with the LFE

Sound isn't just something you hear; it's something you can feel as well. Film audio mix engineers wanted a way to intensify the sound of special effects such as car crashes and explosions, so they came up with the idea of the LFE (Low Frequency Effect) channel. It is designed to give you total control over what sounds come out of the subwoofer in your system.

Let's hear what the LFE channel can do.

1 If the Pan window is not open, double-click the surround control for the Bass Line track.

2 Play your song back from bar 9. During playback, drag the LFE slider to the right.

You should be able to feel the low-frequency sound increase in your room. Now you can use the LFE as an alternative to equalization to pump up the bass in your mix!

3 Click the small button in the upper-left corner to close the Pan window.

Finishing a Surround Mix

Working with music in surround sound is new to almost everyone, even veteran musicians, producers, and engineers. There are no rights and wrongs at this point. The picture you paint with a surround mix can be much more varied than with stereo. Do you create the illusion that the listener is watching a band that's up on a stage, or do you put the listener on the stage, in the middle of it all? Now that you know what all the controls do, it's time to experiment with them. For this section, there is no formal exercise—simply play with your newfound surround toy and see what happens.

Filtering the LFE

Before bouncing your final mix, it's a good idea to remove frequencies higher than what your subwoofer can produce. The signal being sent to the LFE goes over a full-frequency channel, but the frequency response of the subwoofer generally limits what you hear to a low rumble. However, in some consumer 5.1 playback systems, users can indicate in their equipment configuration options that a subwoofer is not present, causing the LFE channel to be redirected into the main speakers—which means the full-range signal of the LFE channel is heard through the main speakers. If that occurred with your song, the consumer would be hearing a mix that you never intended, and this could be quite disruptive to the overall sound of your song. By filtering the LFE output in Logic before bouncing, you eliminate any possibility of the full-range signal of the LFE being heard—regardless of a consumer's configuration.

So, let's go ahead and filter the LFE on your song's output.

1   Select the LFE Output Object.

2   Click the Show EQs check box in the Object Parameter box.

EQ Box

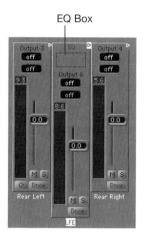

3 Double-click the EQ box at the top of the LFE channel.

This will automatically insert a Channel Equalizer plug-in and open
the Channel Equalizer window.

4 Click the Lo-Pass Filter button in the upper right-hand corner of the
Channel Equalizer window.

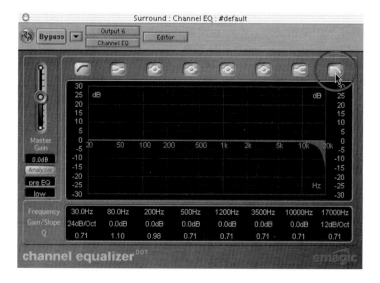

5 By dragging up or down on the setting values as needed, set the Lo-Pass filter setting to 80 Hz, at 24 dB per octave.

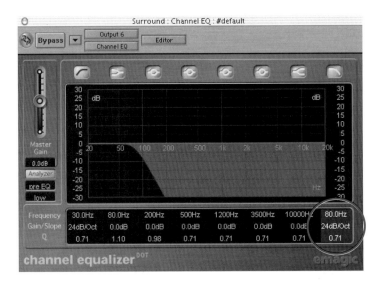

This frequency setting causes sounds with frequencies above 80 Hz to get quieter as their frequencies get higher. The setting of 24 dB per octave specifies how quickly the sounds above 80 Hz die away. You can see this filtering visually represented in the channel equalizer's display.

For an LFE Send, 80 Hz is the most accepted filter point. You shouldn't hear any dramatic change to the sound. Remember, the way a sub-woofer works is to remove the higher frequencies of sound.

6 Close the Channel Equalizer.

Optimizing the Surround Mix Level

It's not possible to maximize the level of a surround mix using the Normalize function as you did in Lesson 14. Because you end up with six separate files, Logic has no way to look across all of them to find the highest level of the group. You can, however, get close to the same result by following these steps.

1 Make sure the master fader is positioned at 0.0 dB.

The master fader affects the volume of signals going to any of the Output Objects in a song. If the master fader is turned down low, then the meters in the surround output masters that you created will read low. Leaving the master fader at 0.0 dB will give you an accurate reading of the levels you are sending to the surround Output Objects.

2 Play your song from start to finish. Look at the clip level indicators on the surround output channels.

3 Whatever the highest level is, simply add a little less than that value to all of the surround output faders. If one or more of your surround outputs clip, then turn them all down evenly until they don't.

In the left-hand figure, the highest peak was on the Right channel at 1.9 dB below 0.0 dB. The right-hand figure shows that 1.7 dB has consequently been added to all the output channel faders, creating a higher level for the file you're about to bounce. It's important that the relative levels of all the channels remain the same, so double-check that the values on all the output faders are the same.

> **TIP ▶** When moving the output faders, select them all first, and then move one of them up or down. This links the faders temporarily to ensure that the fader positions remain the same.

Bouncing for Surround Sound

You've already learned in Lesson 14 how to bounce a final mix when working in stereo. Bouncing in surround sound is basically the same thing, except you have to pay attention to more meters and change one simple setting.

1   Make sure that the fader on the Master channel is at 0.0 dB.

2   Click the Bnce (Bounce) button on any of the surround output channels.

The Bounce settings dialog displays.

3   For the Surround Bounce parameter, select 5.1.

In this song, some channels are assigned to a 5.1 output, and others are assigned to 5.1 w/o center. When you use 5.1 for the Surround Bounce parameter, all output channels and groups of output channels that are part of a 5.1 mix are included in the bounced files.

4   Select a start position of 4 1 1 1 and an end position of 38 1 1 1. As for file formats and bit resolution, those depend on your final destination. Select the appropriate values, and click Bounce.

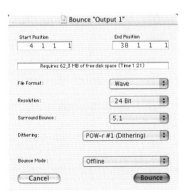

5   Save as Surround Mix. Select an appropriate folder on your drive to store the bounced files.

> **TIP** ▶ Since six different files are going to be created, you may want to create a specific folder to keep them in.

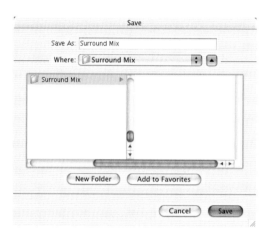

6   Look inside your bounce destination folder to confirm your files.

Notice the extensions that are automatically added to the end of the filename you chose. They indicate which speaker each audio file represents.

Now you've done something that a lot of longtime music and recording professionals have never done. You've created a surround mix!

> **NOTE ▶** At this point, the files you have are not capable of being heard by most consumers. They need to be encoded into a format that consumer playback systems understand, such as DTS or Dolby Digital. Logic does not have encoders built into it. There are third-party programs that can do this. For example, Apple's DVD Studio Pro has a Dolby Digital encoder built into it. This allows you to apply the 5.1 sound track you've created in Logic to your own DVD-Video discs!

What You've Learned *✱ CHAPTER 16 SUMMARY ✱*

✓ There are a variety of surround sound formats. The most common is 5.1.

✓ You must pay close attention to the surround configuration of your audio interface and make sure that you've wired your audio interface correctly with your speakers.

✓ Creating additional output channels is necessary to meter the master levels of your surround mix.

✓ You can use the surround panner to position tracks into desired speaker positions.

✓ There are surround track-output options that can be selected to achieve phantom center positions.

✓ To ensure proper playback on consumer surround systems, filter the LFE output.

✓ You must pay close attention to maximizing output levels before you bounce your final mix, because normalizing a bounced file for surround sound doesn't work as it did with a stereo mix.

Appendix

Apple's Digital Production Platform: An Integrated Workflow

Apple has developed a line of professional film, video, and audio production applications that, taken together, give professionals an affordable high-performance, integrated digital production platform. Each product is recognized as an industry standard in its respective field. When used together, they form a complete pipeline from content creation to delivery.

Here's a brief overview of how the four keystone applications—Final Cut Pro, Shake, Logic, and DVD Studio Pro—work together in a variety of standard production workflows.

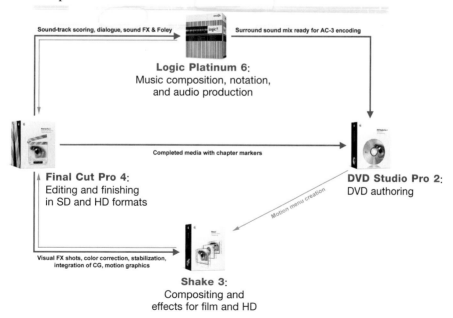

Sound-track scoring, dialogue, sound FX & Foley

Surround sound mix ready for AC-3 encoding

Logic Platinum 6:
Music composition, notation, and audio production

Completed media with chapter markers

Final Cut Pro 4:
Editing and finishing in SD and HD formats

Motion menu creation

DVD Studio Pro 2:
DVD authoring

Visual FX shots, color correction, stabilization, integration of CG, motion graphics

Shake 3:
Compositing and effects for film and HD

It's worth noting that because Apple takes a platform approach to its professional applications, the products also work well with complementary third-party solutions like Alias Wavefront's Maya, Adobe's After Effects and Photoshop, Avid's Media Composer, and Digidesign's ProTools.

Final Cut Pro

Final Cut Pro is a fully scalable nonlinear editing system designed to work with all standard video formats from DV to High Definition. More than just an editing application, Final Cut Pro lets you easily add filters and transitions to clips and play them in real time using an effects engine known as RT Extreme. Real-time color correction, customizable keyboard commands, dynamic and asymmetric trimming, broadcast video scopes, and support for multichannel audio editing, mixing, and output are a few of the features that make Final Cut Pro a great tool for serious editors. Four integrated applications are also included with Final Cut Pro:

LiveType is a powerful title generation tool that lets you quickly and easily integrate dynamic, animated titles, objects, and textures into your video content. All elements are fully rendered 32-bit animations, which can be scaled from DV to Film Academy formats.

Soundtrack is an audio content-creation application that lets you build original, high-quality musical scores for your video. It uses royalty-free *loops* as the building blocks for musical compositions, and includes thousands of loops and sound effects that can easily be arranged to pre-defined markers in Final Cut Pro.

Cinema Tools is a sophisticated relational database designed to track the relationship between original film negatives and their digitized media counterparts. It gives editors and filmmakers the ability to shoot and finish on film and 24P (HD) while using Final Cut Pro for their editing.

Compressor is a high-speed encoding application that gives you an efficient way to convert video and audio content for a variety of distribution formats. Completed Final Cut Pro sequences are exported to Compressor and encoded to MPEG-4, MPEG-2, and other standard formats for distribution on the Web, CD, or DVD.

In the Pipeline

For more robust compositing, special-effects plates can be exported from Final Cut Pro and layered and manipulated in Shake. Audio elements in need of additional processing and mixing can be exported to Logic Audio for sweetening, and rough scores created in Soundtrack can be enhanced by professional composers in Logic. When completed, all treated media can be imported to DVD Studio Pro for professional DVD authoring.

Shake

Shake is a high-end compositing system used to create visual effects for award-winning broadcast commercials and box-office–champion feature films like *The Lord of the Rings* and *The Matrix*. Unlike the timeline-based compositing in Final Cut Pro, Shake uses a node-based architecture. Each operator is a discrete unit that can be plugged into other operators in an incredibly flexible, nonlinear fashion, creating a detailed process tree that leads to the final composited shot.

Like Final Cut Pro, Shake is resolution independent, so it can handle all standard video and film formats. Shake also includes two industry-standard keyers for greenscreen and bluescreen work: Photron's Primatte and Framestore/CFC's Keylight.

Shake is typically used for combining elements from multiple sources into a single image, creating the illusion that everything was filmed "in camera." These elements typically include 3D animation, particles, procedural painting, and live-action plates. Shake's compositing capabilities are complemented by an abundance of color correctors, necessary tools for the professional compositing artist.

One of Shake's greatest strengths is its customization. Almost every parameter in Shake can be linked to another via simple expressions, so it's easy to blur a light source as it gets brighter, or make an airplane fade into the sky as it shrinks toward the horizon. The MacroMaker lets you easily create custom plug-ins. A generous community of Shake users means that dozens of free plug-ins are available for download from www.highend2d.com.

In the Pipeline

In general, any shot that requires multilayered visual effects can be composited with more ease and precision in Shake than in Final Cut Pro. One of the most common shots to be sent to Shake is a bluescreen or greenscreen. While Final Cut Pro has built-in keyers, Shake includes far more sophisticated keying techniques based on color difference and 3D color space technology. Foreground and background contrast and color can be matched, background lighting can be wrapped around the foreground image, and problem edges can be isolated and treated.

Another common use for Shake is footage stabilization and match moving. Shake can stabilize position, scale, rotation, and perspective, salvaging shaky footage that would otherwise be unusable. Using the same technology, Shake can match the motion in a camera shot so that composited elements seem to "belong" in the scene.

Logic

Logic Platinum is a complete virtual recording studio used to create and edit music sound tracks, dialogue, and sound effects as well as to mix and master final audio files (including surround sound). Logic contains a fully scalable mixing console, dozens of effects processors, and the option to add Emagic's world-class software-based synthesizers as virtual instruments. In addition, it is designed with advanced MIDI handling to access external synthesizers, keyboards, and other MIDI-enabled instruments. The software contained in Logic rivals some of the most sophisticated hardware-based recording studios in the world in both audio quality and creative control.

Audio is either imported into Logic in the form of a digital audio file or acquired live by arming an audio track and recording. Once the media is acquired, it can be positioned in a musical timeline, and its pitch and tempo can be modified to match the primary key and tempo of the composition. Typically, levels are then set and automated (for example, fading the electric guitar solo up and down at the appropriate times), effects such as reverb and delay are added, and the final mix is prepared either as a stereo file or a surround sound mix.

Logic works simultaneously with SMPTE timecode, meaning that sounds can be positioned based on events in time, rather than on musical beats and bars. This makes it ideal for work on film and video sound tracks. Video can be previewed in a floating window or viewed as a thumbnail track in order to make precise matches to cuts and significant events in the narrative.

In the Pipeline

There are several ways in which Logic can be used in a film and video production pipeline. The most obvious is in the creation of a musical score. Final Cut Pro's Soundtrack is a great way to quickly create custom royalty-free music, but it can only match the action and dynamics of your visuals to a point. To really finesse the sound track and create a sound bed that includes unique composition and performance by professional musicians, the sound track will need to be ported into Logic.

Logic is also indispensable for working with nonmusical elements in a project. Dialogue in a sound track often needs to be compressed to allow audiences to hear an actor's whispers. Bad pronunciation that could ruin an otherwise great take can be cleaned up by copying and merging consonant and vowel sounds from elsewhere in the audio track. Room ambience can be restored in scenes where overdubbed dialogue had replaced the original audio.

One of the most exciting uses for Logic is the addition of Foley and sound effects, which tend to make or break the professional polish of many movies. Not only does Logic enable you to place and manipulate effects from sound-effects libraries and Foley recording sources, but the virtual-instrument options mean that entirely new sounds can be generated for unique applications: the deep rumble of an earthquake or the throaty whine of a futuristic jet car.

Surround sound mixing is directly incorporated into Logic. Music, dialogue, and effects can all be positioned in a virtual audio plane and animate across that plane relative to onscreen action. So helicopters flying from behind the camera to the front can be accompanied by the noise of their blades starting in the rear speakers of a surround sound system, then moving to the front. DVD Studio Pro includes a Dolby AC3 surround sound encoding system, which can take the Logic output tracks and encode them for distribution via DVD.

Finally, one often-overlooked but significant role for Logic is audio mastering. Sound tracks that sound spectacular on the monitor speakers in an editing suite can sound muddy and distorted when played back on a home stereo or the tinny speakers that accompany most television sets. Logic comes with high-quality audio mastering tools to tame the dynamic range of a sound track so that it is compatible with a wide range of listening environments.

DVD Studio Pro

DVD Studio Pro is a complete DVD authoring platform. It takes video, audio, and image content and combines them into an interactive menu-driven DVD. This can include motion menus, chapter and title access, special features, slide shows, and more. Basically, anything you've seen in a commercial DVD product can be created using DVD Studio Pro.

DVD Studio Pro uses a new intuitive project interface to combine different menus and media into a completed interactive piece. Authored works are designed to meet international DVD specifications, making them compatible with all compliant DVD playback units on the market. With a SuperDrive, finished projects can be burned directly to DVD-R for immediate test and playback. For larger production runs, the project can be mastered to DLT (tape) and sent to a duplication facility.

The application also includes Compressor, a powerful software-based MPEG2 encoding tool, as well as the AC3 encoder mentioned in the Logic section above. In essence, Compressor uses two-pass variable bit-rate encoding to read through the video file, analyze what changed between frames, and then store only the changed information. Using this analysis data, Compressor can encode the footage with a higher data rate for scenes that need it and a lower one for those that don't. The result is extremely high quality MPEG2 video that meets or exceeds the quality of real-time PCI-based professional encoders.

In the Pipeline

DVD Studio Pro is obviously the last step in a production workflow, where media content is assembled for delivery. The DVD authoring may be one of several delivery streams coming from the Final Cut Pro media; others may include video mastering, Web streaming, or even external film edits. One handy feature of Final Cut Pro is its ability to create and export chapter markers for use in DVD Studio Pro.

Other ways DVD Studio Pro and Final Cut Pro can work together include the creation of 4:3 pan-and-scan versions of a 16:9 piece, preparation of multiple-angle clips, and development of complex motion menus. Shake can be used for motion menus, its nonlinear workflow making it ideal for quickly generating alternate motion selection and rollover button states.

Glossary

alias An Object in the Arrange window that mirrors another sequence someplace else. You cannot edit an alias, only a real Object, but any change to the Object will be reflected in the alias. To create an alias, hold down the Shift key when you copy the Object.

arming Enabling a track to be recorded.

Arrow The default selection tool, shaped like an arrow. It is in every window's toolbox.

audio file Any digital audio recording stored on your hard drive. The default storage format for audio files in Logic is Sound Designer II.

Audio Object Audio Objects are found in Logic's environment. They show Logic where to send audio signals. The Audio Object provides a perfect place to tap in to the signal and apply effects. When they're expanded, Audio Objects look just like a channel strip on a standard hardware mixing console.

autodrop To stop and start recording at a specifically defined place—a section that's not quite right, for example.

automation The ability to record, edit, and play back the movements of all knobs and switches, including volume faders and pan, EQ, and Aux Send controls.

Aux An Auxiliary Object, either mono or stereo, in the Audio layer of the Environment. The Aux Object serves as a way to monitor an audio signal in Logic without recording it.

B

bar A measure of music, containing a specified number of beats, that establishes the rhythmic structure of the composition.

Bar Ruler A measurement device that sets and displays the song position, the cycle and autodrop locators, and markers. It is found at the top of the Arrange, Matrix, Hyper, and Score windows.

bit resolution A representation of the dynamic accuracy of a recording.

bounce To combine several tracks of audio into one file.

C

clip (in digital recording) To feed too much signal through a channel, producing a distorted sound. Audio Objects have a clip detector.

catch A window function that enables you to see the positions of recorded events in a song as it plays. The Catch button shows a man walking.

continuous control number (cc#) The number assigned by the MIDI specification regarding audio events or software functions such as volume, modulation, or sustain.

Core Audio The standardized audio driver for a Macintosh computer running OS X version 10.2 or higher. Allows the connection of all audio interfaces that are Core Audio compatible.

core MIDI The standardized MIDI driver for a Macintosh computer running OS X version 10.2 or higher. Allows the connection of all MIDI devices that are core-MIDI compatible.

Crosshair tool This crosshair-shaped tool is used in the Hyper Edit window to select and adjust MIDI events.

Cycle A mode in Logic in which you can repeat a section of a song. To turn on Cycle mode, click the Cycle button in the Transport window. Two locators define a cycle region.

D

dB Short for *decibels,* a measurement that relates the relative change in the volume of audio. Audio Objects have level meters that display playback or input monitor levels in decibels.

digital audio workstation (DAW) A computer that records, mixes, and produces audio files.

digital signal processing (DSP) In Logic, the mathematical process of manipulating digital information to modify sound. An example is in the Inserts area, which assigns DSP effects such as dynamic range compression and delay to a channel's sound.

driver A software program that allows your computer to communicate with another piece of hardware.

E

editor Logic has a multitude of editors to help you compose music. All of them alter the raw input in some way. The primary editors in Logic are the Hyper Editor and the Event List, Sample, and Score editors. You can edit audio regions using the Arrange window, Audio window, and Sample editor.

Environment A section of Logic that graphically reflects the relationships between hardware devices outside of your computer and virtual devices within your computer.

Environment layer A place to organize the Objects in the Environment for easy access. As a general rule, Objects of the same type are usually placed on the same layer.

Eraser A tool for deleting items. When you click a selected item, all other currently selected items are also deleted.

event A MIDI message. The main events in Logic are note, control-change, pitch-bend, aftertouch, and sysex events. MIDI events can be edited in a number of ways.

Event List A list of events and Objects that gives you access to all recorded event data. Thus, you can directly manipulate events and Objects and make precise alterations.

F

Fade tool One of the tools in the Arrange window toolbox. The Fade tool creates a cross-fade when you click and hold the mouse button as you drag across a section where two audio regions meet. You can also drag it over the beginning or ending of a region to create a fade-in or fade-out, respectively.

fader Generally thought of as a volume control found on audio channels. In Logic, a fader can also be an Object that sends out and responds to MIDI events. In this context a fader can be a knob, slider, numerical display, or button.

Finger A tool that looks like a hand with an extended index finger. The selection tool changes from an arrow to a finger to enable you to manipulate events or change window parameters. Different mouse and key commands activate the Finger in different windows.

floating A term that describes a window that's always visible on your Desktop. A window can be opened as a floating window by holding down the Option key while selecting from the Windows menu.

folder An object in Logic that contains sequences, audio regions, or other folders.

G

General MIDI (GM) A specification designed to ensure compatibility between MIDI devices. A musical sequence generated by a GM instrument should play correctly on any other GM synthesizer or sound module.

Glue tool A dedicated tool for merging sequences or Objects.

grid Vertical lines used to map the positions of measures, beats, and sub-beats in various editors.

Hand A tool that automatically appears when clicking and holding an Object with the Arrow tool. It is used to move Objects or events in the editors.

H

headroom Refers to how many decibels are available before *clipping*, or distortion, occurs.

HyperDraw A function that lets you create and edit automation data in the Arrange window by graphically inserting a set of points or nodes, which are automatically connected. Using HyperDraw, you can also make volume and panning changes in the Matrix and Score editors.

Hyper Editor One of Logic's four editors for MIDI data. It is used mainly for creating and editing drum sequences and control-change data.

input monitoring A way to determine which signal to listen to on record-enabled tracks. You can use Auto Input Monitoring to hear a track even when Logic is not recording.

I

insert A way to enhance the sound passing through an Audio Object with a plug-in.

Instrument An Object in Logic's Environment that represents a physical or virtual device that reacts to MIDI information.

key command An instruction to Logic that triggers an action, done by pressing a key or a combination of keys. All of Logic's functions can be activated by key commands.

K

Link A mode that determines the relationship of one window to another. Clicking the Link button activates Link mode. The window now shows the same contents as the top window.

L

local menu The place where the functions of the currently active window can be found.

locators Indicators displayed to the left of the Transport buttons in the Transport window. You can define locator points for the cycle (on the left-hand side) and autodrop zones (on the right-hand side). Cycle locators themselves, somewhat confusingly, are referred to as *left* and *right locators*. The left cycle locator is on the top; the right cycle locator is on the bottom.

Loop A Sequence Playback parameter. When Loop is on, the sequence will repeat until it encounters another Object, the end marker of a folder, or the end marker of a song.

M

Magnifying Glass A tool that enables you to zoom in on any part of the display. Pressing the Control key while rubber-band selecting a part of the window section enlarges the area. You can also activate the Magnifying Glass from other tools by holding down the Control key.

marker Used for indicating and quickly moving to sections of your song.

Marquee tool A crosshair-shaped tool in the Arrange window with which you can select and edit sequences and regions.

menu bar The bar extending along the top of the computer screen that gives options for global functions like opening windows and saving and loading songs. It does not offer access to most functions, which are in local menus.

metronome In Logic, a component that produces a sound measuring the beat. It can be set with a button in the Transport.

MIDI Musical Instrument Digital Interface. It's an industry standard that allows devices like synthesizers and computers to communicate with each other. It controls a musical note's pitch, length, and volume, among other characteristics.

MIDI channel A conduit for MIDI data. MIDI data flows through MIDI ports in channels, and up to 16 separate MIDI channels can pass through each port at the same time.

MP3 A digital coding standard used to compress audio files and distribute them over the Internet.

Multi Instrument An Object in the environment that represents a multitimbral device.

multitimbral Describes an instrument or other device that can use several MIDI channels simultaneously.

mute Used to silence the output of a sequence or track.

Mute tool A tool that enables you to stop an Object from playing by clicking the Object with the tool.

O

Object In Logic, *Object* is general term that can refer to MIDI sequences and audio regions in the Arrange window, or to the graphical representations of elements in the Environment.

P

Pencil Used to draw various types of information in an editor.

plug-in A small software application that adds functions to a main program (in this case, Logic). Logic's plug-ins are typically audio effects processors.

pointer A general term for the mouse pointer.

points The positions in HyperDraw and in the automation editors that demarcate the spots where data manipulation begins or ends.

preferences User settings that are applied to all Logic songs.

punch-in A technique that allows you to interrupt a playback and record audio as the sound is playing.

Q

quantize To correct the rhythm of notes so that they conform to a specific time grid.

R

regions In the Arrange window you will find tracks, which in turn contain regions and sequences. Regions are aliases for parts of audio files. They're subsections of audio files, and they can be as short as a single sample or as long as the audio file itself.

Replace mode An operating state you can activate in the Transport window. The Replace button is next to the Cycle and Autodrop buttons. In Replace mode, newly recorded information takes the place of the old information.

rubber-band A method of selecting multiple items at once. With the Arrow tool, click, hold, and drag the mouse on a window's background. Any item that the rubber band encloses or touches will be selected.

S

sampling rate When audio comes in through your sound card, analog-to-digital converters *sample*, or check, the signal's voltage level. The *sampling rate* refers to the number of times per second a digital audio file is sampled. Logic can record and edit audio at sampling rates ranging from 44.1 kHz (44,100 times per second) to as high as 192 kHz.

screenset An onscreen layout of windows that you can save. Each window retains its position, size, and zoom settings. You can save up to 90 screensets for each song.

scrubbing Moving the pointer back and forth (in a scrubbing motion) while playing back an audio region to locate a specific section.

sequence In the Arrange window you will find tracks, which in turn contain sequences.

Sequence Parameter box A box in the Arrange window where you can edit the playback of a sequence nondestructively.

SMPTE Stands for *Society of Motion Picture and Television Engineers*. These folks set up a synchronization system that divides time into hours, minutes, seconds, frames, and subframes.

solo A way to temporarily allow you to hear one or more selected tracks or sequences without hearing others that aren't soloed.

Solo tool With the Solo tool you can listen to selected Objects by themselves (click and hold the Object).

song The main Logic file that contains all references necessary to produce a final audio output.

song position line (SPL) A vertical gray line on the Bar Ruler and in other horizontal time-based windows that indicates where you are in a song. In Play mode the SPL lets you hear that section of your song. You can position the SPL with the mouse, by clicking the Bar Ruler, or by entering bar numbers in a dialog.

Standard MIDI file A common file type that almost any MIDI sequencer can read. In Logic, you can export selected MIDI Sequence Objects as Standard MIDI files.

step-time Recording notes one at a time in a MIDI sequence.

T

tempo The speed at which a piece of music is played, measured in beats per minute. You can create and edit tempo changes in the Tempo Operations window.

time signature Two numerals separated by a diagonal bar that appear at the beginning of a song. Common time signatures are 4/4 and 2/4. The first number denotes the number of notes in a measure, or bar. The second number denotes a unit of time for each beat. With a 2/4 signature, each bar has two beats; each beat is a quarter note long.

time-stretch To change the length of an audio region without changing its pitch. You can do this in the Arrange window by using menu or key commands.

toolbar An arrangement of onscreen buttons or icons that activate program functions.

track Contains a collection of either MIDI or audio sequences that can be played back over time. Each track has a specified destination where the information will go.

Transform window An editor used to select and modify various aspects of MIDI events according to user-defined parameters.

Transport A window through which you can control recording and playback functions. The Transport buttons are Record, Pause, Play, Stop, and Rewind/Forward.

V

virtual instrument A software element that mimics a traditional hardware sound module.

W

waveform A visual representation of an audio signal; it fluctuates according to the signal's volume over time.

X

x/y element A feature of every window that enables you to move horizontally and vertically at the same time. To engage the x/y element, click and hold on the bottom-left corner of the active window while dragging it.

Z

zoom An action that enlarges (zooms in on) or reduces (zooms out from) a viewing area in any window. The telescopes at the top right of the window or the Magnifying Glass in the toolbox are both zoom tools.

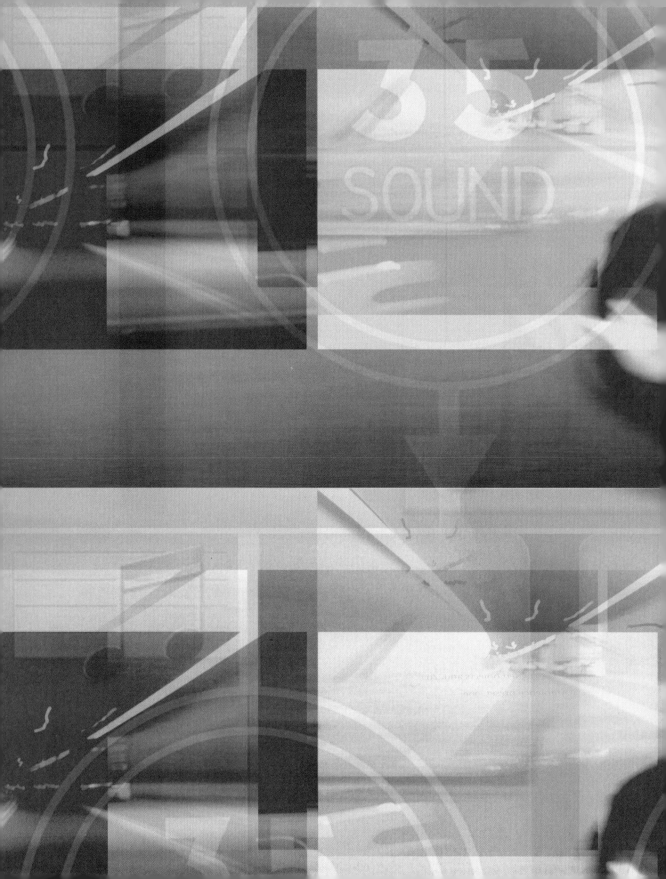

Index

A Message from the Conservatory of Recording Arts and Sciences

Logic 6 Sets New Standard for Audio

By Ben Nauman
Feature Writer

Apple's newly released book, *Apple Pro Training Series: Logic 6*, written by veteran audio producers Martin Sitter and Robert Brock, will set new

Robert Brock in the A Room

standards for individuals interested in creating master audio works. The book will form the basis of the curriculum offered at the renowned Conservatory of Recording Arts and Sciences in Tempe, AZ.

Logic 6 takes users through a step-by-step instruction on how to utilize Logic's software synthesizers, sampler, and digital signal processors in conjunction with producing sophisticated audio creations. Whether you are forming 5.1 surround soundtracks, digital music compositions, or producing your own musical CDs, *Logic 6* will be your guide in a user-friendly fashion.

"I am very happy with the final product Martin and I have created in *Logic 6*," says Robert Brock, head of the Digital Recording Department at the Conservatory of Recording Arts and Sciences. "The refinement and attention to detail in this book will provide

very thorough instruction for audio engineers."

As an established keyboardist, Brock has been an asset to the creation of albums and videos that have been recognized on an assortment of Billboard top ten charts. In addition to his accomplishments as a musician, Brock has been called upon by major league baseball organizations for sound compositions to entertain fans at ballparks across the nation.

Throughout his 11 years at the Conservatory, Brock has had his sights set on raising the bar in the audio engineering industry. Prior to Apple's purchasing of the audio engineering company, Emagic, Brock had been involved with the idea of establishing a certification program for his students to use in their portfolios. With a similar vision, Apple looked to Brock for his expertise in the program.
From this vision, prospective audio engineers will be able to take advantage of the innovative teachings provided by *Logic 6*.

We're really proud of Robert," says Kirt Hamm, Administrator at the

Conservatory of Recording Arts and Sciences. "He's a great example of the fine staff and faculty we have at the Conservatory," Hamm went on to say, "We're already teaching this high level curriculum at the Conservatory. In fact, the *Logic 6* book was in part derived from our program. This will be good for the industry and the students," says Hamm. "After all, it's all about raising the level of professionalism and integrity of our students. Now other colleges will be able to benefit from what we took years to develop. They too will be able to graduate better-trained and better-informed audio engineers."

Logic 6 will bring the Conservatory's number of certifications to seven. Others include Digidesign Pro Tools 135 and 235, SIA Smaart, Waves Plug-ins, T.C. Electronic M3000 and S6000.

For more information about the Conservatory, call 1-800-562-6383, e-mail a request for information to info@cras.org, or write to Conservatory of Recording Arts and Sciences at 2300 East Broadway, Tempe, AZ 85282.

Studio D, the Conservatory of Recording Arts and Sciences all-digital 5.1 Surround Mixing Suite.